The Hollow L
Itsabelle Pati...   ...89

The Sheep Pig. F7b. Radtke, Barbier. 1990
The Sheep Spider. F7b. Barbier, Radtke. 1990

The Hybrid. E5 6b. Radtke, Barbier. 1990

Orange Crush. E6 6b. Peel, Radtke. 1990

Revival. F7b+. Radtke, Peel. 1991
Solstice. E5 6a. Radtke, Ryan. 1991

The Living Dead Extensions. E5 6a. Radtke. 1991

King Rat (pitch 1). Radtke, Ryan. 1991

The Good the Bad and the Ugly. E7 6b,6b,6a. Radtke, Barton. 1992
Three Wishes. E5 6a. Radtke, Metcalf.1992
What God Wants. F7b. Radtke, Barton, Peel. 1992

The Black and White Days. E5 6b. Radtke, Peel. 1992
The Gemini Incident. F7c+. Radtke, Johnston. 1994
Lost in Thought and Lost in Time. F7b+. Radtke. 1994

The Howling. F7a. Barton, Radtke. 1994
The Squealing. F7a. Radtke,Barton. 1994

The Jaws of Grip. F7a. Radtke, Barton. 1994
The Chemistry Set, F7b+. Radtke, Barton. 1995

The Thrivin. E4 6a. Radtke, Barton. 1995
Pillar and Roof Route. F7b+. Radtke, Barton. 1995

The Blue Bus. E6 6b. Peel, Barton, Radtke. 1995

Eat the Onions or the Bitch Gets it. F7b. Radtke, Barton. 1995

Barton, Riley. 1995

A Canvas of Rock

Mark Radtke

2QT Limited (Publishing)

First Edition published 2011 by
2QT Limited (Publishing)
Dalton Lane, Burton In Kendal
Cumbria LA6 1NJ
www.2qt.co.uk

Cover Design by Hilary Pitt
Cover Images supplied by Author
Front cover – Mark Radtke on *Hollow Men* grade 27 Cosmic County,
Blue Mountains of Australia. Photo: Glenn Robbins. 1988
Rear cover – Mark Radtke and Neil McCallum ice climbing in Italy.
Photo: Alan Firth 2011.

Printed in Slovenia on behalf of Latitude Press Limited

The Author has his own website: www.radclimb.com

Distributed through Cordee Limited (www.cordee.co.uk)

A CIP catalogue record for this book is available
from the British Library
ISBN 978-1-908098-00-9

Keep the spirit of adventure alive,
Use the potential it unleashes wisely.

Mark Radtke

Foreword

Dreams that come true lead to other dreams. This could be the motto of my friend Mark Radtke who has spent a lifetime adventure climbing, which he captures here in this fascinating book.

Rad and I grew up less than six miles apart but our paths never crossed as children. I first heard of 'Rad' through a chance meeting with his brother Leon, 3000 feet down the local Grimethorpe pit where we were both working as miners.

Many Polish people settled in the area, following World War II, and they adapted well to mining. They were tough, hard working and loyal, valued camaraderie, and could deal with unknown terrain. Like his father, Rad never worked as a miner, yet over the years I would come to appreciate that he had inherited these qualities in abundance and valued them in others.

What strikes me in this collection of stories is that, for Rad, climbing is a team game; something to be shared in the moment, something to be relived afterwards over a pint. His legacy of hard first ascents in the UK and beyond is impressive, yet he accords the bonds between his partners equal status. We get a real sense of the legend Dave Barton, someone Rad clearly respects, not just as a talented alpinist and adventure climber but as a friend, someone you could trust with your life.

Laid bare here is the cost of adventure climbing, too: the fear, the falls, the crunching of bones. And yet, by guiding us through his emotions, sometimes complex and conflicting, Rad convinces us that it is still worth it. A life lived in the vertical without always knowing the outcome somehow reaches deep into a part of us, touching something instinctive.

Boldly, Rad criticises the recent over use of bolts on some cliffs, on some climbs, pointing to the fragility of British traditional climbing ethics. His point is quite simply that we don't own rock and that we have a duty of care to protect it for future generations so that they may too experience true adventure and freedom as a way to escape the sometimes mundane nature of 'everyday life'. What's impressive is the way he makes these points with gentleness and modesty. Rad shows us his own frailties - his vertigo, his occasional bursts of egocentricity - and this makes him a convincing guide. It is a great read, full of humour and drama, but at the same time it is a wise and important contribution to the ongoing debate of climbing ethics. Where slipping into the comfort zone does not and must not equal progress.

It is first and foremost a climbing book, but it is a very human one, laced with wisdom.

Thank you Rad for sharing the journey so far and never stop dreaming!

Andy Cave
October 2011

Author's Note

It is my hope that this book will be of interest to both climbers and non-climbers alike. The story is semi autobiographical and I have followed a roughly chronological format. In certain chapters I deal with more specific climbing topics and on these occasions you will find yourself doing a bit of time travelling, I apologise for this but it seemed the logical way of dealing with these subjects.

Many activities develop language and terminology specific and unique to themselves. Climbing is no exception. Most climbers who read this book will be familiar with many of the unique concepts and terminology that they encounter in the narrative and for them the language will be self-explanatory.

Non-climbers may be less conversant with some of the nuances and technical terminology associated with the game of climbing. For you, I have included a glossary and some explanatory notes at the rear of the book in the hope that if required, it will provide a further source of reference to clarify these.

Contents

Prologue

First Ascent

*'Climbing is a great game – great not in spite of the demands it makes,
but because of them. Great because it will not let us give half of ourselves,
it demands all of us. It demands our best'.*
Royal Robbins, Advanced Rockcraft

It's late afternoon and a cold wind blows through the gorge. Spray is lifted from the waterfall and carried in erratic eddies towards an overcast grey sky. A middle aged couple making a monumental ascent of the waterfall wince with discomfort as they are caught by a vicious blast of icy water. Their friends wait for them at the bottom, deterred by the adverse conditions currently being experienced by the adventurers above. I smile inwardly and wonder if they will be happy tonight. After a while the couple descend and make a leisurely departure, their voices blending into the sound of falling water and wind as they vanish round the arête guarding the entrance to the gorge.

Today is good in Gordale, cold gloomy and sombre and also relatively free from the countless pilgrims who come here to pay homage to its imposing architecture. I finish tying the two 9mm ropes into my harness and hand them to my climbing partner who methodically clips them through his belay device. His eyes trace the line of our proposed route, which meanders up an initial wall of chancrous grey limestone, and an evil smile begins to touch the corners of his mouth. He turns his head towards me and I detect a familiar glint in his steely gaze and imagine a fire burning behind his eyes. I've seen this fire before. The last time was when he was recounting the tale of a recent incident in a pub which turned a bit ugly. Dave walked away relatively unharmed: some were a little less fortunate. Dave thrives when the odds are stacked against him. I find the fire contagious.

Turning to the rock, the first hold that is gently tested creaks and pulls away in my hand. Dave smiles wickedly as I survey the next thirty feet of loose unprotected climbing. I reassess the situation and make cautious moves

1

upward, inspecting each hold in intimate detail before trusting it with my weight. The climbing is not too difficult, but here I'm treading on thin ice and beneath the ice the water is deep and the current treacherous. As I make cautious upward movements, heartbeats sound loudly in my head. A committing move is made to gain a suspect-looking flake and as my body pivots to the left, my eyes cement the flake in place. I imagine the flake moving, but it's solid and now I breathe easier as I clip ropes into pegs and create a lifeline between vertical and horizontal. A slim groove above looks deceptively easy from below, but enticed into its intricacies by a peg, the reality of the seduction becomes apparent.

Enmeshed in a series of intricate moves, feet smear on flakes that threaten to explode under the pressure and eyes hunt across the rock, seeking holds that will provide access to the sanctuary of the ledge that waits above. Fingers curl round an insecure edge that seems to diminish in size, as muscles contract to levitate me upward. The sound of water echoing round the gorge fades, as all senses are focused by intense concentration. As mind and limb work together in heightened synergy, holds that were previously conspicuous by their absence begin to appear with a regularity that tempts one to run to the awaiting horizontal, but deception still abounds.

Words of caution from Dave interrupt my reverie, as footholds crumble and clatter to the rocky floor below. Deep breaths suppress the adrenaline surge and words circle round my brain like a recording on a closed tape loop: 'Don't blow it now, don't blow it now'. I don't and soon I'm stood on the sanctuary of the rubble-strewn ledge that marks the end of the first pitch.

Once I'm secure, Dave shouts up that he wants to lead the pitch. Understanding his desire, I'm lowered earthward. Back on the ground I relax, mind soaking up the addictive chemicals now coursing through my body. Dave dispatches the pitch with ease, his upward movement only interrupted as he stops to cast loose pieces of rock to the floor. When he reaches the belay the light is fading and it's obvious that we're not going to be able to complete the rest of the climb today. So, happy with what we've achieved, I lower Dave back down the rock face so that he can clean the pitch. In the comfort of the bar we are soon quaffing satisfying gulps of Pendle Witch, an appropriately named brew which we have become painfully acquainted with of late. As the second pint is drained I savour feelings of the 'fix'.

The following day and I'm hurtling round the winding road back towards Malham, keen to get to grips with the rest of the climb. I pull up outside Pete Livesey's café with heart pounding having just taken an imaginary whipper from the huge intimidating roof crack that will form the second pitch of our proposed new route.

Dave is waiting inside the cafe. He looks me up and down. 'Good night?' he asks. The simplicity of the question means that he's already deduced from my appearance how I'm feeling.

I groan. Dave laughs sadistically. I enjoy the relaxing moments as we drink coffee and relate respective tales about the previous night.

Back in the gorge and levels of excitement begin to rise. White chalk-marks trace a tenuous line from the gorge floor up the left wall and bear witness to our activities of the previous day. Mercifully the weather has been kind and above, dry rock bulges with a barrier of overhanging ramparts. A black gash in the rocky cornice, offers hope of a breach through the overhangs. This is the proposed start to the second pitch of our route. I notice Dave examining the brutal intricacies of the roof crack and by the look on his furrowed brow; understand that his thoughts are echoing mine. 'It's going to be hard, the outcome uncertain.'

He turns towards me, smiles and preordains the future with one simple statement, 'Piece of piss.'

Dave reclimbs the first pitch and soon we're both ensconced at the belay. It's an oppressive place with loose rock and overbearing roofs blocking out the sky. The crack above our heads looks alarmingly difficult at close quarters. I quickly check the rack of gear on my harness, carefully noting the position of a couple of crucial looking pieces, and begin to make tentative progress up and outwards.

The first moves feel hard, as eyes scan the rock, searching to detect the friable and avoid betrayal, but here the ground is steep and caution is a luxury. Hands and fingers fight in desperation to gain purchase in the fissure and feet send shards of rock to the floor below. Despite its teeth, the crack offers comfort as wires and Friends are placed within its depths.

I am suspended from hands welded into the rock above my head and with lactic acid threatening to poison forearm muscles. A long stretch outwards from an awkward hand jam and a piece of gear of unknown security is lodged in the crack. Urgently I pull the rope and clip the gear, but it's costly and suddenly I'm airborne.

Dave knows this game well; he's been in this situation many times before. From the belay he's been watching my every move, patient, excited and calm. As I part company with the rock he responds catlike, paying out just sufficient rope to stop me simultaneously swinging into the wall and crashing into the ledge. I trace an arc through the air like a clock's pendulum and on my second swing Dave grabs my harness, pulling me back into the belay.

With the tension broken, we both laugh hysterically; the seriousness of the situation evaporates with the knowledge that the gear in the roof is good and the crack, whilst being desperate, is definitely feasible. After a brief rest, I feel relaxed and climb comfortably back up to my high point. Dave eggs me on with words of encouragement. A strange pirouette on one arm brings the edge of a flake within reach, a slap outwards and my fingers lock onto the edge of the crack; another move and the surreal upside down world returns to the relative normality of the vertical. Lungs draw in huge gasps of air and my heart pounds loudly in my head, pumping blood into swollen energy-starved forearms. I hang motionless from a huge hold on the lip of the overhang, changing hands alternately to shake life back into aching arms. When sufficiently recovered, I move cautiously up the vertical headwall, strangely isolated with Dave hidden in the darkness below, communication drowned by the sound of wind and water echoing from the impending walls opposite. I shout to Dave, hoping that he'll hear me, to get ready for a fall as I make hard final moves to gain the second belay. With feet smearing high I lunge upward, catch a ledge and claw my way to one of the most outstanding belays in the gorge - a rocky perch isolated from the ground below by space, with white walls of limestone spreading in all directions. I fasten myself to the rock and start to bring Dave up.

Dave arrives at the difficult moves below my belay and the fire in his eyes tells all.

'What do you think?' I ask sadistically.

Dave bunches up, and then explodes like an unleashed coiled spring, 'Fucking wild', he gasps, as his fingers lock onto the ledge. A broad grin spreads across his face.

We sort the gear into a semblance of order and Dave, eager to unravel the secrets above, begins to explore the intricacies of the third pitch.

The moves off the ledge are unprotected and the consequences of a mistake here could prove particularly uncomfortable as Dave would clatter down, hitting the ledge and then on past me to end up hanging in space. After a few tentative forays Dave commits himself and gains a bridging position in the slim groove above my head. Suddenly a foothold that he is smearing on explodes. I hunch instinctively, ready to absorb the full impact of Dave's free fall onto the belay. Miraculously he manages to stay in contact with the rock.

'Bloody hell Dave, are you OK?' I shout in concern.

Manic laughter is the only response that I get.

I shake my head in bewilderment remembering tales about his past exploits. I look up, 'Just take it steady Dave.' The comment is pathetically unnecessary, but it eases the tension. As I make the comment the rope begins to tug at my waist forcing me to pay it out, I smile.

After a few minutes Dave shouts down that he's at the top and the remaining rope quickly slithers up the groove. Even with the security of a rope from above, I find the moves leaving the ledge both difficult and exposed. With 150 feet of space below me, I appreciate the manic tones in Dave's laughter. In the groove the game of progress is superbly played, as stone dictates the movements of each hand and foot with choreographed precision. After about thirty feet of absorbing and superbly exposed bridging, I pull onto grassy nettle-covered ledges and scramble up to Dave, who is securely attached to a large ash. A gentle breeze blows through the tree causing the leaves to dance. The air tastes cool and fresh, the damp earth looks rich and fertile, the vegetation unnaturally green. Dave stands motionless beneath the tree, I look at the wrinkled lines spreading from the corners of his eyes and study the burning light emanating from within their depths. A smile touches the corners of my mouth. A grin breaks across Dave's face. I begin to chuckle. Dave laughs. The trees shake. The jackdaws scream. The wind begins to roar.

Chapter 1

Across the Threshold

The shadows where the Mewlips dwell
Are dark and wet as ink
And slow and softly rings their bell.
As in the slime you sink.
JRR Tolkien

I was born in 1960 in the mining town of Hemsworth, youngest of four brothers. My dad was a Polish exile who'd escaped war-torn Europe in 1939. His story was not typical. In 1938 he'd acquired some skill as a glider pilot and although Polish by descent, he was born in Germany. During the early rumblings of World War Two, he was attractive material in the eyes of the German conscription machine. When the inevitable call up papers arrived informing him that he was to join the Luftwaffe, my dad decided it was time to leave Poland.

An adventurous journey across Europe eventually led him to Gibraltar where, like many other exiles, he managed to secure safe passage to England. There, during the closing stages of the war, he joined the Polish Air Force and, thankfully for me, saw only brief active service as wireless operator and navigator aboard Wellington bombers. He was stationed in Lincolnshire and it was there that he met my mother who was serving with the Women's Land Army. They were married at the end of the war in 1945.

Hemsworth is located in the heart of the rich coal seams of West Yorkshire between Barnsley and Pontefract and it was there where my mother, eldest daughter in a mining family, had grown up in the 1930s. When the war finished, my parents returned to my mother's parental village of Hemsworth to start their life together.

My father was well-educated, and during his flight from Poland, he studied briefly at Grenoble in France where he continued to develop his natural talent for languages. He was also a practical man, skilled at working with his hands.

The obvious choice of work for men in post war Hemsworth was coal mining, but my father was astute enough to see the negative aspects of working down the mine. Looking for alternative employment, he was fortunate to get a steady job working as a mechanic and coach builder for a local bakery firm, building and maintaining their fleet of delivery vans.

Although my parents weren't poor, money was at a premium and my brothers and their friends, like most families, invented their own entertainment that generally involved games and adventures out and about. In the 1960s, Hemsworth and the surrounding villages of Kinsley, Brierley, Grimethorpe and Havercroft were all working mining communities, typified by row upon row of red brick terraces and council estates. Despite the heavy urban and industrial landscape the villages were interspersed with pockets of countryside. I grew up on a council estate in the town's west end, which overlooked the colliery in the neighbouring village of Fitzwilliam. A huge black spoil heap, known locally as the muck stack, dominated the village. This was our local mountain.

I had a happy childhood growing up in this environment, influenced heavily both by my parents and my elder brothers. From an early age I was taken on regular forays into the surrounding countryside, under the reluctant care of my elder brothers and their friends. Within walking distance of our house we had a number of areas that could provide plenty of adventure. To the west we had The Ings, which were an area of established woodland consisting of mature trees covering a gentle valley. A small stream flowed through valley, which eventually flattened out at its northern end to reveal an area of sedge and reed beds. It was great natural habitat for wildlife, an island of ancient countryside isolated in a red brick industrial landscape. It also provided great tree climbing and good 'bommy woodin', our local dialect for collecting bonfire wood. To the northeast we had Hagg Wood or 'Aggy' as we called it. Aggy was Hemsworth's version of the Everglades. Huge willow trees grew out of deep pools of rusty coloured water which had been polluted by red ochre and iron deposits from the colliery. Aggy bordered Hoyle Mill Dam, which had been built to hold the black waters pumped from the depths of the coal mine. The squat dam wall contained a small reservoir that was fed at one end by an evil stream of polluted water. The reservoir was known locally as Sally Walsh's Dam, reputedly christened after a despairing individual who drowned herself in the lake. Whether this was true or not, I never found out, but the Dam maintained its reputation as an unsavoury place throughout the '60s and '70s.

One of the gory attractions for us visiting the dam as kids was to see how many dead dogs we could see in the water along the dam wall. On each visit there were often two or three grisly corpses present. Some had met their watery murders in tied and weighted hessian sacks and could be seen through the murky water lying on the bottom of the lake. Others had simply had house bricks tied round their necks and their bloated carcasses could be seen bobbing in the scum on the surface. In the summer the stink would make me gag, but curiosity to see the gruesome spectacle would entice us to the dam wall. The nearby village of Kinsley was the home of the local dog track and we were told that these animals were most probably greyhounds that had outgrown their usefulness as racing dogs. Looking back, it seems unimaginable that people could perform such acts of cruelty, but the reality is that back then that is exactly what some individuals did to their unwanted animals. Their only form of recrimination, their own consciences.

To the south of our house, we had the Cow Mounts and a disused railway tunnel that stretched in inky blackness underground. The Cow Mounts were the spoil heaps from when the railway tunnel was excavated during the industrial revolution. The numerous heaps had the look of drumlins, glacial features that could have been left by the last ice age. They had now been reclaimed by nature and my memories recall a place of escapism, roly-polying down slopes of soft grass and creating other games simply to pass the time.

The Long Dark Tunnel, on the other hand, was a different kettle of fish. It had become disused in the 1950s and the tracks and sleepers had been removed. Each end of the tunnel was guarded by a deep cutting, which added to its sense of mystery and heightened the gloominess of the place. The tunnel itself was about a mile long and was curved, so when you stood at either end you just peered into blackness and literally no light could be seen at its other end. It was reputed that in the centre of the tunnel views of both pinprick entrances were lost entirely and there was a danger of getting completely disorientated. The terror of the place was magnified by local talk of floodwaters, roof collapses and side branches.

The Long Dark Tunnel, Aggy, the Dam, The Ings and the Muck Stack all provided adventures when I was growing up. I was never consciously aware of the lessons that these adventures were teaching me, but I am in no doubt that my early experiences growing up in the 1960s and early '70s had a profound impact on how my life would pan out.

We lived on St Helens Avenue. It consisted of twenty-six semi-detached council houses neatly arranged around an oval area of grass which was called The Patch. In the centre of The Patch was a circle of scorched earth, a year round remnant from the 5th of November, or 'Bommy night' as we called it. All the families on the avenue had kids of varying ages. The norm in those days was to have large families and the biggest clan on our avenue consisted of eleven kids. Despite the age differences, the kids would call round for each other to ensure a big turnout for whatever game was on offer.

A knock on the door would usually reveal the grubby unwashed face of the latest recruit. 'Is tha comin art lakin,' would be asked. This was local dialect for, 'Are you coming out to play.'

'Aye what kept thi', would be the simple response. All the kids would congregate on The Patch and play until they got injured in some way, or were called in by the shouts of their parents.

My least favourite game was football, simply because I had two left feet and was rubbish at it, but we played a whole host of fun, and sometimes sadistic games in which I was able to demonstrate a modicum of talent. British Bulldog was a classic favourite, but we also had Kick Off Can that was a form of hide and seek with a capture and release theme. Johnny Hop Across was a variation on British Bulldog. Hot Rice was a painful form of ball tig. Canon was a form of street cricket played with clothes pegs, a stick and a ball. Whilst Finger Thumb Dumb or Lot was a form of Leap Frog and High Jump combined with a guessing game. Some were day games and some were more suited to after dark. We often thought that we had invented these games, but in reality I am sure that many had ancient roots and had been handed down from generation to generation.

It seemed completely natural to have plenty of freedom to roam around the neighbourhood even from an early age. The threat from predatory adults was still a concern in the minds of our parents however, even in the 1960s. We were constantly warned, 'Never to go off with strangers', and, 'Never accept lifts from people that you don't know even if they offer you sweets'. There was even talk of a 'strange couple of brothers' who lived on one of the terraced streets near us. Despite this we were always off out and about without too much concern and I was usually in the care of some of the older boys.

I started venturing further afield from the age of about six or seven usually in the company of my older brother Nigel and his friends. They were all four years older than me and consequently much bigger. Most importantly their wellington boots were much taller than my own. Much of our outdoor adventuring had seasonal governance. Spring for example, would involve trips to the 'newt pond' to search for aforesaid newts, or to collect frog spawn. The newt pond was a stagnant extension of the swamps that spewed out of Hagg Wood. The circumference of the pond was surrounded by a thick phalanx of bullrushes, but there was an area of clear water towards the centre of the pond and this was where the frogs liked to spawn.

In these early years I was always accused of 'tagging along' by the older boys, so their trips abroad usually had some form of plan to put me off. I recall one occasion when we made our way down to the newt pond. The older boys were taking particular delight in talking about all the foul things that lived in it. I had a vivid imagination and their talk of Horse Leeches and Water Scorpions and the like, would conjure up lots of creepy imagery in my head. I'd also got memories of the dead dogs rotting in Sally Walsh's Dam.

Running across the middle of the pond was an old boundary fence. The posts of the fence were remarkably solid, but the rungs were of varying quality. Some were missing and some were submerged beneath the water. The fence provided our access to the frog spawning grounds in the middle of the pond. The older boys climbed onto the fence at the water's edge and carefully moved out toward the centre of the pond with me in tow. As we slowly made our way through the bullrushes, traversing the rungs of the fence we had to negotiate one particularly rotten section. One of the lads, who was bringing up the rear, suddenly let out a yell as the rung he was standing on broke under his weight. This put an end to any form of retreat, so on we pressed, all the time the murky water inching up our wellingtons. This was okay for my brother and his friends, happy in the knowledge that their feet would remain nice and dry in their tall boots. For me, however, all I could do was look on with an increasing sense of foreboding as I recognised my own fate. Inevitably the dreaded happened and the horrid waters gurgled into my boots much to the mirth and merriment of the others, their master plan complete. All that was left for me was an uncomfortable, stinking squelch home to a final scolding from my mother for getting into such a mess.

When I was growing up in the 1960s, the Second World War never seemed far away, even though it had finished twenty odd years previously. My dad's old Polish flying mates often dropped in and their conversations would inevitably drift into exploits of derring-do in the skies over Europe. Eurek was a bomber pilot in the same squadron as my dad, and like my dad, he was a navigator and wireless operator in Wellington bombers; whilst Eddie was the real hot shot, being a fighter pilot who, during the war years, had tried to impress the women by 'buzzing' the terraced streets of Hemsworth. As well as the parental connection with the war, my two eldest brothers, Leon and Brian, had been born immediately after the war and their formative years had been heavily influenced by its aftermath, growing up in a working class community clawing its way out of post war poverty. The tales and adventurous games that were handed down from the older kids to the younger ones, certainly rubbed off on us in the way that we created and sought out our own entertainment.

War games were a natural way of keeping entertained. Even in the 1960s army surplus equipment was still abundant and we would use this to make the games appear more authentic. We used hardened clods of earth, which we called muck bombs, as improvised grenades. Muck bombs were used to inflict real damage on each other, and also looked good as they exploded in a cloud of grey dust when they hit anything hard. Full-blown muck bomb fights often led to someone or other being injured. Injury seemed to be a natural part of most games. I even remember one occasion where my brother and his mate wanted to test the effectiveness of a trooper's helmet. One of the lads placed a steel British Army helmet neatly on his head. He then purposefully directed my brother to pick up a shovel and hit him over the head with it. My brother followed the instruction precisely and levelled a fine blow directly on top of his mate's head, as the blow struck the lad crumpled to the ground unconscious. What they had failed to take into account in their enthusiasm was that all the helmet's internal padding and webbing had been removed. He might as well have been struck straight on the skull. My brother slapped him around the face to bring him round and they continued the game with nothing worse than one of them suffering mild concussion.

During the '60s the Vietnam War was in full swing and war reports from Vietnam were beamed straight into our house via the television news. Nigel paid particular attention, as rea' combat footage taken in Vietnam would flicker across the black and white TV screen. These reports fuelled his imagination and trips into the depths of 'Aggy' would turn into hazardous missions into the deepest jungles of Vietnam. Prior to a mission, the older boys would equip themselves with 'Bowie Knives', and we'd collect a hatchet from the coal store. We'd then don our wellingtons and head out to Hagg Wood. First we'd find a fallen willow in the swamps. These trees were a good source of sprouting suckers, straight branches that grew out from the main trunk. We'd each select a good looking stem and then spend half an hour or so, fashioning a weapon of choice, usually a spear that could double up as a machine gun and bayonet. The mission would then continue through the maze of trees, streams and ochre coloured swamps, in search of the imaginary Vietcong. The command would then come from the platoon leader, 'Mark, it's your turn to take the point.'

My brother had learned this American GI speak from the TV news reports. Taking the point meant that someone had to lead the column. They were usually the first person to encounter hostile fire, or other evil booby traps, often with dire personal consequences. On this occasion, as the command was called and the boys in front parted to let me take the point, a particularly stagnant-looking pool was revealed. 'There's probably Horse Leeches in there so be careful,' reassured the others.

With sharpened sticks prodding in my back, I was ushered forward into the pool. About halfway across the inevitable happened. Icy, evil smelling water gurgled into my wellingtons, and as I stumbled forward, the thick black mud beneath sucked at my boots. I emerged onto the far bank in stocking feet, soaked to the skin and in floods of tears, with my boots still stuck in the mud in the swamp behind. The others rolled around in laughter. I endured the rest of the day in abject misery, and although this was typical of a trip out with my brother and his friends, it never stopped me from wanting to tag along next time.

By the time I was eight, my eldest brother had a job as an electrician down the pit and Brian, much to my dad's objections, had joined the Paratroopers. The financial burden on my parents of bringing up four dependant children diminished as the two eldest siblings flew the nest. Whilst being far from well off, we had everything we needed. Good food supplemented by fresh vegetables, chickens and rabbits, grown and reared on our allotment. We had clothes on our backs, a car, a TV, and most importantly of all, the luxury of a regular family summer holiday.

When my dad left Poland in 1939, he'd continued his language and philosophy studies for a brief period at Grenoble University before being forced to make his escape from mainland Europe to England. He understood the value of education and had been sorely disappointed when Brian had rejected a place at university for a career with the Army. Not only this, in my dad's eyes Brian's misguided choice of career was compounded by the fact that he had opted to join the Army's elite fighting force as a private, rather than taking an officer's commission. My father was determined that Nigel and I would make the most of our education and whilst mum and dad left the schools to do their bit, at home they actively encouraged us, in every way they could, to pursue and broaden our interests.

Dad had cross-cultural knowledge that set him apart from the parents of our neighbours and he retained an inherent desire to travel. My dad's first trip back to his homeland came in 1962 and my own first visit to Poland came two years later, in the summer of 1964. The biggest pull for my father was to reunite with his family, many of whom had survived the war. Making the long journey through England, Holland, into West Germany and then crossing the Iron Curtain into East Germany left me with lasting memories. In those days the Cold War was still in its icy freeze and the border crossings from West to East Germany and then from East Germany to Poland were still heavily guarded with barbed wire, machine gun posts and armed troops. All this reinforced in my own mind that the last war didn't seem to be so distant. Even though my dad had gone through the long and bureaucratic process to obtain all relevant visas and travel documents, there was always the question that once in Poland, would he be allowed to leave.

Seeing my father communicating with different people first in English, then French, then German, then Polish and then mixing all four languages together was fascinating. The smell of pine resin as we travelled through forested landscapes was new and evocative. The drumming of the wheels of our car as we travelled across East Germany on Hitler's concrete autobahns was accompanied by lessons in history from my dad. We made this pilgrimage again in 1968 and 1974. In Poland, I was acquainted with new uncles, aunts and cousins. I experienced new customs and tasted alien foods. I explored the many museums of Torun, my dad's birthplace, and visited the country's capital, Warsaw. I watched dancing bears in the High Tatra and explored the salt mines of Krakow. It was a world of colour, excitement and exploration. There were always questions to be asked, history lessons to be learned and new experiences to be had. When back home playing around the smoky streets of Hemsworth, I felt I had to put on an act so I didn't alienate myself from the rest of the group, but inside I recognised that I was a bit different from my mates.

Our excursions into the haunts around Hemsworth didn't always start as adventures, although some form of thrill seeking would invariably creep in. One of the seasonal pastimes that was handed down was bird nesting and egg collecting. Even in the '60s, laws had been passed making this activity illegal. West Yorkshire, however, appeared to be stuck in some sort of time warp and people were either oblivious of such laws or simply chose to ignore them. My introduction to bird nesting from some of the boys was a crude hit and miss affair. We would walk along the privet hedges that were commonly grown as boundaries between gardens and then simply burrow our heads into the hedge to see what we could find. Surprisingly, this activity would often yield a Blackbird, Song Thrush or Hedge Sparrow's nest. The motive behind the activity of bird nesting varied considerably between the different gangs of boys. Some were genuinely intent on amassing collections of eggs of different bird species. Some wanted to collect the nests complete with their full clutch of eggs. Others, however, had the purely malicious intent of destroying the nest for destruction's sake alone. They called this pastime ragging. Personally, I deplored this habit and my efforts to dissuade, or educate those who practised it led to fights, bloody noses and black eyes on a number of occasions. As an egg collector, I would remove just one egg from a nest and would rationalise my crime with the logic that the remaining chicks would have more food and stand a better chance of survival. It was during this period that I graduated from the company of Nigel and his friends, and struck up with a group of similar aged peers. It was with this group that I continued roaming the local haunts and our search for eggs led us even further afield. Rather than employing crude hit and miss techniques to identify nest sites, I started observing the behaviour of the birds themselves. I read books to learn about their preferred habitats and subliminally, I gained a fascinating insight into the life of birds.

The Ings contained huge beech, birch and ash trees that I would scale to reach crows, jays or mistle thrush nests. Old industrial or farm buildings provided good nesting habitat for starlings, pigeons and owls. On these excursions I perfected the art of climbing, or rather 'scrimming' up cast iron drainpipes that would give access to the upper reaches of the buildings. By far the most daunting and risky pursuit, however, was that of scaling electricity pylons. These metal giants were the favoured nesting places of Kestrels. Kestrels seemed clever in their choice of nest site, which they invariably located at the end of the arm, very close to the electricity cables themselves.

At first glance climbing a pylon appeared to be a fairly straightforward affair, after all there were purpose built rungs running up the leg of the pylon, put there for the access workers. In reality, climbing a pylon was a bit more complicated and success depended on overcoming a number of challenges or cruxes. The first one was making sure that the chosen pylon was out of view of any prying eyes. There were plenty of signs on and around the pylons stating 'Trespassers Will Be Prosecuted'. I was convinced that being prosecuted amounted to something similar to being electrocuted and wanted to avoid being caught at all costs. The second crux was overcoming an overhanging barrier of barbed wire at twenty feet. The third was dealing with the dizzying exposure as you ascended skyward. The fourth was leaving the security of the climbing rungs on the leg of the pylon and inching out across one of the struts making up the arm of the pylon. The fifth was avoiding getting electrocuted and the final crux was escaping undetected and avoiding the horrible fate of being prosecuted.

I can't remember the exact date, but it would have been around 1970 when a group of us gathered at the base of our identified Kestrel nest site. The nest was on the lowest arm but still about sixty feet above the ground. This was going to be our first assault on a pylon. I enjoyed climbing, but looking up at this monster certainly stimulated lots of self-doubt. I negotiated the barbed wire overhang with the help of a denim jacket cast over the wire thorns. A determined approach with eyes focused on the metal rungs got me up the leg of the pylon and level with lower arm. The next bit of the climb involved lying on one of the struts of the arm and employing a commando-like technique used for climbing ropes slung across rivers. As soon as I adopted this pose, the exposure hit me. I was looking straight down into the faces of my mates far below and I froze, but not only that, I suddenly felt that I was being pulled from the strut to which I clung. I had to shut my eyes tight to block out the sensation of falling and suppress the panic. I focused on the shouts of encouragement coming from below. There was no way that I could go any further and indeed it took all my will and concentration to reverse the route and gain the sanctuary of the ground. About a month later we heard news that a lad we knew from a rival gang had fallen to his death from the very same pylon trying to collect a kestrel chick. We knew the lad pretty well; he'd been crazy about the film *Kes* and dreamed of owning and training a young falcon. I never went near another pylon after that.

My hobby of egg collecting evolved into a real interest in bird behaviour. I gave up egg collecting and deterred others from doing the same. I had started what would become a life long interest in bird watching. I joined the British Trust for Ornithology and was involved in a number of national bird surveys and conservation programmes. My interest in birds progressed to a much wider interest in natural history and a passion for the environment, which endures with me today. It had been a small journey of self discovery. Looking back it is clear that I had formulated some personal beliefs about what was right and wrong and my behaviour changed in response.

I started primary school in 1964 and really enjoyed the first three years. The teachers were both kind and they made the lessons interesting. When I was seven some building work at school meant that our classroom had to be closed. This meant that our year group, which was known as Junior One, was re-housed in the schoolroom at our neighbouring Roman Catholic church. The school room was on the bottom floor below the chapel itself. It was a dingy room cluttered with a combination of church and school furniture. It had a fusty smell tinged with the scent of incense, which filtered down from the chapel above. When we moved to the schoolroom we also fell under the governance of our new teacher. We learned from older pupils that Mrs Walker had a fearsome reputation. She was said to be a strict disciplinarian who dealt out all sorts of punishments, which were often completely disproportionate to any childhood misdemeanour. I quickly learned that the teacher was far worse than any rumours suggested.

Away from the eyes of the rest of the school, she held dominion over us with a regime of psychological bullying and physical violence. She looked like a fat sparrow with a mop of curly black hair shot with flecks of grey. Her podgy face was adorned with flamboyant spectacles and these accentuated her piercing stare. She sat behind a large desk, which was raised on a podium above us, increasing her sense of power and domination. In her desk drawers she had an assortment of missiles. These would be hurled with violent precision at unsuspecting victims if she deemed they were not paying sufficient attention. Her favourite ammunition were sticks of chalk, or the board rubber, but on vicious occasions she would also use a leather bound Rounders ball. Mrs Walker seemed to delight in humiliating individuals in front of the class. One of my particular weak points was mental arithmetic. I dreaded arithmetic lessons with Mrs Walker to such an extent, that I would sometimes be physically sick on my walk into school in anticipation. The lesson would start with the teacher chalking a series of sums on the blackboard. An individual would then be called out to the front of the class and instructed to work out the sums and write the answers on the blackboard. A slow response, or incorrect answer was rewarded with a swift slap. Girls were slapped across the legs and boys were slapped across the face. If the lesson was simple addition or multiplication, I might get away without any punishment, but if it was about subtraction or long division, I would often receive three or four slaps across the face before being allowed to return to my desk. My life in Junior One became increasingly unhappy and to escape the bullying of this harridan, I started playing truant.

Playing truant wasn't easy, boredom could quickly set in and it could get pretty lonely trying to pass a long day alone. Fortunately, a couple of my friends and classmates were as unhappy as I, so we conspired together during school breaks and carefully planned our days off. We were aware that the truant officer patrolled the streets looking for kids bunking off school, so to avoid being detected we used to take a route to school that wouldn't arouse suspicion. Our route took us through the Scotch Estate, which was a natural way to school for a lot of kids, but by taking a concealed short cut we could gain the disused railway cutting that led to the Cow Mounts. The Cow Mounts were inaccessible by road and provided us with a safe haven away from prying eyes. The mounts were a steep array of hillocks separated by V-shaped valleys and we used this terrain to invent various games and forms of entertainment. It was during this period playing truant at the Cow Mounts that curiosity got the better of us and found us standing before the huge circular entrance of the long dark tunnel.

The disused railway tunnel was said to stretch for nearly a mile underground, eventually emerging near the neighbouring village of Brierley. Peering into the blackness we could make out its circular walls lined with smooth black brick. Light penetrated into the gloom for about fifty yards or so, before everything was consumed by total darkness. The only sound emanating from within was the occasional 'plink' of a water droplet falling into a pool. I can't remember who took the first step, but soon all three of us were cautiously moving into the tunnel and stumbling along. As we progressed the light faded. We were torch-less, so we had to move to the side of the tunnel and use the wall to guide us. The entrance slowly diminished in size as we moved further into the depths and although it was still a comforting sight in the distance, it provided no useful light for our eyes. As we felt our way along the wall like blind men, one of the lads who was in the lead let out a yell, he'd lost contact with the wall. So the rumour of side passages in the tunnel was correct. We paused for a quick 'pow wow' to decide on a course of action. On feeling the wall it was obvious that it turned at ninety degrees to the main wall. We mused on the pros and cons of following this side branch. Where would it lead? We might get totally disorientated, lost, or even fall into some unseen pit. We reasoned that if the rumour of side branches were true, then the person that had circulated it must have got back out of the tunnel. We opted to press on. I took the lead, my hand trailing against the wall of the side branch, but after only a few steps my face smacked into another brick wall with a painful thud. When I recovered from this unexpected shock, I carefully followed the wall round. After a few feet the wall turned at right angles once again, it became immediately obvious that the side branch was in fact a small alcove built into the wall of the tunnel. So much for rumours we laughed.

As we continued with renewed confidence, it became apparent that these alcoves had been built at regular intervals throughout the tunnel, but each time we encountered one in the eerie darkness, our imaginations started racing, wondering what unexpected horror we might find lying within. After about half an hour, the pinprick of light that defined the tunnel's entrance had vanished from view. The, plink, plink, plink of dripping water had taken on the sound of a trickling tap and there was no sign of any exit from the claustrophobic blackness.

We pressed on until icy water spilling into our shoes signified that we'd encountered an underground pool. We stopped for another 'pow wow'. We had lost sight of both tunnel entrances, so we reasoned that we must be somewhere near its middle. We already had wet feet, so we continued to probe the pool of water with our feet, feeling along the tunnel wall with our hands and praying that we wouldn't be plunged up to our necks by falling into an unseen, water-filled hole. Thankfully, the water maintained its depth at ankle level and before long a pinprick of light could be seen in the distance, signalling the Brierley end of the tunnel.

We hurried along now and eventually emerged from the gloom into a steep railway cutting. It differed from the Hemsworth entrance. Rather than being formed by steep wooded slopes, the Brierley cutting looked like a U-shaped canyon with steep walls of blocky sandstone and these walls appeared to continue for a considerable distance. We were reluctant to retrace our steps, so we found an area of the cliff that looked to be climbable and scrambled our way out of the confines of the cutting. We made our way back home overland, chatting excitedly about our experience. Inevitably our thoughts turned to the teacher and tomorrow's lessons and this brought us all back down to earth with a gut wrenching bump. I arrived home in a subdued mood. I was frightened of Mrs Walker. I hated the truancy. I felt guilty about telling lies and the way I was deceiving my parents. I was scared, depressed and felt trapped.

Things came to a head in the spring of 1968. I can't recall much about the events. I remember kicking a football around in the churchyard outside the schoolroom. It must have been morning break and I recall that it was a sunny day. The next thing I remember was being dropped off at my house by a police car at about 6 o'clock that same evening. There appeared to be masses of fuss and commotion going on with people milling about. Two teachers arrived at our house from school. When they saw me, smiles illuminated their faces and they put their arms around me, giving me hugs and saying how relieved they were to see me. I was completely baffled by all the fuss. I later learned that no one had seen me disappear from school. When I didn't return to class the teacher had notified the headmaster, who in turn had contacted my mum to see if I had returned home. When I still couldn't be found by late afternoon, everyone started to fear something sinister had happened and the police were notified. Eventually, I was spotted and picked up by the police and returned home in their Panda car. Much to the relief of the school and my parents, nothing untoward had happened, I had simply bolted from school unable to endure the repressive regime anymore. Rather than punishing my behaviour, everyone wanted to know why I had, in their eyes, acted so out of character. I can't remember much about what followed, but my parents and the teachers must have questioned me at length, so they could understand what had forced me to act so irrationally.

After that day, school life changed completely. We were taught by a new supply teacher for the last few weeks of our stay at the schoolroom and compared to the previous months, the time rocketed past. We moved back to the main school as soon as the building work was completed and the new classroom appeared modern and bright, with the smell of fresh paint.

In 1969 something happened that transcended our own adventurous exploits and turned into something with sinister undercurrents. It was a normal Sunday and one of my brother's friends had come over from the neighbouring village of Cudworth. It was the first time he had been over to Hemsworth and Nigel thought it would be a good idea to show him round one of our local haunts. They decided on a visit to the Dam with a walk back through Aggy and I opted to join them. We took a direct route that followed a well-marked footpath and farm track and arrived at the Dam wall. As was typical, we had the place to ourselves and after messing about round the dilapidated sluice gate buildings that were located at the end of the dam wall, we decided it was time to make our way along the bank of the reservoir towards the woods. It was at this point that we noticed the figure of a man about a hundred yards away walking slowly towards us. I don't know why, but the look of the man made us all feel ill at ease. He was walking along a raised bank about twenty yards from the lake shore and to try and avoid crossing paths with him, we took an ill-defined route through boggy ground below the bank. As we passed each other, he paused looking us up and down, 'Weer's tha from?' he called in sly sounding voice.

'Hemsworth,' we replied.

'Wot's tha think tha's doin?' he enquired.

'Going for a walk,' we said.

'Tha shunt be gooin that way, them woods is private,' he informed us with a threatening tone in his voice.

The situation didn't feel good at all. Nigel broke the deadlock, 'Come on, let's get going.'

We started forward, quickening the pace a little. The man just stood his ground at first, but after a few minutes looking back we noticed that he appeared to be following us. At the top end of the lake we had to cross the stream to gain access to the woods, but we knew our way through Aggy better than anyone. The stream was about six feet wide and gushed through a channel which was about six feet deep. The older boys could cross the stream by taking a running jump, but I always struggled to make the top of the far bank. My jump usually landed me above the water line, but I often ended up in the channel itself, having to scramble up and avoid slipping back into the water.

Looking back over our shoulders revealed that the stranger had closed the distance between us. 'Come on,' Nigel urged and broke into jog. Unnervingly we saw the man doing the same. This confirmed our fears, it seemed that our pursuer definitely had some ill intent. Unable to hide our panic, we broke into a full-blown run, 'Make for the stream. We can lose him in Aggy,' Nigel shouted. My brother and his friend were much faster than I and were soon fifty yards in front of me. Glancing back I could see the man closing in. Ahead I saw Nigel, then his friend leaping across the stream and then looking back from the far bank before disappearing into the trees. Panting, I reached the stream, but as I made my run up to the leap I hesitated and in that moment the man pounced. He dragged me into a nearby reed bed and pinned me down. I was lying face down and he was lying on top of me.

'If tha ses owt, tha's dead,' he breathed in my ear. It was then that I noticed he had a knife in his hand. I said nothing.

He kept me pinned down, lying on top of me breathing in my ear. After a few minutes he removed the watch that I was wearing on my wrist.

'If tha ses owt to anybody, I'll find thee and kill thee,' with these words he was gone. I continued to lie there not daring to move, but after what seemed like an age, I got to my feet and looked around. The man was nowhere to be seen. Adrenaline saw me over the stream and sprinting through Aggy, shouting for the other two at the top of my voice. Eventually I caught up with them and we made our way back to our house. At home I recounted the tale to my mother and it was decided that incident was serious enough to be reported to the police.

At the police station two officers sat me down and got me to give a detailed account of everything I could remember about the incident. One officer kept clarifying certain points, 'So the man said he was going to kill you?'

'Yes,' I replied.

'And the man had a knife?' he asked.

'Yes.'

'Other than lying on top of you, did he touch you in any other sort of way?'

'No,' I replied.

'Did he hurt you?'

'No.'

'Would you recognise him if you saw him again?' he asked.

'I think so.'

As one officer clarified various points, the other officer wrote everything down. After about two hours I was given the account to read.

'Do you agree that this statement is a true and accurate account of what happened to you today?' the officer asked. I agreed that it was and was then asked to sign the document.

'Right, now for the next bit,' said one of the officers, 'you'll like this, it's like doing a jigsaw puzzle. It's called Identikit.'

The officer got some boxes out, which contained pictures of various head and facial parts. I was informed that with the Identikit, we could build up a picture of what the man looked like.

'Right what was the man's hair like,' asked the officer. I selected the best fit.

After half an hour we had constructed a face that approximated that of my assailant. One of the police officers drove me back home and accompanied me into the house.

'I think it might be worth picking Mark up tomorrow and driving round for a couple of hours. We think the man is probably local and if Mark happened to recognise him we'd have an open and shut case. Can we have your permission to let Mark help us?' He asked my mother.

'Of course,' she replied.

The police officer picked me up the following morning and we started patrolling the streets. We drove from Hemsworth and headed for Kinsley, which was closer to the Dam than Hemsworth. On entering Kinsley, we took a right turn into an area of rough looking terraces and to my disbelief I saw my attacker slipping into the door of one of the houses.

'That's him!' I said to the officer.

'Are you sure?' he asked.

'Definitely.'

'Right come with me,' the officer ordered. He knocked on the door and elderly woman opened up. 'Is your son at home?' asked the officer.

'No, he's just slipped out of the back door,' answered the woman.

'Can we come in?' the officer asked. The woman nodded and we were led into the living room, it was rather dingy and had an unpleasant odour. An elderly man was standing in front of the fireplace. Above the fireplace was a large oval mirror with filigreed edges and adorning the filigree were wrist watches. I counted about thirty. '

Can you see your watch?' asked the officer. I pointed up to where my black army style wristwatch was hanging on the mirror.

'Your son took this watch by force from this lad yesterday and we think that he's done far worse. We're going to have to take him in. When he returns tell him to stay at home. We'll be back to pick him up this afternoon,' the officer informed the couple.

At the time I thought it was miraculous that we'd caught our man so quickly. Looking back, I suspect that the police probably had some corroborating intelligence about my attacker and so it was no coincidence that we targeted railway terrace in Kinsley. So what of the fate of my attacker? I know he did time, but what he was charged with I never found out. About eight years later, I was standing in our garden at St Helens Avenue, when a man walked past. I went instantly cold and I'm sure the blood drained from my face when I saw him. He looked straight at me, but there appeared to be no sense of recognition at all on his part and he walked on. He then paused momentarily and looked back as if in thought. I made the point of staring directly into his eyes and advanced towards the fence in his direction. He turned and walked briskly on. I never saw him again, but I do speculate that it was probably the like's of him who used to drown the dogs in Sally Walsh's Dam.

It's difficult to summarise in a few paragraphs what life was like growing up in the '60s in a Yorkshire red brick mining community. Having an unusual surname set me apart from other kids from the start. The Continental influence of my father added a unique slant to my experiences, broadening my general outlook and exposing me to new geographical horizons. Clearly there were dangers lurking out there in the community then, as there are today, yet the cultural mindset was less risk averse then, than it is now. There was certainly more sense of community and less sense of fear. Kids were granted much more freedom, both physical and mental, but with this came the challenge of negotiating a minefield of potential hazards. Personally I am eternally grateful for this, because I look back and recognise that what I was given was the power to learn. Not only that, I think that some of my childhood experiences set sparks of excitement burning in my imagination that would always keep personal complacency at bay.

Growing up in West Yorkshire suburbia, I had plenty of opportunity for exciting play, climbing trees and scaling buildings, yet I was oblivious that people climbed rocks purely for pleasure and adventure. It wasn't until my parents started taking us on camping trips to the Lake District that I became aware of mountains and mountain climbing and it wouldn't be until the late '70s that I would take my first fateful steps into the world of rock climbing.

Back in 1966 I was just six years old, and in the Llanberis Pass in North Wales, a young climber called Dave Barton was carving out a little bit of climbing history of his own. Dave had hitched down to North Wales from his home in Lancashire and awaited the arrival of his mates beneath the spectacular crag called Dinas y Gromlech. The Gromlech is one of the Pass's showpiece crags, with vertical black walls a hundred and twenty feet high. In 1966 this crag hosted some of the best hard routes in the country and Dave had come to sample some of these. When his friends failed to turn up on what was probably a historic, but certainly unsung day, Dave made his way up to the Gromlech without rope or partner and proceeded to solo a climb called *Cemetery Gates*. He enjoyed the experience so much that he returned to the base of the crag and soloed one of the country's most famous climbs, *Cenotaph Corner*. This was the first time that the *Corner* had been soloed and was all the more remarkable in that it was Dave's first visit to North Wales. Dave Barton would continue to excel in climbing for many years to come with some fine achievements. In the future my own destiny would converge with Dave's and we would enjoy many fine adventures together even pioneering some fine new rock climbs of our own.

Chapter 2

Lessons in Luck

We start with a state of unconscious incompetence
Then we move to a state of conscious incompetence
Then sometimes gain a state of conscious competence
If we're diligent in pursuit of our goals and have a bit of luck
we might be fortunate enough to experience
a state of unconscious competence.
A personal perspective on the stages of learning.

My own introduction to rock-climbing was unplanned. Initially climbing was like the subtext to a more ambitious plot, but over time this subtext actually became the very narrative of my life. I was no stranger to the great outdoors, throughout my early childhood family holidays were spent camping and caravanning in some of the wilder parts of the UK. These early experiences definitely created an appetite for exploration and at secondary school I got a bunch of mates interested in hill-walking. In our early teens we would go off camping and exploring the surrounding countryside and this progressed naturally into more serious hiking trips.

I recall one of our early camping trips in 1973. Four of us had arranged a week's camping in the Yorkshire Dales, but at the last minute two of the lads cried off, which left Adrian Ledgway and me. I hardly knew Ledge, he was in a different form, but we agreed to go anyway. Ledge's dad dropped us off at Barden Tower in Wharfedale and we pitched our old canvas scout tent by the river at Barden Bridge. The tent was an old single skin variety with two wooden tent poles and a lace up door. We used a layer of polythene as an improvised ground sheet and simply laid our nylon sleeping bags on this. We did our best to peg the walls of the tent to the ground, but the wind still blew through. It was March and during the nights, temperatures fell dramatically. In the morning the inside of the tent would be coated in ice. We spent the nights drifting in and out of shivering sleep, but we were blessed with sunny spring days which we spent exploring our surroundings.

Downstream from where we were camped the waters of the River Wharfe were funnelled into a narrow rocky channel called the Strid. Legend had it that The Boy of Egremont had drowned there in 1128 whilst trying to jump the gorge. His grieving mother, Alice de Rumilly, had founded the nearby Bolton Abbey as a result. The Strid is an impressive feature, as the entire river is forced through a rocky narrow channel about six feet wide.

As Ledge and I peered into the depths of the clear waters we couldn't see the bottom, but we could see that the rocky channel was severely undercut beneath our feet. It was easy to imagine how you could become trapped and drown if you were unfortunate enough to fall in. This proved too much of a temptation for Ledge. 'Come on, I think we can jump this,' he said excitedly. I wasn't so sure, we were only thirteen and the pale face of a drowned Boy of Egremont kept materialising in my head. Ledge picked his spot and leapt across. 'Come on, it's easy,' he encouraged. I followed. We spent the rest of the day jumping back and forth across the Strid each time looking for more challenging jumps. It was basic thrill seeking, but it was all wrapped up with challenge and risk. It gave us a real buzz. That trip cemented a lifetime's friendship between Ledge and me. From that point on school holidays were occupied with camping and hiking trips and the more we did, the more ambitious we became. Whether it was exploring and scrambling around Gordale Scar in Yorkshire or negotiating Striding Edge as we climbed Helvellyn in the Lake District, we were always keen to seek out some method of challenging entertainment. Simple camping trips progressed into hiking expeditions with specific objectives. In this way we explored the Lakeland peaks and the Highlands of Scotland, sometimes covering a hundred miles in a week, always carrying all our kit.

In 1978 Ledge and I finished school and went to our respective universities, but we still got together during summer holidays for increasingly ambitious hiking trips. My brother Nigel had got a job as a teacher and joined us during his school vacations. It was one of these trips which would act as the catalyst and turn me into a climbing lifer.

In 1979 my brother sowed the germ of an idea by suggesting we should try exploring somewhere in the Arctic Circle and after considering a number of options, we decided on the Jotunheimen mountain range of Norway, not exactly the Arctic Circle, but it was glaciated and that held a romantic notion of exploration. As we researched the region and started to plan the trip, the idea of climbing Norway's two highest peaks Galdhøpiggen and Glittertind began to take shape. We recognised that if we were going to be successful, we'd have to cross glaciers and in all likelihood might have to do some technical rock and ice climbing. We'd done plenty of scrambling in the Lakes and Scotland, but other than what we'd read in books, none of us really knew anything about 'proper climbing'.

Over the years we'd learned all we knew about camp craft, navigation, equipment and outdoor survival either by reading up on it, or through direct experience. We'd never had a teacher and it seemed natural to adopt the same approach when it came to rock-climbing. I purchased an instruction manual called, *Advanced Rockcraft* by Royal Robbins, and set about digesting its contents.

Royal Robbins was a legendary American rock-climber who'd pioneered major rock climbs in Yosemite National Park and had been pivotal in the evolution and advancement of rock-climbing through the 1950s and 1960s. His book appeared to contain all the information that we would need to learn how to rock-climb. It was illustrated with neat drawings and funny cartoons that somehow made the required skills all the more accessible. As well as providing technical instruction, Robbins also gave personal insights into the rights and wrongs in rock-climbing. Not just about skill and technique, but deeper stuff about personal codes of conduct and ethics. It seemed that Robbins believed that there were a whole array of unwritten rules surrounding rock-climbing. It wasn't just about getting up a piece of rock; it was also about how a person got up it. Reading between the lines, I got the impression of a man who somehow felt he'd had gained some sort of greater personal insight from his life in the vertical.

Robbins's book suggested that if we were going to learn to climb properly, we'd need a bit of kit. So we made a visit to our local outdoor gear supplier, Crossley Tordoffs in Pontefract. Trevor Tordoff was a highly enthusiastic proprietor, who seemed to have a wealth of knowledge about mountaineering, skiing, caving and most other outdoor activities. He'd organised a trip to the Himalaya's, so we really respected his wisdom. He could also talk the hind leg off a donkey.

'So, you're going to Norway are you lads?' he asked with a knowing look. He then added, angling for a sale, 'You'll need a rope if you're thinking about glacier crossing.'

'Yeah, that's what we've come for,' we said.

'This should do the trick. Lovely new 9mm made by Mammut. I can do this for thirty-five quid,' he said, showing us the rope.

'That sounds OK we'll take one.'

'What sort of tents are you taking?' Trevor continued.

'We've got a Millets three-man tent,' we proudly reported.

'Ooh that won't be strong enough,' he warned, 'I've got some Vango Force Tens that I could do a special deal on.'

We didn't bite.

'So you might be doing some rock-climbing as well?' he asked. He then produced a handful of wire slung chocks. 'You'll need some of these Hexcentrics then.' These were small aluminium devices that could be wedged into cracks in the rock. When used with a karabiner they could form a running belay, or runner. These runners could reduce the risk of falling long distances, but it demanded knowledge, skill and experience to use these devices effectively. Being polite, but eager to get away, I pointed to the chocks, 'I'll take four of those.' He handed over four, number four Hexcentrics, slung on short wire swages.

'We'll think about the tents,' we told him and paid the bill and we were quickly out of the door. With our newly acquired gear, Nigel and I set off to learn how to rock-climb. It all sounds a bit 'Boys Own', but that's exactly how it was.

I was very familiar with the Yorkshire Dales from our many hiking trips and recalled an area above Settle that, from memory, offered plenty of rock-climbing scope. Attermire Scar was an extensive series of limestone buttresses. The main buttress looked impressive, rising to a height of about one hundred feet, but for our first climb we gravitated to a smaller barrel-shaped buttress below the main crag. We geared up at the base with climbing belts, four number four Hexcentrics and our blue 9mm Mammut climbing rope. Nigel and I were both wearing sturdy walking boots. The buttress was steep but was featured with cracks and flakes and looked climbable. I'd studied *Advanced Rockcraft* and felt sufficiently confident in how to use the rope and place the chocks to protect a fall. I tied the rope into my climbing belt, and with Nigel belaying me in traditional style with the rope round his back I set off up a short corner. At the top of the corner I jammed one of the aluminium chocks into a crack and clipped the rope into a karabiner which was attached to the short wire swage. The rock above was steep and I couldn't find any useful holds to facilitate further upward progress. Looking around, I spied some footholds out towards the left and so I followed these. At the end of the traverse, I found another crack which took another chock. A series of flakes led up and left, so I followed these. As I made it to the top of the cliff the tension of the rope on the short wire swages caused the two chock runners to pull out of the cracks and slip down the rope to Nigel at the base of the crag. So much for my rock-climbing knowhow. I tied myself to a large boulder and used a waist belay to protect Nigel as he climbed up to join me. We were both suitably chuffed with our first proper rock-climb.

When I got home, I consulted *Advanced Rockcraft*. Sure enough on page 31 there was a cartoon accurately illustrating why my runners had popped out. I made a mental note of my mistakes. Over the coming weeks we made regular visits to Attermire and started visiting other crags, seeking out bits of rock that we thought we could climb.

I discovered that rock-climbs were recorded and documented in special guidebooks and it wasn't long before I had acquired *Yorkshire Limestone: A Rock Climbers Guide*. The black and white cover photograph depicted a lone climber high on a wall amid dramatic surroundings. The caption inside the guide stated simply, 'The Rebel Gordale Scar'. I found the picture inspirational. Studying the guide on a subsequent visit to Attermire, revealed that the route we had selected for our very first climb was located on the appropriately named Barrel Buttress and was described as follows:

Route No 68. Fantasy – 70 feet Mild Severe. The best route of its grade at Attermire. A miniature classic.

Over the coming months, Nigel, Ledge and I continued on our quest of self-taught learning as we dabbled in the art of rockcraft. We managed two rewarding trips to Norway, one in the summer of 1980 and a repeat trip the following year. Self-reliance was our unwritten credo. Carrying everything we needed, we safely negotiated our way through the rugged and glaciated terrain of the Jotunheimen. As in the Scottish mountains, you can ascend many of the peaks in this region via walking routes, but we deliberately sought out more adventurous routes to the summits.

What we were doing was pretty tame in the grand adventurous scheme of things, but personally we were all operating outside our comfort zones. We managed some rewarding climbs, but I suspect that, unknowingly, we probably had near misses too. I took my first climbing fall whilst attempting to climb a vertical ice cliff on a glacier. The sérac was about fifty feet high and I was climbing using a long walking axe and short ice hammer. At thirty feet I drove a 'Warthog' ice screw into the glacial wall. As I climbed above the screw, my inadequate axes ripped from the ice. My feet remained stuck where they were and I peeled over backwards and shot down the cliff headfirst. Ledge, who was belaying me using a traditional waist belay, managed to arrest my fall. I was upside down with my head about four feet above the glacier floor. Luckily, the ice screw held.

I was still alive. It was a powerful lesson. I'd seen the climb as a challenge and thought I could do it, but I was woefully inexperienced. The old adage, don't try to run before you can walk, seemed particularly pertinent to the art of climbing.

Fantasy at Attermire Scar had been my first real introduction to climbing, but in reality it probably had its seed in some of my exploits as a kid. I had stumbled into rock-climbing through the need to develop a degree of technical competence in the use of ropes as we trekked in Norway. Initial dabbling with climbing reconnected with some deeper need in my subconscious and soon I was well and truly hooked.

The nearest crags to Hemsworth were situated along the Woodhead Pass in South Yorkshire and these became weekend training grounds for myself, Nigel and Ledge. Laddow Rocks and Shining Clough are gritstone outcrops set high up amidst bleak wind-swept moorland. On our visits, save for a few grouse, they were always deserted and had a remote wilderness feel about them. These crags had been climbed on since the early 1900s and when I started repeating routes that had been established many decades before, I found myself speculating about the types of people that these early pioneers were. It kindled an interest in the history of climbing and I was soon reading about the exploits of early rock-climbing pioneers such as Ivar Berg, Peter Harding and Arthur Birtwistle. Climbing their routes appeared to provide some intimate connection to the past and I felt that the climbs that they had left actually gave an insight into their personalities. Even today with thousands of routes under my belt, I still believe that you can gain an awareness of the character of a climber by the signature of their routes.

Fantasy had been my first real lead and over the next two years, I was always eager to take the sharp end on whatever route we attempted. As I became more competent, I fed my hunger for climbing with books. Brown, Bonington, MacInnes, Cassin, Harrer, Wilson and Bonatti, all filled my head with the romance of climbing. Initially, my brother Nigel partnered me but as I became increasingly ambitious and started pushing the grades, he started to lose interest. For him, rock-climbing was all about enjoyment and was just a small part of a bigger outdoor adventure. As my obsessive behaviour grew, his enthusiasm waned. Ledge on the other hand, was carried along by my ambition and together we were soon spending all our free time travelling and climbing, with me selfishly pushing to take the lead.

One weekend would see us on the gritstone edges of Derbyshire, the next camped in the Llanberis Pass in North Wales or at Malham Cove in the Yorkshire Dales. All we had was a guidebook description, or an account written in some book or other and every route was a journey into the unknown, a self taught adventure. Ledge and I were both climbing Very Severe standard from the word go. We had plenty of successes learning our craft during these early years, but there were incidents along the way too.

On one visit to North Wales in 1981 with my brother Nigel, I had a chance meeting with a young climber called Euan McCallum who'd hitched down from the Wirral. We were camped below Dinas y Gromlech, one of the most famous crags in the British Isles. When translated, this means Fortress of the Gromlech, which is an appropriate name since its walls are indeed like those of a huge castle. The crag's central feature is characterised by two striking walls set at ninety degrees. This feature is so perfect, that from a distance it has the appearance of an opened book. The walls are one hundred and twenty feet high and they meet to form an immaculate corner. This corner had been climbed by Joe Brown and Doug Belshaw in 1952 and it stood as a climbing test piece for many years. Today it stands as a monument, symbolising how good Brown and his contemporaries really were. On the right wall of the corner is a discontinuous crack system and this forms the basis of another climb called *Cemetery Gates*. I had done a number of easy climbs on the Gromlech with Ledge and I loved the steep pockety style of climbing. Nigel knew I had designs on *The Gates*, but he didn't feel up to it himself. Talking to Euan revealed that he wanted to do *The Gates*; it seemed that fate was with us. Conditions were less than perfect, with wet streaks streaming down the face, but we were so hyped we made our way up to the deserted crag and enjoyed a fine climb together. In the pub that evening we discussed our ambitions and looked through the guidebook. Under the description for *Cenotaph Corner* it said provocatively. 'A must do climb for all aspiring hard men.' We were both keen to test ourselves on the *Corner* but on this occasion it was pouring like a down spout and would have to wait.

Later that year I made the journey up to North Wales for a short break with my girlfriend. We did a few easy climbs together over the weekend, but the description of 'A must do climb for all aspiring hard men', saw me dragging my girlfriend up to the base of the corner. The crag was completely deserted. It was a grey cold day and there were patches of snow on the ground. I set off up the climb, but unlike *The Gates* experience of the year before, the route felt steep and the climbing technical. I made steady progress up the *Corner*, until I ground to halt towards the top of the climb. I was hesitant and my forearms felt pumped. I managed to clip a peg and make some difficult moves above it. My legs were bridged across the corner and started to vibrate. I was shaking myself off the footholds. I was nearly at the top of the route but panic was giving way to tunnelled vision. Rather than trying to relax, compose myself and make sense of the last moves, I made a desperate lunge for a hold, blew it and was airborne. As my weight came onto the peg I was pulled violently into the rock and my right foot crashed into the wall below. The peg ripped and I hurtled a further thirty feet down the corner ripping gear as I fell. A piece of protection finally held, but the pain shooting up my leg suggested that I wouldn't be completing the climb today.

On the deck I examined my ankle, it had already blown up like a balloon, I couldn't put weight on it and that meant an arduous, hobbling, bum sliding, crawling descent back down the screes to the car. On the drive back to London, I felt sick with pain, but was incredibly thirsty so we called into a Little Chef. I hobbled in, sat down and ordered a glass of milk. As the waitress approached the table with our drinks, she suddenly stumbled and pitched forward drenching me in ice cold milk, the shock of which saw me in one second bolting upright on my injured leg and in the next rolling around on the floor in agony. The waitress didn't know what to do with herself. The diagnosis in hospital later that day was a severely sprained ankle. I couldn't put weight on it properly for two months. The problem with the learning through experience philosophy is that although it's undoubtedly effective, a fine line exists between the power of pain and disaster.

In 1982, Margaret Thatcher's task force was about to set sail to the Falkland Islands and Ledge and I were hopelessly out of our depth in the Alps. We could have easily perished the previous day and now we were stranded on the glacier below the Eismeer station, underneath the south east flank of the Eiger. We'd travelled to Switzerland with aspirations to climb the mountain via the Mittellegi Ridge. Our plan was to gain the Mittellegi Hut perched on the ridge, spend the night there, climb the ridge and descend down the south west flank. Looking back, it is clear that our plan was completely flawed. Our mountaineering experience was limited to two trekking trips around the Jotunheimen Mountains in Norway, albeit in atrocious weather conditions. Yet here we were attempting to climb a 4,000m Alpine peak in winter conditions. To reach the start of our objective, we'd caught the Jungfraujoch train. Our guidebook informed us that at Eismeer a small tunnel, door, and ladder gave access to the glacier and climbers commonly used this.

The Jungfraujoch was built between 1896 and 1912 and for the era was a marvel of engineering. The rack railway follows a tunnel through the heart of the mountain and eventually emerges at a hotel restaurant and observatory perched on the saddle between the Mönch and Jungfrau at an altitude of 11,332 feet. During its construction the tunnellers blasted and dug their way to the outside of the mountain to create holes used to jettison excavated rock and in the process, creating gallery windows. The first one, known as Eigernordwand, overlooks the precipitous North Face and the second one, called Eismeer, looks out of the South East Face. As the train takes tourists up the mountain to the Jungfraujoch, it makes stops at both these stations so people can disembark, temporarily, enjoy the views and take photographs.

Our train came to a halt at Eismeer and Ledge and I summarily disembarked with the rest of the tourists to admire the views from behind thick plated glass. Looking out revealed a winter wonderland of snowy peaks including fine views of the Fiescherhorn. Snow was banked right up the walls of the mountain on either side of the window. If there was an access door it must have been buried beneath metres of snow. Ledge and I were a little unsure about what to do; we had bought one-way tickets to Eismeer and were stubbornly intent on achieving our objective. Looking at the windows we could see that they were locked in place with large wing nuts and we quickly decided that we could make our escape through the window itself. After about ten minutes the guard blew his whistle signalling that everyone should return to the train. Ledge and I stayed put. The guard pointed at us and said in stern German, 'Sie zwei zuruk zum zug bitte,' which I think meant, return to the train please.

'Nine we go out klettern,' I replied in pidgin German.

'Nicht mussen sie zum Zugzuruckkehren,' the guard replied pointing back at the train and starting to show signs of agitation.

'Nine we go klettern Mittellegi,' I said, pointing in the vague direction of the ridge.

'Nicht, nicht, nicht,' the guard's voice was getting higher and higher as he became increasingly agitated. He was glancing at his watch obviously aware that Swiss efficiency was being compromised here. I got my train ticket out of my pocket and pushed it in front of the guard's face.

'Look EISMEER one way,' I said simultaneously pointing at the destination printed on the ticket and then signalling to the window.

With that he threw his hands in the air and stormed off down the tunnel back to the train shouting, 'Sie sind verruckt, sie sind verruckt,' which to us sounded as if he might be saying something to the tune of, 'Aye you're fucked. Aye you're fucked'.

We heard the sound of the train departing and immediately started unbolting one of the windows, as we lifted it to one side a powerful blast of icy air filled the tunnel. We kitted up with climbing harnesses and threaded our rope round an iron bar fixed in the wall and cast the ends out of the window. They landed on the glacier about fifty feet below and in minutes we were both down. We retrieved the rope, put on crampons and started making our way across the glacier in the direction of the ridge. It was hard going as we kept sinking up to our thighs in fresh, deep powder snow. To make things worse, every so often a huge bang would echo round the mountains. We deduced that these must be deliberate explosions designed to trigger controlled avalanches. This process may have been in the interest of skiers, but it certainly wasn't in ours as we played a game of Russian roulette with small, but frequent avalanches as we traversed beneath the South East Face of the Eiger.

After a few hours we reached a place where we had to strike upwards to gain the ridge and the sanctuary of the hut. The climbing should have been relatively straightforward, but with waist deep powder, it was desperate making any upward progress at all. After about an hour's toiling and gaining precious little ground, we acknowledged that our efforts were futile and we'd have to come up with a plan B.

After consulting our map, we decided that an escape down the glacier to the valley looked a feasible option and so we turned tracks and started the steep descent. We made rapid progress and covered several hundred metres, but the angle of the glacier started to become worryingly steep. We were moving together tied to the rope and separated by about thirty feet. Ledge had been blazing the trail out in front with me bringing up the rear. Suddenly he stopped, 'You'd better come and have a look at this,' he called.

I cautiously edged my way down to him. He was stood on a precipice of ice, and below him gaped a crevasse of monstrous proportions, it would have swallowed a small bungalow. Beyond the crevasse was chaos. Huge towers of ice, and yawning crevasses tumbled down the mountain at an alarmingly steep angle. The seriousness of our predicament hit us both with gut-wrenching, palm-sweating reality. Without a word, we turned and began the slog back up the glacier and as we did, large flakes of snow started to fall out of a flat grey sky.

It was now late in the day, the light was fading and the snow was falling thick and fast. It was glaringly obvious that we were going to be spending the night out in the open. Although our Alpine experience was minimal, our camp craft was pretty good. We found an area on the glacier that looked as though it was free from avalanche threat and started digging into a snow bank with our ice axes. After a couple of hours we'd excavated a neat little snow cave that could accommodate two of us lying side by side. We arranged our Karrimats and sleeping bags on the ice and bedded down for the night. We discussed our options for the following day.

'We've got to get back to the gallery window. If we manage to attract some attention then we might get a rescue,' I said.

'Yeah and we might have to pay a big rescue fee. I don't think the authorities will be too happy about us unbolting that window,' said Ledge.

'Well, let's worry about that when we get there. We'll have to run the gauntlet of those avalanches. It was pretty bad today and it wasn't even snowing. If this blizzard keeps up, it'll be murder tomorrow,' I said. With this disconcerting thought we drifted into a fitful sleep.

As dawn broke, we peered out of our hole. It was snowing hard and had deposited about another foot overnight. We had to make a decision, stay put or brave the unstable snow in an attempt to get back to Eismeer. We opted for the latter, roped up and started traversing the steep slope that led to the gallery window. The seriousness of our predicament was reinforced by fresh avalanche debris littering the slopes that we intended to negotiate. Periodically, small, but nevertheless potentially lethal, avalanches cascaded down from the huge face above. If we were going to make good our escape, we'd have to run this gauntlet. We approached the first section of avalanche debris and waited at a reasonably safe distance. With a hiss and rumble snow cascaded from above and thumped into the slope in front of us. After several seconds the avalanche subsided and we set off at a wallowing run across the avalanche cone. As we crossed the cone, we were carried down the slope losing precious height. Trying to race across these danger zones left us sickeningly out of breath and retching for air. We then had to re-climb up the soft unstable snow to regain the height we had lost. We repeated this process four or five times, it was an unnerving, exhausting ordeal, each time thinking that we were about to get buried alive or swept away into the void below. It probably took us about three hours to traverse five hundred metres, but eventually we found ourselves ensconced below the gallery window of Eismeer station.

As we sat on the glacier contemplating how to attract attention, a group of Japanese faces congregated behind the glass fifty feet above us. They were busily taking photographs and seemed oblivious to our frantic waving and shouting and as quickly as they had appeared they vanished from view. A dull rumbling through the mountain, we surmised, was the sound of the train leaving. About an hour later, we detected the dull rumbling again and in due course, faces appeared at the window. This time we were more prepared and had armed ourselves with snowballs which we hurled skyward. We even managed to secure a couple of smiley waves from up above before the faces vanished. After several hours of fruitless results, I turned to Ledge. 'This is hopeless. The only way that we're going to get rescued is by climbing back up and knocking on the window itself.'

Ledge agreed.

The expanse of rock between the window and us was smooth, featureless and plumb vertical. A thin crack did offer the possibility of a way up. It looked like it might be about E1 had it been on a crag in the UK. At an altitude of ten thousand feet and wearing big mountain boots, there was no way that either of us could even attempt to free climb such a route. We got our climbing gear out and sorted through the ironmongery. We'd brought about three or four metal pitons with us. I started to peg my way up the crack. We'd done a bit of aid climbing in the UK, even managing to cross the huge roof of Kilnsey Crag in Yorkshire, but this was different. I banged a piton into the crack clipped a sling to it, stood in the sling and reached up and placed another piton. I clipped into this, but then I had to remove two pitons from below so I could make further progress. The method worked, but it was full of risk. Only having four pitons meant that as I climbed, I had to constantly remove the pitons from below me which meant I was removing any protection that would safeguard a fall. If the pitons from which I was hanging pulled out I would fall to the glacier. It was stressful work. After about an hour, I had inched my way up the crack and gained about twenty feet. Ledge was patiently paying out the rope and giving encouragement when suddenly a rope came snaking down from above. A head then appeared from the gallery window and began gesturing for us to climb up the rope. Ledge quickly lowered me back down to the glacier. We used prusik loops to ascend the rescue rope, unsure of the greeting that awaited us. As I made a relieved entrance back in through the window, I was greeted by the face of wise looking gentleman. He had a mass of curly grey hair and his lined face held a knowing smile. There were no harsh words he simply said, 'Mittellegi.'

I nodded and thanked him profusely, shaking his hand. It was obvious he was a mountain guide. He offered me water from a metal urn and I drank a long draught. I hadn't drunk anything since setting out early that morning. When Ledge arrived, the guide escorted us back to the train. We said our goodbyes to the guide at Eigergletscher station and then continued by train back to Grindelwald, reflecting on how absurd and naive our plan had been. We'd unwittingly put ourselves at considerable risk and, at face value, had achieved nothing. We left Grindlewald with our tails firmly between our legs and considered heading for the warmth of the Mediterranean.

Before leaving England I had bought a guidebook called *French Rock Climbs*, it had been compiled and written by Pete Livesey. Pete was a pivotal figure in British rock-climbing and was captivated by the concept of 'free climbing' which, in its simplest form, is using no more than hands and feet to climb up the rock. In the 1970s Livesey pushed the frontiers of free climbing into the stratosphere and pioneered new routes of the highest quality and calibre throughout the UK.

During this period, Pete Livesey and friends exported their free climbing ethic to France. In the south of the country they discovered some truly spectacular crags with huge sweeping walls of white limestone, sometimes over a thousand feet high. Warm temperatures and perfect solid rock, meant that the climber could dispense with the encumbrance of bulky Alpine gear in favour of lightweight rock-climbing kit. This was a perfect playground to climb rock purely for its own sake.

Livesey is sometimes credited with introducing the concept of free climbing to the French, but in truth pockets of French climbers had recognised the challenge and value of free climbing for years. Parisian climbers had practised free climbing on the sandstone boulders of Fontainebleau since the early 1900s. Perhaps a more realistic perspective would be that during the 1970s, Livesey acted as an influential catalyst highlighting the quality and scope of free climbing possibilities that existed across France.

I gained some direct evidence to support this theory many years later. I'd been on a climbing trip to the south of France with Jerry Peel, Mick Johnston and Chris Gibb. We were on our way home and decided to stop off for a day's climbing at Saussois, a popular limestone crag in northern France. There was a good auberge at the base of the crag which served fine cuisine. After a fine meal and a bellyfull of wine the banter was flowing. Suddenly Gibby piped up, 'There's a geezer over there who keeps looking at me and I think I recognise him from somewhere.' Gibby stood up, puffed his chest out and swaggered over to the team of French climbers who were sat near by, 'Do I know you?' he asked a leather-faced French guy with long greying hair.

'You are a friend of Livesey?' prompted the French climber.

'Aye, I remember now, you were here the day that Livesey freed *L'Ange* weren't you?' said Gibby.

'Yes,' admitted the French man, but then he went on, 'but Livesey wasn't the first to free climb *L'Ange*, it was Droyer.'

He was referring to the talented home grown climber Jean Claude Droyer. Determined to defend British honour and keep the record straight, Gibby entered into a heated debate. Neither Gibby nor the ageing French rocker would back down and eventually both protagonists retired from the argument still convinced in the belief that their respective countrymen had made the first free ascent of *L'Ange*. Who is credited with the first free ascent of this climb is probably incidental. What is important is that the free ascent of *L'Ange* took place on a crag popular with Parisian climbers and without doubt, the word would have spread quickly. The fact that a visiting British climber had made a free ascent of such a landmark route in the early '70s, would surely have ruffled a few feathers. It was evident from the emotive exchange that took place in the bar, that the French climber was protecting national pride. It was apparent to me that this guy at least wanted one of his own to be credited with the move towards the free climbing ethic. It was indicative of the passion that climbers had for such a futile pursuit. Whilst I doubt that Livesey was responsible for introducing 'free climbing' to the French, I do not doubt that he was one of the catalysts that opened up the eyes of the world to the quality and scope of free rock-climbing potential available outside the Alpine arena. I also think he cemented the concept in the minds of the Continentals that rock-climbing was a worthy endeavour in its own right.

In the immediate aftermath of our Eiger fiasco, warm French rock seemed very appealing and leafing through the pages of Pete Livesey's guide, *French Rock Climbs*, revealed a crag that sounded idyllic. Free camping on herb-scented terraces below the crag, good bars and a range of routes from big multi-pitch excursions to shorter single pitch routes. We left Switzerland and headed off towards Nice in search of Saint Jeannet.

We spent the next week or so enjoying some fine French rock climbs. Most of the routes seemed more like traditional British affairs. They tended to follow natural crack lines, but unlike Britain where you had to protect the routes by placing your own nuts and chocks, most of the gear was *in situ* and consisted of pitons and the odd bolt.

An old memory from that trip sticks with me today. After a good day's climbing we headed to the bar for some well-earned refreshments. The bar was buzzing with a group of French guys and their gorgeous looking girlfriends. We deduced that they were climbers since one of them was trying to impress the others by performing a feat of one-arm pull-ups from a beam. They were like no other climbers I had seen, lean and athletic, with tanned bodies and ripped muscles. They looked us up and down scornfully. We ignored them at first and ordered beer. After a while, curiosity got the better of them and one of them shouted over in English, 'What do you make of your Great British Navy declaring war on Argentina?' he seemed to be mocking us. We hadn't seen a paper or heard the news in over two weeks.

'I didn't know they had,' I replied.

'Ah oui, they are already sailing,' retorted the French guy.

'I don't agree with Thatcher's policies,' I confessed. He waved us over and we joined them. They seemed intrigued that we had travelled so far. We related our experience on the Eiger and told them about Livesey's guidebook. They were disparaging about the Alps.

The French guy continued, 'We have some great Alpine faces, but even routes like the South Face of the Dru are like the Autoroute du Soleil in summer.' He was referring to the notorious French motorway that becomes full of French tourists as they travel to the Med for their summer vacation. We got the drift of what he was saying.

'No,' he declared, 'the Alps are for the old men. This is the future,' he pointed at his comrades. 'See him,' he continued, pointing at one of the group, 'he has just climbed F7b.'

It meant nothing to me, but I indicated my approval with a thumbs up to the guy. We continued chatting to the climbers for some time, as the beer flowed their arrogance seemed to increase.

I retired to my tent. The French rock stars' prophecy echoing round my head. The guys were certainly passionate about their climbing, but they also seemed to want to sweep the achievements of their predecessors under the carpet. I found this disturbing. Ledge and I had enjoyed our brief stay in the South of France. The cuisine, wine and culture were most appealing. Climbing on the sun-kissed crags had been enjoyable and certainly not without challenge, but as we made the long drive back to England, memories of the routes we had climbed at Saint Jeannet seemed to fade and blur into each other.

Over the coming months, rock-climbing started to become an all-consuming passion. One of my climbing bibles at the time was a book called *Hard Rock*. It was a collection of evocative essays about great British rock-climbs and had been compiled by Ken Wilson. It featured the writings of the crème de la crème of British rock-climbers. They articulated their experiences, through poetic, candid and sometimes gripping prose. It was illustrated with magnificent and revealing black and white photographs. This book was my mentor during the early '80s. I would read and then reread the essays it contained and study the photographs trying to glean whatever I could to increase my chances of success on the routes that book described.

I never kept a diary, but like many climbers I did try and keep a record of what I had climbed by ticking guidebooks. I used *Hard Rock* in a similar fashion. Most of my ticks in *Hard Rock* during the early '80s were against those climbs from Yorkshire and Derbyshire, ones that were fairly local to me. Despite this, I'd also managed to tick climbs from as far afield as Scotland, The Lakes, Wales and the South West.

One of the gaps in my *Hard Rock* CV was a local route called *Elder Crack* at Curbar Edge in Derbyshire. *Elder Crack* is an overhanging slit about eight inches wide and seventy feet long. Climbing such a feature requires special technique and this technique is only acquired by climbing such features. The 'chicken and egg', which came first, scenario, springs to mind. My experience of climbing off widths was limited to an overhanging crack on the Old Man of Hoy that I'd climbed a few months earlier. In *Hard Rock*, Geoff Birtles opens his essay about *Elder Crack* with the following sentence, 'There are plenty of excuses for failing on *Elder Crack*, but few for not trying.' So on a crisp, sunny, autumnal day, I found myself looking up at an evil, overhanging chimney. I recall that we'd partied till late the night before and my head was thumping with a hangover. I climbed the easy lower section and fiddled a runner into the bowels of the cleft. Birtles talked about swimming up the crack and employing the gritstone udge to facilitate upward progress. I think I probably used all these techniques as I thrutched, slid and floundered my way upwards. Eventually, I found myself wedged in the crack above the overhang, sweat pouring down my face, brain throbbing to bursting and utterly spent. My only runner was hidden in the depths of the crack about eight feet below me. Try as I might, I could make no further progress, rescue from above was inconceivable and I knew I was in for it. The feeling was horrible. It wasn't like a sudden or unexpected fall. On this occasion I had plenty of time to visualise what was going to happen. I closed my eyes and fell out of the crack hoping that my token runner would stop me hitting the deck. As the rope and runner took my weight I was whipped into rock ledges just above the ground, I hit with my feet and felt a searing pain shoot up my leg. I was out of action again for another two months.

These early incidents didn't curb my desire to want to push myself on routes. On *Cenotaph Corner* and *Elder Crack* I'd let my heart rule my head, I'd put the accelerator to the floor and run out of gas just when I'd needed that extra bit to get to the top. During these early formative years I'd had a few scrapes and without knowing it, I'd probably had one or two lucky escapes. Whether it was a blessing or a curse my ambition and passion for climbing remained intact. One thing I did recognise was, that if I was going to climb harder and remain unscathed, I still had a lot to learn. I couldn't afford to live on romantic notions of grandeur alone. I'd need to work at it.

Top left: Mum and Dad's wedding photo 1945. *Photo: Radtke family collection.*

Top right: Me in the High Tatra's of Poland, 1964. This was the first of several trips to my father's homeland. *Photo: Bernard Radtke.*

Bottom: Looking towards Fitzwilliam Colliery from our allotment in Hemsworth in the '70s. *Photo: Mark Radtke.*

Norway 1981. **Top:** Adrian Ledgway in camp in the Hurrungane region. Ledge and I tried to climb the big wall of Store Ringstind in the background, but after about 200 feet climbing up steep slabs, incessant rockfall forced a retreat. *Photo: Mark Radtke.*

Bottom left: Nigel below Galdhøpiggen. We took a line directly up the face via the two snow patches and an easy ramp line. Was it a new route? I doubt it, but we had the whole glaciated cirque to ourselves and it felt like we were pioneering. *Photo: Mark Radtke.*

Bottom right: Early ice climbing practice. About to make the cardinal mistake. *Photo: Nigel Radtke.*

Top: Ledge descending the glacier below the Mittellegi Ridge of the Eiger. March 1982. *Photo: Mark Radtke.*

Bottom Left: Dave Barton descending the Eiger after a successful, but storm bound ascent of the North Face in 1971. Note the hawser laid ropes.
Photo: Martin Burrows-Smith.

Bottom right: Laddow Rocks in 1982. Leading *Twin Eliminate* E1 5b. *Photo: Nigel Radtke.*

Ledge on the classic free abseil descending from the summit of the Old Man of Hoy, Orkney in 1984. *Photo: Mark Radtke.*

Top left: Dave Kenyon on Fawcett's *Butch Cassidy*, E4 6b in the early '80s. 'The Chimp' was an extremely talented climber, quiet, understated and bold. His Malham route *Raindogs* done in '86 is still a sought after benchmark F8a. *Photo: Mark Radtke.*

Top right: Martin 'Basher' Atkinson making an early repeat of Fawcett's *Scrittos' Republic*, E6 6c, Millstone Edge. Atkinson together with a group of like minded individuals started applying new levels of professionalism to training which translated into some ground breaking achievements on the rock in the mid '80s. *Photo: Adrian Ledgway.*

Bottom: From left to right - Andy Cave, Dave Barton, Greg Rimmer, Mick Johnston, Christian Waller, Jerry Peel, Chris Gibb, Dave Green with Sean Myles climbing. *Photo: Mark Radtke*

Top left: Ledge in action on the Livesey classic *Foil* E3 6a. *Dinas Gromlech, Llanberis Pass. Photo: Mark Radtke.*

Top right: Ledge on the Pink Floyd inspired *Heart of the Sun*, E2 5b. Baggy Point, Devon. In the mid '80s, we were just mad for rock, one weekend would see us in the Peak District, the next in The Lakes and the next in North Wales. *Photo: Sharon Horry.*

Bottom: En route to the Verdon in 1984. Sharon, Ledge, Me and Ian Cooksey. *Photo: Mark Radtke*

Verdon exposure. Ian and I climbing the upper section of *Chrysalis* F6c.
Photo: Adrian Ledgway.

Ledge cast adrift on *Necronomicon* F6c. *Photo: Mark Radtke*

Chapter 3

Northern Soul

*Twin competencies that mobilize people to seize
opportunities and allow them to take setbacks
and obstacles in their stride.*
Initiative and Optimism

1984 was an important year for me. Whilst studying for my degree in Applied Biology I'd specialised in subjects that gave me the best chance of employment. I'd spent a year in Cambridge working for one of the UK's large agrochemical companies and felt confident that I'd be able to find work in the area of chemical research and development. The downside of this career choice was that most of the agrochemical companies were based in the arable flatlands of East Anglia and the South East and these areas were about as far away from any decent climbing as you could get.

It came as a great surprise, and with much relief when I landed a job with a Bradford-based chemical company. A H Marks had its own research and development department and I was appointed as a Field Trials Officer. The job suited me down to the ground. I had full responsibility for the annual trials programme. Most of the work was outside and involved travelling all over the North of England. I was fortunate to have a boss who gave me the autonomy and freedom to run the programme as I wished, providing I delivered good results. Shortly after getting the job, I moved to Halifax and this meant that some of the best crags in Yorkshire were on my doorstep.

I quickly learned that there were two important social centres for climbers. The Richard Dunn Sports Centre was located about two miles from my work. It was named after Bradford's famous boxing son and contained a purpose built climbing wall. West Vale was a revered gritstone quarry and was located about four miles from my house in Halifax. In the early '80s both these venues were significant training grounds for climbers from across Yorkshire and Lancashire.

Climbers had always recognised the benefits of training to improve performance but this often amounted to doing more climbing to gain greater fitness. In the 1970s certain individuals started adopting more scientific and dedicated approaches to developing technique, power and stamina. The benefit of this was immediately evident as rock-climbing standards were raised in quantum leaps.

Established rock-climbs, like track and field records, have reputations, and like athletes of track and field, climbers are intent on breaking these records, often testing themselves on the most difficult routes of the day. Such routes are called 'test pieces'. *Cenotaph Corner* provides a good reference to illustrate the concept of record breaking in climbing. In the 1950s it had the hallmark of a test piece. It had taken the ability of one of Britain's best to climb it and would-be suitors were eager to see if they could mirror Brown's achievement. In 1952 the *Corner*, with its grade of E1, stood as a benchmark for others to aspire to. In 1979 a new breed of climber in the form of Ron Fawcett climbed the blank wall to the right of the *Corner*. He had named this climb *Lord of the Flies*. An indication of how standards had risen since Brown's era, were revealed in its grade of E6. *Lord of the Flies* contained challenges that were six times greater than *Cenotaph Corner* and the reality was, that in the early 1980s, *Lord* had taken centre stage as the 'must do route for all aspiring hard men'. When I climbed the *Corner*, it had long been relegated to the status of a 'Trade Route' and even ascents of *Lord*, whilst still significant were not exceptional. Climbing routes like Brown's classic were viewed as 'run of the mill' for any moderately enthusiastic rock-climber.

Many climbers are content to climb within their grade and their aspirations never transcend the desire to climb trade routes. This doesn't mean that climbing is without risk or challenge, it simply means that the climber has a feeling of being in more control. Others, however, are intent on pushing themselves hard. This often means operating outside personal comfort zones. This can mean dealing with greater uncertainties and elevated risks, but success can often bring immense levels of personal satisfaction. It can also lead to major advances in what is possible. Whether *Lord* actually represented challenges that were six times greater than the *Corner* is questionable. When I eventually climbed *Lord* myself, I had an easier time on it than when I had first tried the *Corner* seven years earlier. The challenge in a climb is subtler than a number can represent, it often comes down to the shape you're in when you set foot onto the route. What sticks with you is the journey that the climb takes you on. This said, I think it's also important to recognise that the more competent you become then the number of climbs that you are at liberty to attempt increases exponentially.

When I moved back up north I had a big appetite to satisfy and began training to appease the hunger. The Richard Dunn wall made use of one of the building's containment walls. It was about a hundred and fifty feet long and provided excellent fingery climbing. The right-hand section was a vertical concrete block wall that attained a height of about thirty feet. The blocks were inset with natural stone holds of varying shapes and boulder problems and traverses could be contrived at will. It also provided the opportunity for some exciting soloing. This part of the wall adjoined the main sports hall and the underside of the sports hall's concrete seating area had been fashioned into a large roof about twenty feet long and fifteen feet wide. The middle part of the wall had been made out of poured concrete, it was about fifteen feet high and featured several arêtes, a chimney and an off width crack. The left-hand side of the wall was also made of poured concrete and contained a small but significant overhang littered with tiny edges, finger pockets and a finger crack. The room doubled as the sports centre's weight training facility and housed a range of free weights and weight training machines.

I became a regular Dickie Dunn aficionado in 1984. Over the winter months the routine would be Tuesday and Thursday evenings and if the weather wasn't fit enough to climb outside, weekends as well. On wet Sunday afternoons the wall would be flooded with locals from Bradford, Leeds, Huddersfield and Halifax. A 'wired' character with wild curly hair and round rimmed glasses would bounce around the wall, demonstrating multiple one-arm pull ups from finger holds on the overhanging wall. His name was Duncan Drake, he was a fierce traditionalist who valued danger and adventure. The Lancashire team of Greg Rimmer, Mick Ryan, Dave Kenyon, Malc Haslam, and Big Ronnie Marsden would drop in to perfect their quarry pioneering techniques.

The schoolboy team of John Dunne, Andy Jack, Dave Pegg and Jason Myers could always be found *in situ* almost living at the wall. Inspired by the older generation, but intent in making their own mark in climbing history, these young locals embarked on sadistic training regimes. John in particular devised gruelling circuits. Intense tendon ripping problems on the overhanging wall were interspersed with frenzied attacks on an overhanging Bachar ladder strung to the ceiling. These were followed by power pulls on the weights machine, during which two or three other climbers would hold John down on the bench so he could pull double his body weight. Repetitive dips hauling muscle-ripping weights would be followed by one-arm pull downs, it would then be back to the wall to sample a series of delightful rock overs, single dynos, double dynos, traverses and roof problems. All four of these young lads would go on to have an important impact on climbing in the UK by establishing impressive new climbs of their own.

Walls were few and far between in the early '80s and rock-climbing was definitely a minority sport by today's standards. At walls like the Dickie Dunn it would not be uncommon to brush shoulders with any number of climbing luminaries. One such climber who was a frequent visitor to the wall was Jerry Peel. JP was an accomplished rock-climber with hard new routes to his credit. He lived in Bacup in Lancashire and had started climbing in the '60s on his local gritstone crags, Hugencroft and The Bridestones. These windswept moorland craglets were quite diminutive only attaining an average height of about fifteen feet. The rock had been sculpted by searing winds over the millennia into smooth and rounded forms and although small in stature, presented climbers with considerable technical challenges. Characterised by a dearth of positive usable holds for hands and feet, it meant that considerable skill, power and technique had to be applied in order to climb them. These rocks had proved attractive to local climbers and some strong local traditions had been born at The Bridestones. Early pioneers included the legendary mountaineer Don Whillans, and locals such as Rod Valentine, Barry Rawlinson and Dave Barton had used these rocks as convenient training grounds to develop strength and technique for greater things. Their competitive natures soon saw individuals trying to outdo each other and bouldering at The Bridestones became an activity in its own right. The tradition of climbing at The Bridestones was very much a hand-me-down affair, with apprentices learning from masters, and then going on to outmaster their masters. Jerry Peel was of this mould and although an excellent all-round rock-climber, he enjoyed bouldering as a unique and independent sport within the broad spectrum of climbing. Don Whillans had even given Jerry the official stamp with his acerbic observation, 'Aye, Jerry, you're just another one of them little bloody hill men'. In the early '80s, Jerry Peel was undoubtedly one of the UK's modern bouldering pioneers.

Other Dickie Dunn regulars at this time were Joe and Gary Healey, masters from the Wirral. Whilst Jerry was a gritstone aficionado, Joe and Gary had perfected their technique on the famous sandstone quarry of Pex Hill. They had developed immense finger strength. All were highly talented and fiercely competitive, but Joe in particular had a Scouse wit to match his climbing prowess. They would delight in trying to burn each other off, perfecting a move that no one else could execute and establishing new problems on the wall. The craic was fierce, the rivalry intense and the camaraderie roguish, but through all the antics, boundaries of possibility were being realised on a primitive wall and, more importantly, outside on real rock.

It was during this period that I first met Ian Cooksey. Ian was studying at Huddersfield Polytechnic but hailed from Cumbria. It was obvious from watching him on the wall that he was a natural rock-climber. He was strong fingered and moved with effortless grace. Ian had served his apprenticeship during the late '70s, where, biting at the heels of modern Lakeland pioneers like Pete Whillance and Ed Cleasby, he had climbed many of the modern Extremes that adorned the mountain crags of Cumbria. He even sported a '70s style rock star look with long black curly hair and a droopy moustache. It was clear from the outset that Ian's talents were considerably greater than my own, but rather than showing arrogance born out of superiority, he was laid back, relaxed and encouraging, and we hit it off immediately. Over the coming years we developed a strong climbing partnership, which was based as much on mutual cultural interests and on a strong thirst for travel and adventure as it was on our passion for climbing.

As well as providing an excellent physical workout, climbing at the wall could also be quite a harrowing affair. The floor was solid concrete so falling off, particularly on some of the hard highball problems, was not an option. I remember one occasion when John Dunne wanted to demonstrate one of his latest test pieces. His latest problem involved a tenuous series of moves culminating in a desperate rock over at about fifteen feet. There was a gymnastic session taking place in the hall next door and the gymnasts were using crash pads. John strolled into the hall and dragged a pad to below his problem. He was in mid demo, when one of the sports hall officials spotted us with the mat. He immediately walked over, read us the riot act for misuse of equipment, and promptly removed the mat. Such was the concern for health and safety at the Richard Dunn climbing wall in the early '80s.

Visiting the wall became an addictive obsession; watching my peers solving cutting edge problems; honing our own abilities by trying to repeat a Peel rock over, or Healey arête; hearing news about the latest new routes that were being done from those who were doing them; sharing beta about the next test pieces that people were going to attempt and thrashing our bodies on a JD circuit. The scene felt fresh, exciting and above all inspirational.

As winter turned into spring our attention turned from the wall to West Vale. West Vale nestled above an urban landscape of redundant cotton mills and Victorian stone terraces. It had been carved out of the hillside to provide stone for the buildings that it now overlooked. What had been left were sheer walls of smooth quarried grit about twenty feet high. Its walls were daubed with paint and graffiti and it epitomised urban climbing. The quarry was about two hundred yards long and was littered with edges and small cracks that provided sustained and technical climbing. The ground below the walls was flat and grassy which meant that the only risk associated with a fall was that you might land in a pile of dog shit. This meant that you could climb until your forearms totally pumped out and you could simply not hold on any longer. This was excellent for developing endurance, an attribute so essential for pushing the limits on 'real' crags when a fall could have hazardous consequences. These traverses weren't natural phenomena, but had been manufactured by West Vale's discoverer and early pioneer, an unforgettable character called Alan Stevenson aka Heavy Duty.

Heavy Duty was a gritstone enthusiast who had unrivalled nervous energy. Alan's hyper character had reputedly resulted from one of his other pastimes, dancing the nights away at a famous club called the Wigan Casino. The Wigan Casino was the North West's Mecca for people addicted to a unique brand of music known as Northern Soul. Individuals would travel from all parts of the UK to indulge their passion for this brand of music and dance, and to boost their endurance often used liberal quantities of amphetamine sulphate. Heavy Duty was no exception to this rule, but whether this led to his 'hyper' character I'm unsure. I suspect he was simply hyper by nature. I first met Alan whilst out bouldering with Ian Cooksey at Halifax Rocks and he had taken an immediate liking to us.

Heavy Duty was at his best on spring evenings when the warm sun illuminated the graffiti-covered walls of West Vale and the throngs would arrive. It was not uncommon to have twenty or so climbers adorning the walls of the quarry making their way crabwise back and forth across the various traverses. Heavy Duty loved to hold court. He'd stand in the middle of the quarry, dispensing advice to one climber about how to complete a section of a traverse, whilst simultaneously chastising another for using an illegal hold on another boulder problem. At the same time he'd be enthralling others with some ripping yarn or other. As well as being loud and talking at a phenomenal rate Alan had a nervous tick and used expletives with gay abandon as part of his natural vocabulary.

On one occasion he was giving Ian Cooksey and me a tour of the quarry's many up problems. We started at a smooth wall at the right side of the quarry. 'Right lads, try this fucker, this is one of mine.' Alan showed us a thin crimpy wall with two tiny undercuts. After climbing the problem wall Alan gave us an enthusiastic, 'Well done lads,' and with a twitch of his mouth he pointed out the next problem, and added, 'What about this twat? This one was first done by Al Manson.'

And so the session went on with Heavy Duty pointing us at problem after problem. As the evening came to a close Heavy Duty guided us towards the left side of the quarry.

'Try this fucker,' Alan said with a particular gleam in his eye. 'I've not seen anyone repeat this.'

'Who did this one, Alan?' I enquired, keen to continue the history lesson.

'Bendy Man did this fucker,' Alan pronounced with an air of reverence in his voice.

'Who is Bendy Man?' I asked genuinely curious about the identity of the aforesaid.

Alan looked at Ian and me, his mouth twitching like a rabbits nose. 'You don't know who the fuck Bendy fucking Man is?' he asked in a shocked voice, and then quickly added before we could answer, 'Bendy Man! Bendy Man? You don't know who fuckin' Bendy fuckin' Man is? It's Rob fuckin' Gaw fuckin' Thorpe, that's who fuckin' Bendy fuckin' Man is!'

Ian and I just doubled up in laughter. I've never met anybody since who could intersperse expletives between words in single sentences with such aplomb.

Although I'd not met Rob Gawthorpe I'd read about some of his ground-breaking exploits. He had done several significant first ascents in Yorkshire, including a free ascent of the first pitch of the main overhang at Malham Cove. In 1984 this was a visionary piece of climbing which would influence people's attitudes to climbing on Yorkshire limestone throughout the '80's and '90's.

West Vale and the Richard Dunn wall made a difference to my own attitude to climbing which started to reveal itself in my own ability. This wasn't just the product of a rigorous training regime, but more the result of mixing with inspirational climbers and roguish characters alike. These people were testimony to what was possible, they inspired, they encouraged, and they provided competition. Heavy Duty was a colourful likeable rogue, and I even named a new route in his honour:

Oh No! It's Heavy Duty 30 m E4 5c Three stars
Crowden Great Quarry
1st Ascent Mark Radtke and Adrian Ledgway.

It would have been the mid '80s, I guess, when I opened the door of my house and squinted out into a bright spring Halifax morning. A local climber called Dave Green stood in the yard. He was gently bouncing up and down as though he needed to release some bottled up nervous energy. He had a beguiling smile on his face and I knew instantly that he had some devilment up his sleeve.

'Good morning Rad, I hope you're up for some adventure,' he said.

'Come in Dave, I'll make you a brew.' I could sense the inevitable.

I was introduced to Dave by Heavy Duty and like Heavy Duty, Dave had been a regular at the Wigan Casino and had a similar pent up energy. When I first met Dave I found him pretty aloof, almost arrogant. He had a reputation as a talented climber with a penchant for thin bold climbs. He possessed an air of quiet superiority. Dave was certainly a cool cookie and could hold it together when the climbing got hard. I'd held his ropes and watched him in action on some notoriously bold routes. I'd also had days out with him when all we did was solo route after route. He didn't suffer fools gladly, and benchmarked the competition with how ballsy he considered their climbing to be. He loved nothing more than stepping into the breach where other climbers had failed.

Initially, going out climbing with Dave was always a stressful affair for me. I knew that by hook or crook, he'd manoeuvre me into a situation where ultimately my eyes would be out on stalks. The downside of climbing with Dave was that it was usually a downright scary affair. The upside was that as a result of climbing with him I had a string of bold E5s under my belt. I also felt that I'd earned his respect, and on the rock at least, he almost treated me as an equal.

We sat down for a brew and I asked, 'What do you fancy, Dave?'

'Well you know you've always wanted to do *Rebel*, so I think we should go to Gordale,' Dave replied.

I'd always liked Gordale, I'd explored this fantastic limestone gorge on camping and hiking trips as a kid and it had always held a fascination for me. Only a year or so after I'd started climbing I was drawn into Gordale with Ledge. On that occasion we did a route called *Light*. At the time it was graded Hard Very Severe or HVS and the first pitch gave us real hell. I only managed to climb it after numerous yo-yos. On the way out we noticed a pair of climbers ensconced high up on the left wall of the gorge and decided to sit down and see what they were up to. We recognised the two climbers as the legendary Ron Fawcett and Chris Gibb. They were on a climb called *Rebel*. Gibby, as he was called, was belayed in a little cave about seventy feet above us. As we watched, Ron climbed from the belay and followed what looked like a ridiculously steep groove line above. He moved swiftly up the groove and paused momentarily at a roof at its top. He then climbed out left and started up what looked like a blank wall. He was now about sixty feet above Gibby who was paying out the rope from below. It was an impressive spectacle and looking around we noticed that a sizeable group of tourists had gathered around us to watch. It was interesting listening to their banter.

'Who's that up there?' asked one.

'I don't know but he's mad,' replied another.

'Dad look up there,' said a kid, pointing his finger.

'Yes son, that's Spiderman,' said his dad in a knowing tone.

Just at that moment there was a loud and protracted, 'Fucking... Hell!' from above. I looked up to see Ron flying through the air, before coming to a halt eyeball to eyeball with Gibby in the belay cave. Ron was dancing around like a marionette on the end of the rope and Gibby was suspended in mid air having been pulled skyward off his belay. Both were laughing hysterically.

One of the female tourists piped up, 'How disgusting, I don't think there's a need for language like that.'

Ledge looked at me, 'What the fuck does she expect when someone's just taken a sixty footer? Oh bother?'

We quickly deduced from the conversation that ensued between Ron and Gibby that a hold had unexpectedly snapped off. Such was the nature of climbing in Gordale. Ron was soon back on the rock and this time got to the second belay without incident. As we sat there another guy walked into the gorge and waved up to the climbers above. Ron was on the third pitch by this time. Suddenly he retrieved something from the crack. He shouted down to the guy standing near us, 'I can't believe this Ashley, I've just pulled a wooden wedge out, it looks pretty new as well. I can't believe that people are still pegging this route!'

Ron had made the first free ascent of *Rebel* a few years earlier and had given it a grade of E5 6b. He seemed a little bemused that someone had still resorted to aid climbing it.

The new arrival called Ashley turned his attention to us, 'What have you lads been up to?' he asked.

'We just did *Light* that's all,' I informed him modestly. Ashley looked at us and I detected that he was recalling something from his own past.

'Good effort lads, it's a fantastic route that, how did you find it?' he said.

'Bloody desperately harder than any HVS that we've done before,' I told him.

'Aye, well they can be funny grades in Gordale,' Ashley informed us.

Back in my living room, in Halifax, Dave Green and I were planning the days proceedings and I asked Dave, 'OK Dave, if I do *Rebel*, what do you fancy?'

'We'll do *Mossdale Trip*,' replied Dave, 'I'll lead the main pitch and you can do the short top pitch.'

We arrived at Gordale and made the short walk up to the scar. No matter how many times I made this walk, I was always blown away with the magnificent scenery. Nearby Malham Cove was spectacular, but it was on full view. Even as you drove along the road towards Malham village you could see it. What I liked about Gordale was that it kept its secrets hidden until the very last moment. It was only when you rounded a short arête, guarding the entrance into the gorge proper, that its full magnificence was revealed. It was like stepping into the inner sanctum of some huge Gothic cathedral.

As Dave and I rounded the arête, we could see teams in action on the right wall. Greg Rimmer, familiar from his jester-like red and white tights was halfway up *Cave Route Right Hand* and Dave Kenyon, an unassuming but extremely talented climber from Lancashire, was trying the neighbouring *Defcon3*. Both these routes had been free climbed by Ron Fawcett and at grades of E6 and E7 were two of Yorkshire's finest and hardest rock-climbs.

After shouting a hello to the lads, we geared up and Dave led off easily up the first pitch of *Rebel*. I followed and then set about tackling the second pitch. Dave had done *Rebel* previously and was able to offer advice and encouragement, 'Just commit to the first bulge, clip the peg and go for it. It's okay when you do it and then you're in.'

I took a deep breath and went for it. Dave's advice proved sound and after a bit of a fight at the roof near the top of the groove, I was soon at the belay. Dave followed through and led the third pitch. At the top of the crag we coiled the ropes and then returned back to the gorge floor.

We went over and had a chat with Greg to obtain some beta on *Mossdale Trip*. *Mossdale* had been climbed by Pete Livesey in 1977 and followed a steep shattered wall for about a hundred feet. It didn't really follow any obvious features so to climb it you had to rely on good route finding. The rock was less than solid and required a confident but cool approach. The route suited Dave's temperament perfectly. Livesey had named the route as a memorial to a notorious caving disaster that had resulted in the deaths of several cavers in the nearby Mossdale Caverns. Livesey was meant to be involved on the day of the fateful trip, but had been called away. The name gave an indication of the seriousness of the route. Since 1977 it had only had a couple of repeats, but Greg had done it recently and in the last few months, it had received several ascents. Greg reassured Dave, 'Climb up the blunt arête and you get some bits of gear, then move up left and you'll find a peg. You've then got to run it out for about thirty feet to another poor peg. You can back the pegs up with a couple of small wires. From there you get to better rock and some more gear. There's a hard section to get to the belay ledge, but this is protected by a good thread runner.'

Dave thanked Greg for the beta.

'What about the top pitch?' I asked Greg.

'Oh you just follow your nose, take the obvious line.' Greg said.

I consulted the guidebook and the description appeared to be at odds with the information that we'd just got from Greg. The route was graded E6 6b, but Greg made it all sound so easy.

Dave led off and climbed the pitch in his cool methodical style and after about forty minutes shouted down that he was safe. I followed the pitch. Safe on the end of the rope, I could simply enjoy the absorbing nature of the climbing. I arrived at the belay and congratulated Dave on a fine lead.

'Where do you think the next pitch goes?' I asked.

Dave had taken a belay at an obvious spot on a vague ledge. The guide advised taking a belay way over to the right, but Dave had decided that this would cause too much rope drag.

I opted to tackle a steep thin crack directly above Dave's' belay. I launched into the crack, it was steep and deceptively technical and only wide enough to accommodate finger tips. I fought a tiny runner into a small slot and made another desperate move up. I was using everything I had in the tank and could feel the gas running out. Suddenly my fingers popped and I was flying through the air. I waited for the runner to arrest my fall, but it didn't happen. The runner had ripped and I flew past Dave head first. I sped down the wall for about fifty feet an involuntary scream echoing round the gorge. When I finally stopped, the other guys who were climbing shouted up anxiously to see if we were okay. Dave was doubled up in agony, my full weight had fallen directly onto his belay. He shouted down that he thought he'd done something to his hand. I was pretty shaken up myself, but after we'd calmed down, I reclimbed back up to Dave. His hand was ballooning up, so we rigged an abseil and baled out. I drove Dave down to Airedale Hospital where an X-ray of his hand revealed a neat crack right through his index finger.

'Thanks a lot, Radtke. I'm supposed to be in Chamonix next week,' Dave complained.

I later learned that the finish I had tried was in fact unclimbed and would later form the finish to a climb called *Sweet Hereafter* by Martin Berzins. The guidebook description reads:

Climb the crux of *Mossdale* but rather than moving right to the belay climb straight up the thin crack (hard) pulling out left to a tree.

A couple of years later I had the pleasure of leading *Mossdale Trip* myself, I was starting to add new routes of my own to the crag and considered myself a true Gordale devotee. At the time I was asked by *On The Edge* Magazine to write a piece about Gordale. This is a short section from that article.

To the right of *Face Route* a magnificent ocean of white rock, devoid of features and cracks rises out of the rubble strewn floor and soars skywards. When seen in the afternoon sunlight this vast expanse of shattered limestone provides a temptation for those in search of adventure. No bolts intrude to interrupt your concentration. Holds are studied in intimate detail, tested carefully and gently weighted. Progress is slow, no savage pulls, no random slaps or snatches. No room for error, just cautious, calculated movement, mind and body in total symbiosis. An occasional rusted peg appears momentarily and then slips away into the void below – temporary psychological comfort, as the mind concentrates, the body obeys and all doubt is suppressed. This is no place for doubt. This is the *Mossdale Trip*.

Looking back, I think that this single paragraph sums up what rock-climbing came to mean for me before the advent of sport climbing would take many of us in a new direction.

Chapter 4

Verdon Vertigo

Every experience that we have an emotional reaction to,
No matter how subtle, seems to be encoded in the amygdala.
Joseph LeDoux. The Emotional Brain

In 1982 filmmaker Sid Perrou produced a documentary called *The Fingertip Phenomenon*. It was a natural extension to Sid's successful series of TV programmes called *Rock Athlete* and painted a picture of modern rock-climbing against a canvas of the Verdon Gorge in the south of France. Its stars included Ron and Gill Fawcett with Jerry Peel to support Ron on some of the harder climbs and Chris Gibb in charge of sound recording. When the film was broadcast on UK television I watched it in awe and knew that I had to climb there.

The Grand Canyon du Verdon, as it is known in France, is a title that suggests a bit of over exaggeration, but when I gazed upon its vastness and breathed in the scented Provence air for real in 1984 I wasn't disappointed. The Verdon is an immense gorge carved into the rugged limestone hills between the medieval town of Castellane in the east and the sleepy village of Moustiers in the west. The gorge proper starts at the appropriately named Point Sublime, where sheer walls of white and yellow rock plummet over a thousand feet vertically from the rim of the gorge to the river below. From here the river weaves its way westward, between these immense walls, for around fifteen kilometres until it merges into the lake which it feeds, the turquoise waters of Lac de Saint Croix. A small road runs along the edge of the gorge and viewing balconies called belvederes allow tourists to soak up the spectacular scenery. Some of these belvederes offer great vantage points to view proceedings and climbing can sometimes have a goldfish bowl feel about it as gawping spectators look on.

The Verdon was brought to the attention of the Brits by early visits from Pete Livesey, John Sheard and Ron Fawcett in the '70s. Subsequent articles and photographs in the international climbing press soon spread the word and by the early '80s the Verdon was a truly international climbing Mecca. A number of factors combine to elevate the area to world-class status. Its grand scale offers obvious appeal. The sheer exposure of the climbing and space between your feet can provide both gut-wrenching anxiety and a true sense of liberation, depending on your disposition, and the rock itself is as near to perfection as you can get. The original pioneers approached the crag in the traditional way. Early routes were climbed ground up and follow natural crack and chimney lines. In between these natural features are huge sweeps of smooth grey limestone. From a distance the rock looks blank, but nature has worked in the climber's favour. Acidic rain over the millennia has dissolved little pockets into the carboniferous limestone that accommodate fingers and toes perfectly. In certain areas these pockets are present in sufficient numbers and adequate combinations that they can be linked together for hundreds of feet and it is these tracks that modern climbers have exploited to produce some spectacularly beautiful climbs. Finally, there's the Mediterranean climate with late spring and early autumn providing perfect weather conditions. However, the weather shouldn't be underestimated, storms can balloon up out of nowhere. I have been in the Verdon in the middle of summer when freak conditions have left the surrounding hills plastered in snow and climbers, caught out unexpectedly, have been struck by lightning and killed.

Establishing new routes from abseil has allowed pioneers to be quite selective in their choice of line and many routes favour only the best quality rock. This approach means that many of the newer routes avoid sections of poorer rock and actually start several hundred feet above the gorge floor. Often the start of a climb is simply a couple of bolts stuck in a blank-looking piece of rock halfway up the gorge wall. Rather than climbing up from the ground the start of these climbs are gained by abseiling in from above which can be an unnerving affair. Starting at these hanging belays feels something akin to being cast adrift in a vast ocean, only here one is surrounded by a sea of steep grey limestone.

Easter 1984 saw Ian Cooksey, Ledge, his girlfriend Sharon and me making the long drive down to the south of France. We only had a week and had a hit list created from what we'd seen on *The Fingertip Phenomenon,* an old copy of *Mountain* Magazine, a poster of Ron Fawcett on a route called *Necronomicon* and the cover of *Climber* magazine that featured one of Ian's mates making a free abseil into a route called *Luna Bong.*

On our first foray into the gorge, Ian and I stood at the edge of the abyss hoping that we'd located the right spot for the abseil and were nervously psyching ourselves up for the long decent down the walls of the gorge.

'If Danson did it, we can do it,' Ian was emphatic, 'and anyway, he said that the abseil in is scarier than the route.' Ian was referring to his mate who had climbed *Luna Bong* the year before.

Dealing with exposure is a natural part of climbing; having air beneath your feet is part of the buzz. Usually the exposure increases the higher you climb, but it's a gradual process and psychologically you acclimatise to the sense of space as you climb. The Verdon experience is very different. Here as you prepare to abseil into the void, the full exposure slaps you straight in the face; a thousand feet of air and sheer exposure instantly beneath your feet. Weirdly enough, I suffer from vertigo and get completely gripped when I stand near the edge of a cliff or in other exposed situations. Once I'm on a route and climbing, the reeling sense that I'm being pulled into the void evaporates. Psyching up for a Verdon abseil was always a big thing for me and Ian's comment of, 'the abseil is scarier than the route', was far from reassuring.

'Come on Ian, let's just get on with it,' I said, trying not to think about the sickening drop below our feet. Ian clipped his ropes into his abseil device, slid over the precipice and was gone. A few minutes later a distant 'Safe' echoed up from below. I took a deep breath and followed Ian into the void.

Necronomicon started from a hanging belay about sixty metres down and climbed perfect rock for two pitches. It was reputed to be about E4 6a and the picture of Ron on it in the poster made it look superb. I got the first pitch. The rock was rough grey limestone, and was so perfect it could have been sculpted, but I soon forgot about the romanticism as I fought my way up an unhelpful finger crack. I managed the pitch, but only by the skin of my teeth. Ian followed and led through to the summit. It was a short climb but its length was compensated by the quality of the climbing and its superbly exposed position.

Next day we opted for a route called *Chrysalis*, which had featured in *The Fingertip Phenomenon* and looked sensational. We had been told that the route weighed in at a grade of E3 6a and we thought it should be well within our abilities. I girded my loins and began the abseil down the wall of the canyon. After about a hundred feet I spied a couple of bolts winking at me. I clipped myself into the belay and awaited Ian's arrival. We pulled the ropes down after us. It felt like we were cutting an umbilical cord, severing our lifeline to the world above. Ian slid off down a second abseil. After some time he called me down. As I slid down the ropes the grey slab of wall suddenly changed into overhanging yellow limestone and I was hanging in space.

'I think we've fucked up here, it took all my effort to swing back into the rock,' Ian said as I joined him at the belay, 'there's no way that that's E3 6a, it looks desperate.'

I surveyed the rock above us and agreed with Ian's assessment. 'Well we'll have to give it a go. Otherwise the only way out is down,' I replied.

I tied on and started work, but it was useless I was way out of my league. 'Lower me back down Ian, you can have a go,' I shouted, but Ian declined the offer, and trapped, we decided to bail out hoping that we'd be able to continue abseiling down and get to the gorge floor. It would be a long and uncomfortable hike out especially in tight rock boots, but if we made it to the loop road at the rim of the gorge we might hitch a lift back to La Palud before nightfall.

Below us was a large terrace covered in trees and it looked like we'd get down to that without too much difficulty. We began abseiling again and made the terrace. Some bushwhacking through the dusty scrub brought us to the edge of the cliff again and we spied what looked like an abseil descent route to the base of the gorge. Further abseils and we were back on Terra Firma with the prospect of a long walk.

A stony path runs along the base of the gorge from Point Sublime and eventually rises up the canyon side to emerge at a place called Les Malines. We located the path and started the foot-numbing hike out. My rock boots were brand new and very tight. After several hours being fastened in these vice-like torture devices with the sun beating down, my feet were swollen and in agony. As we stumbled along the path a runner approached us in the opposite direction, he stopped for a chat and we explained our predicament.

The French guy suggested that he could help us out, 'I run to Les Malines, I ave ze auto zer. If you run wis me, I give you a lift to La Palud.' With that we started what I can only describe as a run in hell. With gear jangling round our waists, ropes tied to our backs and our water long since gone, it would have been a bit of a shocker in trainers, but in rock boots the pain was almost unbearable. Our helpful friend was also a bit of a task master. Inevitably we'd fall behind and I'd be thinking, 'Thank God for that, at least when I get to the road I'll be able to take these damn boots off. I'd rather walk to La Palud than endure this.' But as we'd round the next bend he'd be there waiting for us and tapping his watch, 'Allez, allez, Messieures, you must be quick.' In this fashion we stumbled along the rocky path, like cripples, in a bad dream. Eventually the nightmare ended as we made Les Malines. The following day I examined my feet, they were bleeding at the heels, the soles were badly bruised and my big toe nails were completely black, but at least my new Firé rock boots were broken in. A week later both my big toe nails fell off and when they finally grew back they were only attached by a small section of skin near the growing point and that's how they have remained to this day.

Undeterred by our previous misfortune we returned to *Chrysalis* a few days later. We'd done a bit of research and discovered that the lower pitches still required some aid and it was the upper two pitches that went at about E3 6a. This time we didn't overshoot the belay and enjoyed some brilliantly exposed pockety wall climbing on perfect rock.

During the '80s I made many trips to the Verdon. They were great times spent in fine company. In those days La Palud was a simple, rural Provençal village, surrounded by lavender fields and still free from any of the trappings that tourism encourages. There were two bars, a restaurant, a tobacconist, a bakery, and local shop. A simple campsite at the top of the village provided our home, it was owned by an eccentric farmer called Jean Paul. If proceedings ever got a bit rowdy, or out of hand, Jean Paul in true wild-west fashion would emerge from his house, shotgun in hand, and let off a couple barrels into the air to quieten things down and let people know who was the boss.

Apart from the local inhabitants, La Palud was buzzing with climbers from all over the world. Development in the gorge was at its peak and the climbing scene felt fresh, with a real spirit of pioneering adventure about it. It was commonplace for regular guys like ourselves, to brush shoulders with some of the world's finest. There was always a healthy faction of Brits present. Whether it was man of the moment Craig Smith shaking off our hangovers as he blasted Frank Sinatra's *I did it My Way* out of his van, or Mick Lord Johnston holding court in the bar, there were always stories to be told and mischief to be had. I remember on an early visit bumping into a rather shy young climber from Derbyshire, 'Aye up Simon what did you get done today?' I asked.

'*Pichenibule*,' was his reply.

'And how did you find the bolt ladder?' I asked.

'Well I flashed it, so I don't know what all the fuss was about,' was his modest response.

Pichenibule had been brought to notoriety in Sid Perou's film *The Fingertip Phenomenon*. The climax of the film shows Big Ron free climbing and falling off a particularly hard section of the route. It is evident from the film that this was a challenging piece of climbing even for Ron. It seemed incredible to me at the time that this young climber from Derbyshire could be so dismissive of a route with such a fearsome reputation. But the climber who had flashed the route with such ease was none other than Simon Nadin. Simon would go on to demonstrate his talent to the climbing elite, by winning the international indoor climbing competition series to become the world's first official climbing champion. With hindsight it is easy to reconcile Simon's comment, 'I don't know what all the fuss was about.'

Talk in the bars and on the campsite often revolved around who had done what and which were the latest must-do routes, everyone enthusiastically sharing info and waxing lyrical about this route and that. Further details could be obtained by consulting a newly published guidebook to the Verdon, together with the new routes book, both of which were kept in the bar. In this way people built up their hit list for the trip. A route called *Necropolis* was brought to my attention in this fashion. We'd had a particularly wine-fuelled night and were looking for a fairly stress-free climbing day.

'Yeah, *Necropolis* will just do the trick for you,' said Clive as we sobered up over coffee and croissants. He continued enthusiastically, 'It's just one abseil in, there's a nice F6b pitch to warm up on, followed by a couple of F6c pitches. The last pitch has got a thin tricky section, but then you move right and follow a VS crack to the top. It's about E3 6a overall.'

Great! We were sorted and decided that we would do it as a three, Ledge would get the first pitch, Ian the second, and I'd lead the third.

The climb went off without a hitch until it came to my lead. I wobbled my way up a tricky wall and was pleased to get to the traverse that led to the easy VS crack. About fifteen feet above me I could see a bolt in the groove-cum-crack and so I pressed on upwards, thinking to myself, I'm climbing really shit. I cursed my over enthusiastic intake of red wine. I got to the bolt above, but with a real struggle.

Ian and Ledge were heckling me from below, 'Come on what's up with you? It's only VS.'

The way ahead looked deceptively easy but I was finding the climbing desperate. It was much steeper than it looked from below, and where I thought there should be huge finger sinking pockets, there were just shallow dimples and an unhelpful crack in the back of the groove. I was trying to make it to another bolt, sweating, shaking, and clawing my way upwards while a constant stream of piss-taking came from the lads below. Eventually, I got up level with the bolt, but couldn't take a hand off to clip it. I started to really shake and it was a real fear shake. My last protection was about fifteen feet below and if I blew it here I could see that I'd slam into the slab after taking a thirty footer. Somehow, I managed to get a karabiner into the bolt just before I shook myself off the rock completely. I grabbed the bolt and got the ropes clipped in. I was relieved, but cursed my ineptitude, 'That's it, if I can't climb VS after a couple of bottles of wine I'm giving up,' I shouted down.

'What, the wine or climbing?' was the piss taking reply. At the top of the route, I was gratified to watch as both Ledge and Ian had a similar struggle to myself on the VS crack.

Back in camp, Ian and Ledge were eager to recount the tale to Clive, but I was able to have the last laugh, as Clive explained, 'You didn't traverse far enough right, what you did was the *Andropoulis* finish that gets F7b.' He went on, 'Have you seen Spider's back? It's a right mess! He took a big pisser off it earlier in the week and smashed right into the slab.'

John 'Spider' Mackenzie was a very good climber and a Scottish hard man to boot. I took some consolation from my recourse to grabbing the bolt.

The Verdon experience always took you on a mental journey and a day in the gorge was guaranteed to leave your body flooded with an intoxicating mix of endorphins. At the end of the day this heady mix was usually fuelled with copious quantities of cold beer and warm red wine. Groups would gather together around camping stoves, eating and telling stories long into the night. On one such evening Ledge and I returned to camp after a great route. Its name was the antithesis of the actual climb itself. *L'Ange en Decomposition* or The Decomposing Angel was a magnificent hundred metre climb that provided sustained and beautiful moves up an ill-defined pillar. At that time it was regarded as one of the best climbs of its grade in the gorge. We'd started on the climb late in the afternoon to avoid the heat and had actually topped out in darkness. Our friend Billy Lukin from Australia had fortunately abseiled down the last pitch and illuminated our exit by head torch, we'd cut things fine. Needless to say Ledge and I were buzzing when we got back to camp and, true to form, got stuck into the beer and wine. A group of like-minded climbers slowly gravitated to our encampment for the impromptu party. Legendary Verdon pioneer and French rock star Jean Marc Troussier was in town and had taken up residence in his little caravan in the corner of the campsite.

As our party subsided into tales and story telling, the French rock star emerged from his caravan and began chastising us, 'How long you gonna talk, one hour? Two hour? Three hour? I have an important redpoint to make tomorrow.' We just cracked up laughing. Troussier simply put his hands in the air, uttered a cry of despair and retired back to his caravan, disgusted at both our behaviour and our irreverence.

The following evening as we sat quaffing our customary beers, one of the lads who'd been partying with us the night before came over to recount a tale, 'I had a bit of a laugh today, I was climbing near where Troussier was trying his new route. It looked desperate and he was having a bit of a rough one on it, so I shouted over, 'Hey Troussier, how long yer gonna take? One hour? Two hour? Three hour?' I don't think he was amused.'

Looking back, the mid '80s Verdon scene was pretty unique. Different nationalities were literally thrown together in a couple of small bars and on a tiny campsite. Different attitudes, styles and approaches to climbing were debated in the bars and demonstrated with some audacious ascents on the rock. Some climbers came for the sheer adventurous nature of the place, but it was also a forging ground for pushing standards and not just the grade. Some extraordinary feats were accomplished, like Phillipe Plantier's free solo of *Frères Caramels Mous*, which featured F7a climbing with hundreds of feet of space beneath his feet. The Verdon definitely opened up people's imaginations and broadened their horizons. I am sure visiting climbers of all nationalities took new ideas, attitudes, and beliefs back home with them, with influential consequences.

I remember Ian Cooksey and I bumping into boy prophet Mick Johnston at Kilnsey Crag in Yorkshire. Mick had just come back from an extended trip around the south of France and he'd had a particularly successful time in the Verdon, racking up a comprehensive list of impressive routes. At the time I only knew Mick as a passing acquaintance, our paths had crossed on several occasions, but we both displayed the guarded behaviour that competitive climbers who don't know each other very well sometimes demonstrate. It was pretty apparent from Mick's appearance that his Verdon experience had done more than simply boost his climbing ability, it had influenced his cultural attitude towards climbing and even perhaps his own self-image. Mick struck a dashing figure. He sported long hair, dyed red, and adorned with some strategically placed beads. In his ears he wore elaborate fishing fly earrings and pranced around in neat black and green stripy Lycra tights. He was making a fashion statement. Not a 'look at me I think I look great', sort of statement. He was, in my opinion, stating where he placed himself in the grand climbing pecking order. Ian and I on the other hand, with our long hair, droopy moustaches and white sports socks, pulled over the ends of our Ron Hills, communicated quite a different image. We were still stuck in the past.

On that day at Kilnsey Crag, our apparent differences could have exaggerated the guarded suspicion that we held for each other, but things took a different turn. A little route called *Ground Effect* had brought us together and was now the focus of our combined attention. It had been climbed a couple of years earlier by Pete Gomersall and typically, for hard routes of the era, was graded at E5 6b. For us, this simply meant hard, but not quite cutting edge. *Ground Effect* was characterised in typical Kilnsey fashion, by an initial section of steep rock that led to good holds and some runner placements. Above these initial difficulties, lay an impending groove protected by two *in situ* threads. If my memory serves me correctly, we all managed to boulder the initial fifteen feet of the route out and were able to ascend to the good holds and retreat back to the ground with relative ease. I can't remember who decided to tie on and go for it first, but whoever it was, retreated unashamedly after scrutinising the fragile slivers of rock that supported the crucial threads protecting the crux.

After this initial failure each of us took the opportunity to impress the other, but after the sharp end had gone round full circle, we decided it was all a bit too scary. This incident had cut through egos and had broken the ice. As we started reminiscing and telling tales of past exploits, we recognised that we shared much more in common than is apparent at face value. Mick talked at length about many of his adventures and some roguish exploits in the South of France and concluded with a barbed statement, 'The route for you lads in the Verdon is *Surveiller et Punir*, best route in the gorge, if you get going well enough you might flash it, like I did.' The egos might have been deflated, but the competition was still fierce.

The following year we were back in the Verdon with *Surveiller* at the top of the hit list. On this occasion however we would be denied the climb. We learned that Jean Marc Troussier had removed all the bolt hangers and used them to equip another new route. Perhaps it was pay-back time for taking the piss out of him the year before. This seemed to be perfectly acceptable to many, since a new climbing practice was now being adopted. Rather than abseiling into the gorge and pulling the ropes down afterwards, it was becoming popular to simply top rope the upper pitches of routes, just selecting those with the hardest moves or most homogenous climbing. Extra long ropes were now being used and climbing teams would lower each other down the gorge and simply belay from the top. Teams adopting this technique justified it by suggesting that they were able to select the best and hardest pitches and also maximise the amount of climbing they did. This appeared to be the norm for routes like *Surveiller*.

For me, the Verdon experience was about the commitment of going over the edge, often into the unknown, cutting off retreat when you pulled your ropes down afterwards. Even though bolts were used to protect the routes, they were often spaced by today's sport climbing standards and routes still had a very adventurous feel. This new practice of top roping seemed to me to be trying to turn the gorge into something that it was not and it left a bad taste in my mouth. It would be the last time I would visit the Verdon for many years.

Back on home turf in England, the memory of *Ground Effect* kept gnawing away at me. Failure can be a hard thing to bear and it wasn't long before I was once again scrutinising the beguiling threads that would hopefully stop you hitting the ground if you fell. This time, I was able to throw caution to the wind, make the crux moves and wobble my way to the belay and then breathe a very big sigh of relief. Unsurprisingly, both of my compadres were also drawn moth-like to *Ground Effect's* flame, and with craft and cunning they also escaped unharmed. Since then I, like them, have visited Kilnsey more times than I can remember, occasionally trying new challenges, but more commonly repeating and re-repeating many of the excellent routes that have become our favourites. For me however, *Ground Effect* never allowed such familiarity, and judging by the lack of traffic that the route saw, I suspect the same applied for most other people as well. That was the state of play up until 1999 when, whilst on a familiar visit to Kilnsey, I was surprised to see a line of shiny bolts adorning the groove of *Ground Effect*. Interestingly enough, the person who'd added the bolts to *Ground Effect* was first ascensionist Pete Gomersall himself, who twenty years earlier deemed that bits of nylon tat, threaded behind flimsy bits of rock would be 'all reet'. My initial reaction to this was to be a little saddened, knowing that the mental game gambling with those suspect threads would be consigned to pre-history and the age of the climbing dinosaur. Contrary to my own feelings, I suspected that to most climbers it would be a welcome and progressive move. The rarely done *Ground Effect* would now become a popular classic that could be enjoyed by many. It was proof of how the idea of sport climbing, seeded over a decade previously, had taken permanent route in the UK. It also illustrated how people found climbing far more appealing when it was presented as a purely physical sport.

It would seem that humans have an inner need to climb. I think that subconsciously we associate climbing with danger. Even when rock-climbs are bolt-protected and safe, parts of our brains are still triggered into thinking we are in danger. Our rational brain knows it's safe, but those bits linked to emotions and survival are still given free rein to flood our bodies with hormones and endorphins.

This theory has more credence when the background of the climber is considered. A climber who learns the trade in the traditional way, has to deal with real risk and in doing so amasses a bank of stored memories and experiences that generally associate falling off with real danger. When the same climber moves into sport climbing mode, those same stored survival instincts still kick into play. I speak from experience here. When I first started climbing on bolts in the Verdon, I held the irrational view that the bolts were unsafe and was still very fearful of falling off. Even today when sport climbing, the irrational falling fear can kick in. Stored memories learned through powerful experience can take considerable unlearning. Perhaps the modern wall-born sport climber doesn't have to deal with such unlearning, but I suspect that the fear is still present as part of their inner psyche. If this is the case then it might give an insight into sport climbing's popularity. The risks are greatly reduced yet it is still found to be a thoroughly thrilling experience. Our brains trick us into thinking we are really courting danger and perhaps this is part of its powerful appeal.

Chapter 5

The New Wave

*Against the vast grey sweep they were
like peacocks in a concrete zoo.*
Gill Fawcett 1987

Ledge and I entered the café in Malham village. A bespectacled face appeared behind the counter. His curly grey hair was tied back in a ponytail and a straggly grey beard fringed his welcoming smile. It was Pete Livesey.

'Hello lads what can I get you?' he asked.

'Two coffees please Pete,' I replied.

'Are you two going up to Gordale again?' Livesey enquired.

'We are,' we stated in unison.

'And what're you going to do this time?' he continued.

'We thought we'd have a go at *Jenny Wren*,' I told him.

Pete came over and joined us at our table, 'You two like your adventure don't you?' he then continued on a different tack before we had time to answer, 'Have you heard about that young kid down in Wales. I believe he's just done a new route at Pen Trwyn. I heard that he put ten bolts in seventy foot of limestone. What do you make of that?'

Livesey was referring to a climb called *Statement of Youth* that had just been done by a young rock-climber called Ben Moon. The way that Livesey emphasised, ten bolts in seventy foot, suggested to me that he thought these bolts somehow undermined or discredited the route. The name, however, appeared to have a powerful underlying message. It wasn't just a throw away name, it appeared to be deliberately conceived, very much like the route which it described. To me, it suggested that Moon was sticking two fingers up at the old guard and saying: 'Here I am, I'm here to stay and this is what the future looks like.'

Climbers like Moon and his contemporaries were eating up established climbing test pieces and wanted new challenges. Influenced by what the French were achieving across the Channel, these climbers began to model the style of the Continentals and to some, this appeared to contradict or undermine traditional climbing values that were upheld in the UK.

'Mm, ten bolts does seem a bit excessive,' I agreed, 'but it's still reckoned to be desperate. It gets E7.'

Livesey concluded his ethical line of questioning with a matter of fact statement, 'Well personally, I can't see how a seventy foot climb with ten bolts in it can be graded E7.'

At the time, I was unaware of the facts surrounding Ben Moon's route and was completely oblivious about the phenomenal nature of his achievement. The reality was, that by climbing *Statement of Youth*, Moon had established a route in the UK whose standard of difficulty was as great as any of the routes of a similar type that were being done internationally. It was also some of the first evidence to illustrate how approaches to rock climbing in neighbouring Europe were being imported back into the UK.

Livesey redirected his attention to Ledge and me and, with a knowing smile, said, 'Well you'll not find any bolts on *Jenny Wren*, so don't fall off.'

Pete Livesey and John Sheard first climbed *Jenny Wren* in 1971. Unlike some of the aid routes that Livesey was attacking around this time, *Jenny Wren* followed an intricate line unique to itself. It was two hundred feet long and meandered across the left wall of Gordale Scar in three exposed pitches. The line could be traced from the safety of the gorge floor, but once you set foot on the route it was apparent that the challenges ahead were hidden from view.

The first pitch set the scene perfectly. A creaky groove seduced you upwards. The climbing was never desperate but suspect rock and sparse protection made total concentration mandatory. The groove led to a cave belay on a narrow rubble-strewn ledge. Overhangs adorned with loose and unstable flakes of rock thwarted any hope of escape upwards. The place had a sense of decomposition and decay. Ledge and I sat in the cave sorting gear. The way ahead was out leftwards round a blind arête and into the unknown. It looked blank and uninviting. I set off, arranged a token runner in a small crack and started probing the shattered wall to try and find useful holds. There was eighty feet of space below my feet, no obvious runners and Livesey's words, 'don't fall off,' were circling round my head like a Tibetan mantra. The only thing egging me on was the knowledge that other people had made this journey. Eventually, after hesitant probing, a slight variation in hold combination allowed a stretch left round the blind arête. My fingers locked onto a good flake and I was making steady progress leftwards over increasingly solid rock. I arrived at the belay, an oasis set in sea of white limestone, and hung myself from some ancient pieces of ironmongery. The third pitch was the crux of the climb. It continued up and leftwards linking technical pieces of bold climbing with subtle features that offered hope of protection and the possibility of rest. *Jenny Wren* is a subtle route; the way ahead is never obvious, and runners have to be placed with craft. It was classic Livesey. The rock may be dubious and the line tenuous, but the quality of the climb comes not from purity of line, or excellence of moves, but more from where it takes you mentally. For me the experience of *Jenny Wren* and many more Livesey classics that I enjoyed always resulted in complete mental and emotional immersion. These climbs absorbed body and soul. Climbing them was almost a meditative process. Routes like *Jenny Wren* connected with something in my psyche. They gave me a fleeting sense that I was free to choose my own path and destiny. It was a feeling of mental liberation.

Over the summer of 1985 some contentious issues were buzzing around the Yorkshire scene. Rock-climbing, or at least people's approaches to it were changing. Talk at the Richard Dunn wall suggested that passions were running high.

'Fucking Gomersall. What the fuck does he think he's fucking doing placing fucking bolts in *Frankie*.' Heavy Duty was having a rant and Ian Cooksey and I listened as he continued, 'It's one of the best fucking routes I've done, I really risked my fucking neck on that fucker. Anyway he's not going to get away with it. I'm going to chop the fuckers. If he wants to do it free let him do without the fucking bolts.'

Heavy Duty was referring to a route at Kilnsey Crag called *Frankie comes to Kilnsey*. He had made the first ascent of this blank-looking sheet of grey limestone with Duncan Drake. At the time Alan Stephenson, Duncan Drake, Dave Green and a few others were pushing the standards of aid climbing on Yorkshire limestone. They were attacking increasingly steep and featureless areas of rock, employing protection only where the rock allowed natural placements. These routes were technically extreme, very bold and psychologically exhausting undertakings. *Frankie* was no exception and its A5 grade gave an indication of its technical difficulty and seriousness. Even though Alan had employed aid, a fall taken on the climb would have had serious consequences. Clearly, Heavy Duty had pushed the boat out on this route.

At the time aid climbing appeared to be totally at odds with what real rock-climbing was all about. Raising the standards of free climbing by eliminating direct aid on former artificial routes is where the scene considered it was at. Aid climbing was definitely perceived as unfashionable, out of vogue and was even viewed as a retrograde step in the overall scheme of climbing development.

Pete Gomersall was an excellent climber and prolific new router. He was one of Pete Livesey's boys and had established some significant new routes throughout the country. He was not averse to bold scary climbing either. In 1980 he added Yorkshire's first E7 with his ascent of *Death Wish* at Blue Scar. Gomersall had free climbed *Frankie*, but not without the addition of three expansion bolts. This action would protect you from a potentially lethal fall and reduced the risk to a level that Gomersall deemed acceptable. Listening to Heavy Duty's tirade, I could see his point. In Heavy Duty's eyes Gomersall had stripped away the adventurous psychological challenge of the climb and in his view this was a retrograde step and a violation of ethics. On the other side of the coin, Gomersall had shown that it was physically possible to dispense with aid by climbing the route free. In his mind, this was a superior form of ascent. It was a scrap over principles.

As promised, Heavy Duty summarily chopped the bolts and returned his climb to its former glory. Martin Berzins, another influential climber on the Yorkshire scene, was next to rise to the challenge. Martin was a staunch upholder of traditional ethics and was even dubbed the self-proclaimed protector of Kilnsey. He free climbed *Frankie* relying on natural protection only. Martin had his critics however and despite a spirited attempt to set the free climbing standard straight, the style of his ascent was deemed to be flawed and was discredited by both aid men and free climbing purists alike. The bolts were replaced and the route became briefly popular. In 1987, Martin Berzins chopped the bolts and made a ground up free ascent of *Frankie*, but despite this, fashion still prevailed and the bolts became a permanent fixture. Up until that point, when artificial routes were freed, they still relied on the original gear for protection. By retro bolting *Frankie*, Pete Gomersall had set a precedent. Parodies of this little scenario would continue to play themselves out over the coming years.

As well as a melting pot in which ethical skirmishes raged, the Yorkshire climbing scene was fed by the egos of some fiercely competitive individuals. During one June day in 1985, Ian Cooksey and I were one of many teams climbing at Kilnsey. We were intent on making a free ascent of *The Superdirectissima*. Rob Gawthorpe had transformed this former A3 aid climb into an E5 free climb in 1980 and it was now a classic rite of passage Kilnsey route. Ian and I lay siege to our chosen objective and this kept us busy for several hours. Kilnsey was unusually busy that day and well-known teams were attacking some of the harder test pieces. Looking down the crag towards the North Buttress we could see Martin Berzins and Chris Sowden laying siege to a wildly overhanging route known as *Dominatrix*. They were intent on ridding it of its remaining aid points. It was a spectacular sight watching the silhouetted climbers repeatedly taking falls from high on the route. Also present that day was Ron Fawcett, who was obviously on fire as he cruised up and down the crag rapidly dispatching hard route after hard route. It was also pretty apparent that he was eager to get on *Dominatrix*. As the afternoon progressed, so did Ron's impatience as he loped up and down the crag like a hungry dog, periodically checking on the progress being made on Dominatrix. There was definitely not going to be a friendly 'Fancy a go Ron,' from Berzins and Sowden. In fact they occupied the route all day making sure that Ron didn't even get a sniff at it. Eventually, at the end of a long tension-filled afternoon, Berzins clinched the first free ascent of what would become another major classic free route. If my memory serves me correctly, Ron made a swift second ascent shortly afterwards. Competition for new routes was fierce.

In the '80s a day's climbing at Malham usually started with breakfast at either Livesey's or the Beck Hall café. One such day in '86 saw Danny Morgan and I enjoying a brew in Livesey's. Pete joined us at our table for a chat, 'What's all this then, Danny, part of a Black Pudding Team meet?' Our host directed the question at my companion in a dry almost mocking tone. Livesey had taught Danny whilst he was studying for a degree in Outdoor Education at Ilkley College and the pair knew each other pretty well. Livesey continued, 'There's been a steady trickle of your lot in and out of the café all morning. You've just missed Jerry Peel, he's gone up to the Cove. He said that there's lots of new route activity going on at the moment.' Before Danny had a chance to reply Pete directed his gaze at me, 'I didn't know you were a member of the Black Pudding Club. I thought you were of sterner stuff than that.' I didn't reply genuinely, confused by the comment.

'Anyway, what are you up to?' Livesey pressed. Pete had retired from climbing in preference for fell running, but still retained an interest in how climbing was developing particularly in his own back yard.

Danny informed him of our intentions, 'We're going up to the Cove. We've heard that people are putting up some short bolt routes that just finish at lower offs in the middle of nowhere, so we're going up to check it out.'

We finished our coffees and exited the cafe.

'What was all that stuff about a Black Pudding Team meet?' I asked Dan.

'Oh that was just Livesey's way of taking the piss out of me,' Danny replied. Danny Morgan was originally from Bolton and he talked with a Lancashire burr. Competitive to the end, Livesey was a master at weaving his Yorkshire sarcasm into friendly banter. Black Pudding Team meet was his little way of stressing the traditional Yorkshire-Lancashire divide. It was a subtle put down. Danny was not without a rapier-like wit himself. He had the knack of quickly identifying and exposing character flaws in most people he met. He was especially adept at it with climbers, particularly those who tried to take themselves a bit too seriously. He knew he was no match for Pete Livesey though. I first met Dan in Chamonix in 1983, but later, I discovered that like me, he was living in Halifax. He was also a mutual friend of Ian Cooksey, so days out on our local crags often saw us climbing together. I enjoyed his company. He was laid back and mellow and had even earned the nickname of Steady Dan.

Malham Cove, like neighbouring Kilnsey, had been a forcing ground for rock-climbing development in Yorkshire and by the mid '80s ascents were being made that were significant by national standards. The Central Wall of the Cove was an uncompromising sheet of compact white limestone, both steep, and to an untrained eye, looking pretty blank. This wall had been scaled by artificial means in several places in the '60s. In the early '80s pioneers like Ron Fawcett and Rob Gawthorpe had pointed the way by making free ascents of some of these spectacular former aid routes and now they were heralded as some of the hardest and best rock-climbs in the country. Climbers fresh from European travels soon recognised the potential of opening up previously unclimbed areas of rock by placing new expansion bolts. These actions were catalysts for an intense period of rock-climbing development.

As Danny and I approached the spectacular limestone amphitheatre that is Malham Cove we could see that certain areas of the crag were festooned with climbers. It looked like a grey canvas onto which an artist had splattered dots of different brightly coloured paints. Many appeared to be sitting or standing, some were hanging motionless from the rock and one or two appeared to be inching their way upward, or were being lowered back down the rock face. Most of the coloured dots were congregated on a large ledge near the base of the cliff. This ledge formed a natural walkway under the very centre of the Cove. Above the walkway, overhanging white and grey limestone stretched skywards for two hundred and fifty feet. It was this area of the Cove that had been the focus of our earlier conversations in Livesey's Café. Climbers of the day had taken to wearing Lycra tights. These stretchy skin-tight garments allowed the legs good freedom of movement that was essential for modern athletic climbing. Garishly coloured tights also showed up spectacularly well in magazine photographs and in the mid-80s, Lycra had become the fashion statement of the day for cutting edge rock-climbers. I don't know who coined the name for the ledge beneath the central wall, but the Catwalk, as it became known, was based on a humorously insightful observation.

As we gained the right-hand side of the Catwalk, Danny was greeted by Jerry Peel, 'How're you doing Dan?'

'Have you met, Rad?' said Dan introducing me. I'd bumped into Jerry on one or two occasions and whilst I didn't really know him, I was fully aware of his technical brilliance on the rock.

Jerry was a painter and decorator by profession. I remember having a conversation with a young and impressionable John Dunne in which he revealed the secret of Jerry's climbing prowess. 'You know why Jerry is so strong and has got so much stamina, Rad?' he asked.

'Go on then, John, give us the secret,' I urged.

John promptly revealed his pearl of wisdom. 'He uses his work to train, he paints ceilings using two brushes, one in each hand, and that gives him awesome stamina.'

As we stood passing the time of day with Jerry, Dan cast his gaze over towards the left hand side of the Catwalk. 'Is that The Arm over there?' Danny was referring to Mick Lovatt, who was making short work of some blocky overhangs. 'What's he on, Jerry?' enquired Dan.

'That's a new route of Rimmer's, he did it last week, *Appetite* I think its called, E5 6a, all on bolts. Micky Ryan has also bolted some new stuff up.'

'What's The Chimp on?' Dan nodded in the direction of Dave Kenyon who was tackling a blank-looking wall above the centre of the Catwalk.

'That's *Seventh Aardvark*, another bolted route,' Jerry replied.

'What are you going to do, Jerry?' asked Dan. We looked across the heaving Catwalk.

'I don't know, there's every man and his dog here, I think I'm going to go upstairs and have a go at *Obsession*,' Jerry said.

'Any recommendations, Jerry?' we asked.

'*Yosemite Wall's* good,' he said.

'Yeah I did that last year, I thought it was hard,' I told Jerry.

'It's very busy today, so I'd just see what you can get on,' advised Jerry, and then he said. 'See you later,' and he was off.

Dan and I made our way along the Catwalk. 'How come you've got nick names for everyone, Dan?' I asked.

'Well most of them are earned by reputation. Watch Kenyon climb and you'll get the gist,' he replied.

'What about Lovatt, is he called The Arm because he's so strong?' I asked.

'Oh no, you've got to be après climbing with Mick to understand where he gets his nickname from.'

As we wandered across the Catwalk we bumped into Mick Ryan. Mick was a bit of a radical thinker, he liked to challenge entrenched attitudes and loved playing Devil's advocate. Mick appeared to fully embrace the Continental ethic of sport climbing.

'What's this Mick?' I pointed at a line of new bolts that finished at a lower off at about fifty feet.

'Oh it's a route of mine, I did it last week. *Consenting Adults*, about F7a. Do you like the name?' Ryan asked.

'And what's this?' I asked again, pointing to a route just to the right that was evident from a disjointed ladder of old bits of ironmongery.

'That's *Free and Even Easier*, about E5,' he replied.

Dan and I geared up and prepared to do battle, and a battle it proved to be. We each made little desperate forays up the route. With each foray we'd get to a high point, clip the rope into a bit of gear and lower back to the ground. The other person would tie in and then essentially top rope to the high point and then try and make further progress. In this fashion, we eventually managed to get to the top of the route. The frustrating thing was, it wasn't really the top of the route it was simply a place where things got ridiculously steep and free climbing was no longer an option. Once we'd got the route sussed we pulled the ropes and tried to climb the route from bottom to top, clipping gear as we went. The climbing was certainly physically demanding but at the end of the day I walked away feeling a little bit deflated. I didn't have the buzz of the adventure. What's more, I hated the crowds. It felt as though I'd been climbing in a goldfish bowl. As a kid I'd suffered from claustrophobia and my Catwalk experience resurrected similar feelings.

Over the next few years Malham Cove became one of the UK's big arenas for change. Ethics were debated more than ever and with heated frenzy. Fitness, attitude and new approaches brought rapid rewards for a new wave of climber. Around this time the concept of competition climbing was taking off in Europe. This introduced new elements into the rock-climbing melting pot, mainly in the form of commercialism. Gear sponsorship, money and fame were attractive carrots for up-and-coming young climbers who often existed primarily on their dole money. This undoubtedly influenced the attitude and beliefs of some, that sport climbing was the way forward. Malham started attracting some of the best climbers from far and wide. A hard-core team of Peak-based lads became regulars. Ben Moon, Chris Gore, Ben Masterson, Jerry Moffat and Mark Leach started to make their mark, repeating the latest new routes and adding test pieces of their own. This also stimulated anger in some quarters, whose protectionist instincts wanted to resist the inevitable winds of change. As well as the visitors, locals were also grabbing a fair share of the action, including a young John Dunne. John would prove to be a controversial figure on the climbing scene as he pushed the standards of modern rock-climbing skywards. Over the next decade John established cutting edge routes throughout the country.

In 1994 I was asked by *On The Edge* magazine to write a mini biography about John and his achievements. Whilst researching this article, I interviewed some of the influential climbers who were on the Yorkshire scene during the Malham boom years. I have included some extracts from the article here since they give some insight into the prevailing attitudes that were in evidence during the mid '80s:

Mick Lovatt remembered the period well.
'I teamed up with John in 1986, we did a lot of climbing together between '86 and '87. John amassed an impressive list of first ascents and early repeats. In a way he was a victim of his own enthusiasm, he could be quite abrasive and would wind people up simply by the way he did things. He'd warm up on *Raindogs* F8a, redpoint his latest project and then do laps on *Obsession* F7b+. People just didn't understand how keen he was. Despite his achievements he never seemed to get the credit that he truly deserved. When he did *The Well Dunne Finish* there was more news about the jump from the top than the actual quality of the route'.

At the age of 17 John was keen to stamp his authority unquestioningly on the crag and produced what he considered his first masterpiece. Ironically the turn of events surrounding the climb would cast a cloud over John that would never truly disappear:

John described events surrounding his ascent of *The Maximum*.

'Alan Watts was over from America and had just done a really rapid ascent of Jerry Moffatt's route, *Revelations* which was E7 7a, really a benchmark F8a. We started working on *The Maximum* together. There's an obvious slot on the crux which when you look at it now it's obvious to undercut this to get the pinch. At the time, however, the lower part of the route was often wet and through naivety or lack of new route experience I was getting the pocket with my right hand and undercutting a vague edge to do the crux. Alan tried the route over four or five days using the same sequence as me, but couldn't do the move and thought it was definitely harder than *Revelations*. When I finally did the route, I thought it was harder than anything else I had done at that time, so between us we reasoned it must have been E8, or F8b, or whatever. I have to admit, however, when you're young and after sponsorship and things, you do push the big numbers. Then up walks Mark Leach, puts two and two and together and does the crux using a different sequence and downgrades the route to E6. I think it did me a lot of damage that incident, because for years after it stuck in people's minds. Every time I did a new route, doubt was cast over its difficulty. Looking back, I wonder what the hell I was doing, but it would be interesting for someone who's done everything at Malham to try *The Maximum* using the same sequence that I used. I think they'd find it quite hard'.

When John completed *Magnetic Fields* F8b in 1987, the big number had finally arrived at Malham. Despite this fine achievement new rumours were soon flying around Yorkshire. This time the accusing finger was incriminating John as a thief and stealer of routes. John admitted to making the first ascent of someone else's project at Kilnsey, but maintains that this was a genuine mistake, thinking that it had already been climbed:

Steve Rhodes who was active in Yorkshire at the time recalled the events.
'I bolted up the line that ultimately would become *Predator* F8b, but only up to the hard section. At the time I had just joined the fire service and it was clear that I was going to be off the scene for a while. John asked me if he could work the route and I agreed that it would be okay. John was very fit at the time. He'd do things like *L'Obsession* F7c+, *Obsession* F7b, *Herbie* F7c+, and *Main Overhang* F7c+, one after the other at the end of a full day's climbing. At the time I was just about managing to redpoint one of these routes in the day. When he

did *Predator* there was no animosity. I never felt as though he'd stolen it. It was the media and gossip mongers who spread the rumours and stirred the shit up'.

I am sure that the primary motivation of most top-flight climbers was still centred round challenge and the desire to push the boundaries of the sport. However, I am also convinced that during the mid-80s, personal attitudes were also being fed by commercialism and media exposure. Whether these climbers liked it or not, their actions were sending out messages to the broader climbing community, who often looked on through the pages of glossy magazines. Many climbers started to turn their backs on their traditional climbing roots in favour of the emerging modern game. There was a subtle change in emphasis. Advocates of the new sport appeared to value the physical and aesthetic challenges of climbing. On Yorkshire limestone at least, the adventurous element, with its associated risks and uncertainties, seemed to be falling out of fashion.

Every generation feels the need to make its mark in history, whether it is music, fashion or science. The concept of sport climbing enabled a visionary few to take climbing into ground-breaking areas. They pushed the boundaries of physical possibilities and left some of their predecessors awestruck. After all, they were free climbing sections of rock that had been previously declared impossible. They were true pioneers and history shows us that they were influential in shaping rock-climbing culture. New achievements were defined and measured more than ever before with the grade. Climbers had a long tradition of pushing the physical side of the sport, but always recognised the significance of an ascent, that coupled hard physical climbing with bold mental control. It seemed that now, the number alone was becoming the holy grail of rock-climbing and those in search of it were at risk of losing touch with the element that, in my opinion, actually breathes 'soul' into a rather irrational pursuit. To quote a good friend of mine and simple climbing observer:

'There are rock-climbers around today who will only venture onto a route if it is fully protected with bolts, clearly it's their prerogative, but in a way they are Hollow Men.'

Chapter 6

A Step in The Light Green

'And Frankie kicked a mine the day that mankind kicked the moon,
God help me he was going home in June'.
John Schumann

I'd been living in Halifax for about eight months, there were stacks of crags on my doorstep and I'd slotted naturally into the local climbing scene with its quirky characters. My job was going well, so I decided to take the plunge and bought a stone terrace in the town, which was on the market for £12,500. In 1984 I was on a salary of around £7,000 a year, the house seemed a big financial commitment, but I wasn't particularly materialistic. Mates, travel and climbing had become the focus of my life.

The house was a stone's throw from the local crag, a moderate gritstone edge called Woodhouse Scar. It was home to some good bouldering and short solos and it made a great training combination with West Vale. After work, I'd nip to Woodhouse, solo about fifteen routes and then drive round to West Vale and traverse till I dropped. I thought I was training hard, but it was a pretty mediocre regime compared to what many were doing. I remember making visits to the Peak District around this time. We'd arrive at crags like Raven Tor and Stoney Middleton psyched for routes, only to find the likes of Martin Atkinson and Chris Gore using the crag as an outdoor gym. These lads were part of the New Wave, and they were really embracing sport climbing in the UK. They weren't new to climbing, however. The likes of Gore had been around the scene for years and was well-respected as a strong climber with a long track record of hard routes under his belt. They'd have a Bachar ladder rigged up to the crag with top ropes down some of the harder routes. The ladder was an innovative training method devised by American visionary and soloist, John Bachar. Essentially it was a rope ladder that was rigged under tension at an angle of about eighty degrees. Training consisted of climbing from rung to rung on the underside of the ladder. It was effective in training upper body strength and the ability to do one-arm lock-offs.

We'd look on as these 'Peakys', as we deridingly called them, would do laps on the routes not only climbing up them, but also reversing all the moves back to the ground. They'd then work out on the ladder and repeat the whole process. Personally I found their behaviour on the crags quite arrogant, but I couldn't deny that what they were doing was pretty impressive. It was clear that climbers like Atkinson and Gore knew what could be achieved with innovative training methods. They were adopting a professional approach to their sport that hereto had not been seen.

This period in climbing history also coincided with the emergence of commercial competitions and a number of leading British rock-climbers started competing at international events. Prize money for the winners of competitions wasn't to be sniffed at, but equally important, even for those who didn't make the podium, were the sponsorship deals that could be secured as a result of the high profile media exposure and PR. For the first time in the UK there seemed to be a real possibility of earning a living as a sponsored rock-climber and this was an attractive proposition for the gifted few, or those willing to work at it.

There appeared to be a transition in the marketing tactics of gear manufacturers during this period. New names endorsing various products started to replace the old guard. Domestic climbing magazines became littered with adverts portraying the exploits of what seemed to be a new breed, and whether intentional or not, these climbers continued to influence the evolution of the sport. I think that some of this influence had a powerful and really positive impact on rock climbing in the UK. Martin Atkinson pushed the standards forward in the Peak District with routes like *Mecca* F8b+ at Raven Tor and in Yorkshire with the likes of *Supercool* F8a+.

Even the likes of Mark Leach, with his dogged determination, would demonstrate what was possible at Malham and at Kilnsey. Despite their inspirational efforts it would take years for the mainstream to catch up. Malham and Kilnsey in Yorkshire, Raven Tor in the Peak District, Pen Trwyn in North Wales, all yielded cutting edge, world class sport climbs which stand as inspirational achievements even by today's standards.

During the '80s I drew my own inspiration from books and tales told at the wall. Climbers would extol superlatives about one particular route, or relate epics that they'd had on another. This led us on a quest up and down the country targeting famous climbs, or seeking out the next logical challenge. It became apparent that there were some marked regional differences between grades of climbs, particularly on the mountain crags. This disparity was particularly evident when we compared grades of routes between North

Wales and Cumbria. I remember one season in the mid '80s. I'd been getting fit by doing a lot of climbing in the Lakes ticking my way through the E3s and E4s. A burning ambition of mine at the time was to lead *Right Wall* on my old favourite crag Dinas y Gromlech. Pete Livesey had established this classic route in '74, it was a masterpiece of climbing that followed a meandering line up the wall right of *Cenotaph Corner*. It still held a challenging reputation for an aspiring E5 climber like myself. So one weekend saw Ian and me camped by the Gromlech boulders in the Llanberis Pass, looking up at *Right Wall*, each inwardly speculating whether we were up to the challenge. I broke the silence, 'Come on Ian, I'm going for it.'

A couple of hours later I was standing at the top of the climb buzzing with the joy of success. It felt like a breeze compared with some of the Lakes E4s that I'd done earlier that season. I loved North Wales and its sheer diversity. The accessible roadside crags of The Pass and Tremadog, the mountains and of course the sea cliffs of Anglesey.

It is Dave Green to whom I owe a debt of thanks for introducing me to the delights of Anglesey. It was 1988 and Dave was on my case.

'Come on Radtke, you don't know what you're missing get yourself down here, there's some amazing stuff being done,' he said.

Dave had moved to North Wales and he shared a house with his girlfriend, Gerry, they lived in Deiniolen. Dave had slotted in nicely to the Llanberis scene, which was fuelled by a heady mix of wild partying and adventurous climbing.

So the following weekend saw Dave and me at South Stack, overlooking the Irish Sea. As I stood at the cliff top breathing in the salty air, Dave interrupted the cacophony of gulls.

'Right, Rad, I've got the perfect warm up for you,' he wore a familiar enigmatic smile as he spoke. An abseil later and we were stood beneath an overhanging wall of shattered rock that bristled with overhangs.

'I've done it before so you can have the main pitch. It looks daunting but the climbing's steady,' he declared.

We swung leads up the cliff in three spectacular pitches. *The Moon* was my first Gogarth route and I was addicted. Next day saw us at the base of North Stack, looking up a smooth wall of white quartzite. My stomach was a veritable butterfly house.

'Well, Radtke, you've been talking about it for years. You've got an audience at the top of the crag so you can't back out now.' Dave's ultimatum was final. He then continued, 'Once you clip the bolt, you make a couple of sequency moves on small edges and you're in. All you've got to do is keep your head together as you run it out to the top. If you blew it there you'd be seriously close to the deck, but you're not going to blow it are you?' Dave was speaking from experience and I took his wisdom on board.

I set off up the lower wall and my nerves subsided as positive holds appeared out of the blank-looking canvas of rock. It was a delicate climb that required careful evaluation and precise movement. It was a perfect piece of chess play. Think through several moves in advance, evaluate the risk, execute the planned sequence, re-group and repeat the process. This is how I played *The Cad*.

Next on Dave's agenda was a route called *Heart of Gold* that took an impressive line up *Left Hand Red Wall*. The original line had been climbed by legendary pioneer Mick Fowler, but a more direct line had been climbed by Paul Pritchard a couple of years earlier and Dave was intent on making a second ascent of *Heart of Gold Direct*. We abseiled into the route only to find that a pair of local climbers had beaten us to it. A young Ber-iste by the name of Ben Pritchard was just starting to second the first pitch, his partner already hanging from a belay up and right of our position. We bided our time until they had vacated the hanging stance and then I set off up the first pitch. It climbed over strange rock that had a fragile biscuit-like texture, very different to the rock on North Stack. Dave followed and then quickly dispatched the second pitch in his cool steady way.

The regional grade anomalies didn't always work in your favour, however, and at times the tables tipped the other way. Not long after my first Anglesey experience I was back in the Lakes with Bolton climber Geoff Hibbert. Geoff was an unlikely looking rock-climber, more akin to a musical rock star with his huge stature and shoulder length hair. Nonetheless, he was massively enthusiastic and doggedly determined. Over the years he had steadily plodded away, ticking hard routes across the UK and the Alps. He had an offbeat sense of humour and was a real practical joker, but underneath this easygoing façade, he was also fiercely competitive. But above all he was good company.

Our target for the day was Raven Crag in Langdale. The centrepiece of the crag is a smooth shield of rock protected by roofs that have to be breached from below and overhangs that stifle escape above. The left side of this shield is guarded by a steep groove line, which is taken by a climb called *Trilogy*. Another climb called *R n S Special* sneaks boldly across the shield in an exposed position. Someone had told me that *R n S Special* was an easier version of *The Cad*, so I had this firmly in my sights. Geoff wanted to do *Trilogy*. I had climbed this previously and seconding Geoff up it would provide a pumpy but safe warm-up. It seemed that we had the perfect day lined up.

Geoff fought his way up *Trilogy* in fine style and after following the route, it was my turn to do battle with *R n S Special*. I gained the shield and placed some runners to protect the next section of the climb. I tried to evaluate the moves out right, but unlike *The Cad*, the way ahead was not at all obvious and it took some tentative probing before I was able to commit to a sequence. The climbing was insecure and balancey and as I made tenuous moves right I was aware that I was leaving my runners and protection well behind. I'd done my research and knew I was heading for a good hold where a runner could be placed. I could see the hold out right, but couldn't work out how to get to it. My runners seemed miles away and I started to lose focus as the thought of a big sweeping fall began consuming my concentration. I pushed these unnerving thoughts back, by looking at the hold and visualising the runner placement that I knew would take all the pressure off. With this I committed myself and thankfully my fingers curled round the hold, but rather than being filled with a sense of relief, I was greeted with horror. It looked like half the hold had broken away and with it the runner placement. A fall from here would be disastrous. An internal dialogue fired up in my brain like two different people arguing with each other;

'Fuck, fuck, fuck, you've blown it now.'

'Calm down, calm down, calm down, relax, you're gripping that hold as if it's a micro edge

'I'm going to die, I'm going to die!'

'Look you're on a jug, you can stand here all day.'

And so the mind games went on for what seemed like minutes. Eventually, the calming dialogue grew louder and the panicking voice inside my head subsided. I started to rationalise my position. I shouted down to Geoff, 'The runner placement's gone, I'm completely committed here, I think I can see how to make the next moves, but if I blow it, I think I might deck it.'

Geoff shouted back up, 'You'll take a big un, but I think you'll be okay.'

I was strangely calm now and in what seemed like a disembodied state of mind, I left the sanctuary of the jug and made some sketchy moves to easier ground.

What a trip! I'd expected it to be a stroll compared to *The Cad*, but I'd been right at my limit, it had felt a full grade harder than *The Cad*. So much for the reliability of the grading system. I later learned that someone had taken a fall on the route and had, in fact, broken the hold and ripped the runner placement. It might have even been Chris Gore himself.

Although I loved travelling around the country and pitting myself against established classic routes, I'd also developed a bit of an interest in putting up new routes of my own. I did my first new route in my first year of climbing. I'd just completed one climb and noticed what seemed a better looking line just to the left. The guidebook revealed that no route was described. I wondered why no one had thought to climb that piece of rock and set to work leading it. It was only VS, but I felt that I had accomplished something different completing that climb. That little obscure VS sowed the new route bug in me. A couple of my new route highlights were associated with a small gritstone quarry in Yorkshire.

Heptonstall Quarry is a fine sunny crag overlooking the Calder Valley in Yorkshire. Climbing at Heppy didn't start until the 1950s, but over the years it has attracted the attention of some notable rock-climbers who have produced some excellent quality routes. The quarry's most famous and perhaps best climb is the aptly named *Forked Lightning Crack*. This route follows a striking off width crack that splits an overhanging wall of smooth yellow rock. It's an impeccable feature and was first led by Don Whillans in 1961. It has the great man's signature all over it, blatant and uncompromising at face value, yet more subtle on closer acquaintance. Even today with modern camming devices to protect it, it still commands respect and is one of the quarry's must do routes. Through the 1970s and '80s the local team of Jerry Peel and Barry Rawlinson added some excellent climbs to the quarry. In 1974 Pete Livesey and Al Manson added a tough route with their aptly named *Hard Line*, and Ron Fawcett and John Syrett got some of the action when they added the hard finger cracks of *Demerara* and *Brown Sugar*. Even Steve Bancroft from the Peak managed to sneak a new route in. In 1983 Jerry Peel had climbed a hard problem up a blank looking section of rock on the *Thin Red Line* wall. He'd called the problem *Badlands*. It featured technical boulder problem type moves and mirrored his character. Unfortunately the route finished halfway up the crag where it joined the traverse line of a HVS route called *Pulpit*. Above the traverse a dark and brooding headwall streaked with green algae reared for another thirty feet. The headwall was steep and uncompromising and although featured, it looked pretty improbable from a climbing perspective.

When I moved to Halifax, Heppy became one of my local crags and I systematically worked through the routes until I'd virtually ticked the crag. I developed a regular soloing circuit. I'd start on *Curving Crack* VS, move onto *Senility* HVS, then do *Bulls Crack* HVS, and finish by doing *Thin Red Line* the quarry's classic E2. By 1987, Heppy felt like a second home and it was about this time that Ledge abseiled the headwall above the *Pulpit* traverse and declared that he thought it was definitely climbable. Ian Cooksey and I were keen to have a look and tried the moves on a top rope. We both agreed with Ledge's verdict and what was also encouraging was that it looked like the climbing could be protected. There were places for a couple of pegs and an eye that would take a tied off cam. We were really fired up; snatching such a plum from under the noses of the locals would be a real coup. The only problem was, that we'd made plans to spend the following Easter week in Pembroke. We were due to leave the following day, so the route would have to wait until we got back.

The Pembroke trip was probably a blessing in disguise. It was still early in the season and Pembroke was always a great place to get going. We got plenty of mileage in and by the end of the week we'd managed to tick several E5s. I was also tormented with new route paranoia, and as we'd left telltale chalk marks on our proposed line at Heppy, we were worried that someone might sneak in before us. There were some strong and talented locals operating in the area. Jerry Peel was still very much on the scene and the likes of Mark Leach and Mick Johnston were also Heppy aficionados. We just hoped that their attention was focused on the limestone. Leach in particular was very strong. The following year he would establish *Cry Freedom* F8b+ at Malham and would be dubbed, The Human Fly, with his free ascent of Kilnsey's main overhang.

The Sunday on our return from Pembroke saw Ian and me standing below the sunbathed quarry walls of Heppy. Our route paranoia proved unfounded. I abseiled the line and hammered in two pegs and we set about the siege. I was first up, but kept falling off, trying to get up to the second peg. After about an hour I gave up and Ian took over. Ian had similar misfortunes to me, but was looking stronger than I and with a really determined effort, linked the moves and managed to clip the second peg. The effort had cost him, however, and he powered out and fell off. It was my turn to take over. This time I won through and managed to gain the ramp line at the top of the headwall. I threw a leg up onto the ramp and in this position was able to place a tied off Friend in the eye-like slot. It was a pumpy position and as I fought to make the final moves, I blew it and fell. It was Ian's turn to get the glory. He tied on and fought his way upward. One half of me was willing him on, the other half secretly hoping that he'd blow it. He made the ramp and then started the rock over that would give him the first ascent, but he started to shake and just as he was about to get the finishing holds he fell. My turn again and I was lucky enough to win through. Ian grabbed the second ascent on his next attempt. We'd put a lot of effort in and it had taken us most of the afternoon to get up thirty feet of rock. A first ascent photograph appeared as a full page spread in the July edition of *High* magazine. In Neil Foster's rock notes it stated:

> On Yorkshire grit Mark Radtke completed the superb, *A Step in The Light Green* E6 6b, above the Pulpit Traverse.

There was no mention of Ian. In reality the ascent was a combined effort, but to the onlookers I had created the route, such is the power of the media in writing history.

People often asked me how I came up with the name. At the time I was listening to an Australian folk band called Redgum. The band had a big hit with a song called 'A Walk in the Light Green'. The song was about Australian soldiers who served in Vietnam. During the war the Americans used a herbicide, called Agent Orange to defoliate huge swathes of jungle. The theory being that they would be better able to observe the movements of the Vietcong with the forest canopy removed

Areas of defoliated jungle were designated as light green areas on maps. During mission briefings, troops on the ground used these maps. If they were being deployed into a light green area, they knew that there would be limited ground cover and that in all probability it would be laced with land mines. In other words a walk in the light green was going to be a tough mission. I didn't think I could dishonour the bravery of these servicemen by stealing A Walk in the Light Green as a name for a meagre rock climb. *A Step in the Light Green* seemed a little more acceptable. Perhaps it should have been A Tip Toe in the Light Green.

A few years after Ian and I had climbed *Light Green* I recall bumping into Dave Pegg at the Ambleside climbing wall. At the time Dave was area correspondent for *On the Edge* magazine and I'd just read his latest new routes report for

Yorkshire.

'Sounds like Jerry Peel's new route at Heptonstall was a good addition, Dave,' I said.

'Yeah. The thing is, I don't think he actually did it,' replied Dave.

'How come?' I asked.

'Well, I was there when Jerry and Mick were trying it on a top rope. They looked like they were really on for it. They even said that it was called *Orange Crush*. When I left I naturally assumed that they'd led it, so I reported it as being done. I later found out that they didn't have any pegs to protect it. As far as I'm aware they haven't been back to do it.'

I'd never describe myself as a fiercely competitive person but a couple of days later I was back at Heptonstall with a top rope down the bulging arête immediately right of *Light Green*. After working the line for about an hour, I'd put together a sequence of moves that enabled me to climb the route, but only just. There was a horizontal seam that would take a couple of pegs, but a fall when making the final slap for a good hold at the top of the arête would leave you dangerously close to some big ledges near the base of the cliff. I left the quarry at the end of the evening excited and apprehensive at the prospect of leading the route. There was no question in my mind what I was going to do. I'd bumped into Jerry Peel on a number of occasions and he'd always suggested that we should get out and climb together. I picked up the phone and dialled Jerry's number, 'Is that Jerry? Hi it's Rad. You know the route at Heppy that was reported recently, did you do it?' I was straight to the point.

'No we just put a rope down it and had a play on it,' replied Jerry.

'Well, I've been on it this week and I think I can do it, I was just wondering if you'd like to join me and we can do it together?'

'No problem Rad, I'll see you at Heppy at one o'clock,' he told me.

'Can you dig out a couple of pegs Jerry? I'll bring my selection as well, see you later.'

In the quarry we soon had a rope down the arête and I placed two pegs side by side in the horizontal seam. This would be the only protection on the route. We warmed up on *Thin Red Line* and then set to work on the new route. I was first up, keen to demonstrate the sequence to Jerry. Steep moves on good holds gained the pegs, but then a technical sequence followed to gain a thin flake, a powerful undercut off this gained better holds and eventually the top. They were brilliant moves, but on my lead attempt I failed to connect with the good hold from the undercut and fell. I handed over to Jerry. He climbed coolly, cruising the sequence that I'd shown him, but just as he was making the long span off the undercut, the flake exploded and he was airborne. On inspecting the rock the flake had completely gone leaving nothing but a faded scar. It was back to the drawing board. If we were going to climb this route, we'd have to figure out a new sequence. Jerry went back up and after playing around, figured out a new way up the arête a metre or so to the right. It wasn't quite the quality of the original sequence, but provided an alternative key to the lock. Jerry came down and handed me the ropes, 'It's all yours go for it.'

I climbed the route and got to the jug, but I was pumped. The last move required a strong lock-off, or a dynamic slap. I didn't feel strong and rather than focusing on a well-aimed slap, I was thinking about the fall and its consequences. I tried the move, but it was a weak willed affair. I came to halt a couple of feet above the ledges. It was a re-run, in reverse, of *A Step in The Light Green* and true to form, Jerry cruised to glory. I got it next time, but not without a little bit of a heart flutter as I fumbled the last moves.

'Why did you want to call it *Orange Crush?*' I asked Jerry.

'Oh I just liked the R.E.M song that's all,' he replied.

It is known that Agent Orange contained dioxin and it has been suggested that use of such defoliants was an undercover tactic for using bio weapons. This herbicidal warfare programme was even known as Operation Ranch Hand. Vietnamese studies after the war suggested that 4.8 million people were exposed to Agent Orange with 400,000 suffering premature death, cancer and children born with severe birth defects.

I mused on Jerry's name and reflected on Operation Ranch Hand. Was it all coincidence, or had fate had played a card?

'Well I think it was christened *Orange Crush* so *Orange Crush* it should remain.' I said.

Doing that new route cemented a climbing partnership and friendship that would see Jerry and I sharing some fantastic adventures together for many years to come.

A few years later, Jerry and I were back at Heppy, but this time Dave Barton was with us. There was a thin break that crossed the *Light Green* headwall that offered the possibility of a traverse from *Pulpit Route* into *Orange Crush*. This was the object of our attention.

'Do you think we should put a rope down it for a look first?' I suggested. Dave scotched the idea immediately, 'No. On-sight ground-up on this one,' he declared.

Like all climbers Dave has a style unique to himself. I think it reflects his personality. He adopts an up or off policy, regardless of the situation. Once he's fully committed to something, there's no going back. That's not to say that he doesn't exhibit caution. Over the years I've learned that Dave has a powerful intuition. There have been many occasions when I've turned to him and he's acknowledged my own feelings with a simple, 'Come on Rad, let's get out of here, things just don't feel right.'

When rock-climbing, he climbs fast, anything he latches onto no matter how small, he pulls on.

On this occasion Dave obviously thought the portents were good. He tied in and made short work of *Brown Sugar*, the route that gave access to the tenuous traverse line. After arranging some protection, he started the technical climbing across the headwall. Dave was on form at the time and we could tell, from his cursing and grunting, that the climbing must be pretty tough. After about ten feet we got the telltale, 'Watch me here, Jerry.'

He made a swift reach right for a thin edge, but failed to hit it and in the next moment Dave was flying across the face in a huge arcing pendulum. Luckily he didn't hit anything and when he came to a halt, he uttered the single command, 'Down.'

Jerry lowered Dave to the deck and took over for round two. He climbed in his inimitable style, considered movement, precise footwork, totally cool under pressure. He crossed the headwall smoothly, completed the route and untied. Dave pulled the ropes and tied in, eager for some more excitement. With a bit more fire in his belly Dave stormed across the headwall, barely breaking sweat. I was content to second the route and retrieve the gear. It was a bit of a contrived route to nowhere, but in a world where the opportunity to pioneer new ground continues to diminish, it gave the three of us a fleeting sense that we'd done something that was outside the normal run of the mill, and, on this occasion, that's all that mattered.

The '80s were certainly an exciting period for me. Everything felt new and fresh. Crags were visited for the first time, new friendships formed, personal boundaries were stretched and I learned a lot along the way. There was always something to aspire to. Curiosity is an inherent trait of mine, whether externally manifesting itself in wanting to look round the next corner, so to speak, or internally dealing with risk. It was curiosity that led to my interest in new routing. It seemed to satisfy something creative in me and would continue to play an important part in my own climbing.

Chapter 7

Phoenix in Obsidian

Working out a line which wends a serpentine way up an obscure face, or through apparently impassable overhangs may be an act of brilliant creativity which over shadows the quality of the climbing on the route.
Royal Robbins

Looking back over the brief history of rock-climbing we can recognise that its development has been largely bound up with the human urge to explore. Unlike other sports, no one deliberately set out to write a rule book that clearly defined the parameters of the game. As climbing evolved people recognised that it was an expression of human endeavour and that certain achievements represented the spirit of that endeavour. Respect was born out of the simple appreciation of the skill and mettle that climbers demonstrated in fulfilling a basic human characteristic to explore and rise to a challenge. Unwritten principles emerged and these promoted behaviours that supported the very human spirit of adventure. These principles became embedded as respected traditions which in turn acted as the rudder, guiding climbing on a course that was acceptable to most participants.

As sport climbing started to take root in the UK certain individuals held the view that some long established traditions were being violated. Such was the passion that, on occasion, conflicting views spilled over into open confrontation. In 1987 the ethics police were in action again in the form of Duncan Drake. Another version of the Kilnsey *Frankie* saga was unfolding only this time the focus of the conflict was a route in Gordale called *Supercool*. *Supercool* was an aid climb originally created by Lakes climbers Rick Graham and Andy Hyslop in 1980. The route had minimal fixed gear and the name gave an indication of the mental state required to climb it.

Martin 'Basher' Atkinson had already made his mark in Gordale with free ascents of the neighbouring *Hangman* and *Pierrepoint*, and in doing so had created two magnificent free routes. Atkinson's attention was now drawn to *Supercool*. This was a different kettle of fish, however. Unlike other aid routes hereabouts, there was minimal fixed gear, or scope for good natural protection. Atkinson considered that the only feasible way of free climbing this wall would be to employ bolts as protection. Duncan had other ideas.

I remember one evening at West Vale, Duncan was in hyper mode and was ranting, 'I met Basher at Almscliff on Tuesday. I went straight up to him and said, "What's all this about bolting *Supercool*, haven't you got any balls or what?" He tried reasoning with me saying that there's no way that *Supercool* would go without bolts. I just said that he'd lost his bottle, but he insisted that he was as bold as anybody. So I said, "Come on then let's prove it." So I soloed *Wall of Horrors*. "Come on Basher show me what you've got," I said, but he wouldn't do it. So I soloed it again. I soloed it three times, but he wouldn't take me up on it.' Duncan was clearly very angry.

Basher went on and placed bolts on *Supercool*, but tried to keep the adventurous nature of the climb alive. He spaced the bolts, so that real commitment was required to climb between them, particularly towards the top of the climb, subsequent ascensions experienced some spectacular falls. During this period rumour circulated that on one evening while Basher was trying the route from below, Duncan was abseiling down from above threatening to chop the bolts such was his passion to preserve *Supercool* as a bold aid climb.

In the end Duncan's efforts proved futile, the quality of the free climb that Basher produced was exceptional and the bolts remained. A few years later even more bolts were added because climbers thought that the run outs and massive fall potential on the route were unjustified. Today *Supercool* represents the best of Yorkshire's sport routes and in my opinion would hold its own in terms of quality on the international stage. So what does this little episode tell us? Simply that Duncan was passionate about what he believed in, and brave enough to stand up for those beliefs. He didn't just sit back and talk about it, he actively demonstrated by his controversial and sometimes adversarial actions what he stood for. Looking back from today's world of politically correct attitudes, Duncan's actions might be seen as a little unorthodox. He was genuine in defending his beliefs, yet his demonstrations ultimately yielded naught. Maybe a silent majority were being caught up in a newer, more appealing form of climbing and that held sway. Rather than giving Duncan the metaphorical pat on the back for his efforts, people either said nothing, or gave each other the, 'he'll get over it', sort of nod. Even though this was a minor little episode in rock-climbing's evolution, I think subliminally, it had significant ramifications in Yorkshire.

The fact that Basher and *Supercool* came out on top perhaps reinforced popular opinion of the day. At the time he was mixing in some pretty influential climbing circles that included top-flight climbers from the Peak District. These climbers were seen to be leading the way in terms of modern rock-climbing. Whether intentional or not, they were role models to many. Basher's achievements were exonerated whilst Duncan was demonised as an out-dated maverick. I knew Duncan pretty well and understood where he was coming from. He wasn't trying to preserve *Supercool* as an aid climb, he was simply of the opinion that eventually someone would come along and climb *Supercool* free without recourse to bolts. In his view that was upholding the long tradition of British climbing and when such a time occurred it would represent a real 'raising of the bar' in climbing standards.

Today, characters like Duncan are a thing of the past. He certainly had an edge. One of his favourite party pieces was a little show that he often put on in Pembroke. At St Govan's Head there's a popular E3 called *The Butcher*, which climbs a steep little arête. The crux of the climb involves making a long reach to gain a jug at about two thirds height. Duncan would hang around until the area was busy with climbers and then proceed to solo the route. When he got to just below the jug he'd start to shake and gibber to deliberately draw attention to himself. He'd then lunge up to the jug, cut loose with his feet, hang from one arm and start beating his chest with his other hand, indicating that he'd given himself and his audience a heart attack. He'd then climb to the top of the route, laughing his head off.

I recall climbing with Duncan in Huntsman's Leap one year. I had just climbed the first pitch of *The Minotaur*, which finishes at a small cave below the top of the cliff. As I arrived at the cave, I was surprised to find another climber ensconced at the belay. He was an unkempt character wearing a threadbare woolly jumper and two odd rock boots. He also had a rucksack with him. It was the unmistakable Crispin Waddy, an active pioneer particularly in the South West. A rope led off up the next easy pitch indicating that his partner was up above and Crispin duly followed leaving the rucksack to be hauled up afterwards. As I brought Duncan up the climb, Crispin started hauling the rucksack up the cliff with disastrous results for us. As it made its way up the pitch above us, it started a veritable avalanche of earth and debris, which cascaded onto me and then down onto Duncan. A stream of abuse echoed up from the depths of the Leap which culminated in, 'WHEN I GET TO THE TOP OF THE CRAG I'M GOING TO RIP YOUR FUCKIN' HEAD OFF!' Duncan arrived at the belay in about five minutes flat. His face was covered in dirt and without a pause he sprinted past me saying, 'I'm going to kill 'im.' When Duncan got to the top Crispin, was nowhere to be seen. I climbed with Duncan on and off over subsequent years, but then lost touch with him.

Several years later I met him in Gordale, 'What are you going to do?' I asked.

'Dunno,' was his casual reply.

'Have you done *Revival*?' I asked.

'Yeah, but I didn't like it.'

'Why not?' I pressed

'I dunno, I just thought it was pretty crap route,' he replied.

Revival was a new route that I'd climbed with Jerry Peel in 1991. It took a sweeping line up the right wall of the gorge. Like the neighbouring *Supercool*, the rock that *Revival* covered lacked natural gear placements so to protect it I had placed about twelve bolts. At F7b+ it was by no means cutting edge, but most people rated it as a good and worthwhile route. Perhaps Duncan's comment was his way of having a dig at me for placing bolts. He was edgy till the end.

Climbing new routes is a fundamental element of climbing. It brings life and evolution into a pursuit that, at face value, lacks tangible goals and outcomes. The concept of climbing a new route is like trying to answer the oft asked question, why climb at all? This has been debated at length, but maybe the answer is plain and simple. It's innate within us, part of our evolutionary past.

On the subject of new routing, I know climbers who search for unclimbed rock so that they can simply satisfy their urge to explore. Others seek to break records and push boundaries of possibility. Some use new routes to judge their competition. A new route can stand as a statement. It can be used to broadcast a personal point of view, or express a belief or value. A new route can be left as a legacy to be judged by others. Despite a nebulous array of possible motivations, when boiled down I think that the new routing game, for me at least, is a form of self-expression that provides a brief sense of self-fulfillment.

Climbers often choose to climb those routes that give them the most pleasure and I think this is linked to their particular style and, sometimes, personality. Lakeland climber, Pete Whillance, was an avid new router during the 1970s and added many fine routes to the mountain crags of Cumbria, Wales and Scotland. As I became familiar with Whillance routes I started to appreciate that they often had a particular feel about them. Routes like *Top Gear* in the Lakes, *The Long Run* on North Stack wall at Gogarth and *The Naked Ape* in Scotland tackled improbable walls. Protection was often well-spaced

On *Face Route* in 1984. This must-do introduction to the delights of Gordale Scar is a product of the Livesey and Sheard 'free climbing' vision.
Photo: Adrian Ledgway.

Right: Making the first ascent of
A Step in the Light Green E6 6b in 1987.
Photo: Jane Cooksey.

Left: World champion Simon Nadin
having some fun in Font early '90s.
Photo: Mark Radtke.

Top left: Starting the crux of *Spacewalk* E4 6b, Aonach Dubh, Glen Coe belayed by Billy Lukin. *Photo: Eddie Turner.*

Bottom left: *The Minotaur* E5 6a, *Huntsman's Leap*, Pembroke. Crispin Waddy is just visible in the top right of the photograph. *Photo: Jane Cooksey.*

Top Right: On *Strapadictomy* Froggatt Edge in 1985. This was a classic 'rites of passage' route in those days. Ian Cooksey belaying. *Photo: Adrian Ledgway.*

Bottom right: Mick Lovatt, 'The Perfect Man', epitomises 'the climbing lifer'. A keen activist on the northern rock scene for over thirty years. Mick emerged from a strong culture of traditional climbing, but fully embraced the bolt and pushed standards of sport climbing in Yorkshire. Captured here in 2009 in his fiftieth year, enjoying a fine F7b+ in Majorca. *Photo: Mark Radtke.*

Right: Roy Healey getting ready for the 'crux' sequence on Gomersall's route *Ground Effect* at Kilnsey. This route used to have quite an adventurous punch to it. The steep and technical section above Roy was originally protected by two fragile threads of unknown security. In the old days the physical challenge of the route was multiplied by real fear. The threads are still there, but the addition of bolts mean that executing the climb is now a simple exercise in athletics. Why risk your neck when you can have another convenient way of 'working out'?
Photo: Glenn Robbins (2011).

Left: Pete Gomersall (left), Roger Hindle (centre), Jerry Peel and my daughter Lauren. Gommy is another example of a talented climber who's experienced the full gamut of cutting edge extreme climbing. At heart he is simply a pragmatic person. When he placed bolts in Heavy Duty's bold aid route *Frankie* and climbed it free it simply amounted to the logical way forward.
Photo: Mark Radtke.

Chamonix days mid '80s.
Posing for the camera on a fairy tale summit. *Photo: Chris Frost.*

Chamonix days mid '80s.
Frosty above the Vallée Blanche enjoying the Voie Classique, Pointe Lachenal.
Simon Bolton brings up the rear. *Photo: Mark Radtke.*

Frosty enjoying steep slab climbing on *Super Dupont* F7a, South Face of the Aiguille du Midi. *Photo: Mark Radtke.*

Frosty climbing solo and heading for the couloir on the North Face of the Tour
Ronde, February 1986. *Photo: Mark Radtke.*

and the climbing was intricate and absorbing. The more Whillance routes that I climbed the more I wanted to climb. These routes left the impression on me of what the man himself might be like. I had the pleasure of meeting him on top of the Old Man Of Hoy in the early '80s. Frosty, Ledge and I were climbing the classic original route on the stack. Whillance and well-known Scottish climber, Murray Hamilton, were preparing a new route on the stack that was going to be used during a live climbing television spectacular. As we sat on the summit, Pete Whillance emerged from the other side of the stack. Frosty asked Pete to take a photograph of us, and said, 'You're Pete Whillance aren't you?'

He came across as an unassuming and rather reserved character, but I also detected a sense of mischief burning in his eyes. 'Aye lads,' he replied, 'You should have got here yesterday, an army team had an epic. They must have been pretty incompetent, we recovered three brand new ropes and a heap of Friends, I reckon we salvaged about three hundred quid's worth of booty.'

The TV broadcast duly went out. It featured Whillance and Hamilton climbing their new route and legendary veteran Joe Brown climbing the stack with his daughter. A lot of people still remember that programme and can still quote Zoe Brown on the summit as she looked into the camera and said, 'Beam me up, Scotty.'

Whillance and Hamilton christened their route, *A Few Dollars More*.

I started new routing almost as soon as I started rock-climbing in earnest. The curiosity in me asked why hasn't anyone been up there? With that I set about climbing my first new route, and from then on I recognised that you didn't necessarily need to be at the forefront of climbing to put up new routes. You simply needed an inquisitive eye. *A Step in the Light Green*, the route that Ian Cooksey and I established at Heptonstall, was born out of curiosity and a bit of self-belief. Maybe the reason that potential routes sometimes get overlooked is, in part, the result of assumption.

Imagine the following scenario:

Pete Livesey has just done the first ascent of *Hard Line* in Heptonstall Quarry and looks at the headwall that will eventually become, *A Step in the Light Green*. Maybe he says to himself, mm a bit too steep that, or thinks, no real line to it, and so he dismisses it. Then Fawcett and Peel come along, and eyeing the headwall think to themselves, well Livesey's bound to have had a look at that, and if that competitive bugger hasn't done it, it must be desperate. In their turn they consolidate the route's improbability. Then Johnston and Leach come along and look up at the headwall. These two are of a different generation, but still respect their mentors.

Leach turns to Johnston and says, 'You know, I was at The Bridestones with Jerry the other day and he's still the master on grit.' With this simple statement, they subtly put a personal mental block in place and walk away.

Then Ledge comes along abseils down the line and declares, 'It'll definitely go.'

Suddenly in my mind climbing that headwall is a real possibility, and bang, a week or so later the route is in the bag. Livesey, Fawcett, Peel, Johnston and Leach were all far more capable than I of climbing that piece of rock, but the fact is, Cooksey and I climbed it, whereas they didn't. Clearly I'm hypothesising here, but maybe the reason that we climbed the route and the others didn't, was simply that our imaginations were not troubled by preconceptions and we challenged assumption. I think this is a useful lesson that can be applied to life more generally. Imagine what we could achieve if we focused on possibility, rather than allowing preconceptions to cloud our judgement and impede progress.

Imagine Basher Atkinson looking up at *Supercool* and declaring, 'You know with some bolts to protect this wall I think I'll be able to climb it free, but do you know what, if standards continue to rise, someone might come along and solo this in the future. So rather than climb the route now with bolts, I'm going to make a point of view clear to everyone, that it should be left for the future.'

I'm not arguing the right or wrongs of placing bolts here, but more how the actions of influential people shape our future. Indeed I followed Basher's lead myself when I created the route, *Revival*. My own internal dialogue went something along the lines of: 'The rock is loose and snappy, there's no natural gear placements, no one will ever want to risk their neck on a piece of rock like this, bolts are the only way forward here.' If truth be known there was something else driving my thoughts and actions, the selfish desire to be first.

An inquisitive imagination has definitely been behind many of my new routes, but that's just the start of the process. For me the process of new routing adds another dimension to the whole game. Climbing a new line for the first time satisfies a personal need to be creative. I am more of a conceptual rather than detailed thinker. I am the sort of person who can look at crags and can see caricatured faces peering back at me. When I look at clouds I instantly turn them into creatures and other worldly things. Conceptualizing new routes can follow a similar process. The route *Revival* is an example of this. Many routes are instantly recognisable, they follow natural features in the rock, such as a crack, or an arête, or a corner. As such they are usually obvious and stand out as striking lines. *Cenotaph Corner* is a supreme example of this and once seen is rarely forgotten. Some of its neighbours by contrast, are much more subtle. It takes more imagination and a discerning eye to link the features and pockets together to form the line of *Right Wall. Revival* was born like this. I remember at the time of its ascent, Mick Ryan and I had teamed up and were beavering away in Gordale. We'd just finished our chores at the end of the day and were keen to get back to The Lister Arms in Malham, for a well-earned beer. Just as we were leaving the gorge, we turned to look back to admire the scale and geology of the place. This was never a conscious thing that we did, it was just the magic of the crag. I'm sure it was this same magic that inspired artists like James Ward, J M Turner, and David Hockney to capture it in their fantastic works of art. On this occasion, as I dallied at the entrance to the gorge a particular light fell across the right wall and as it did, I could visualise an imperceptible line of weakness that arced like a crescent across the rock face. I illustrated the line to Mick by tracing the line with my finger in the air, but he couldn't see it.

'I'll take your word for it, Rad. I didn't believe you when you when you spotted *Solstice*, but that has proved to be a good route.'

As we drank beer in The Lister Arms I was already visualising what it would feel like creeping across that huge expanse of unclimbed shattered limestone. I was buzzing with excited anticipation. That evening I was on the phone to Jerry Peel, who had become my regular climbing partner. He was familiar with my enthusiasm and in his own words knew that I had an eye for a line.

At the end of the following day I'd inspected the route on abseil and was of the opinion that it would go. I took the plunge and, armed with a Hilti battery drill, I placed about twelve expansion bolts in the forty metre-long first pitch, and two pegs in what would form a short second pitch. We started to do battle, but it proved to be a hard-fought one. The crux section was particularly problematical. I kept blowing one move, but could then get back on and make the belay in one. Jerry on the other hand could climb through the crux, but then would pump out and fall off higher up. After a couple of days trying the route, I started to think that I'd created a bit of a monster. What's more Jerry appeared to be getting fitter. It came to the crunch on our third day. I'd had a couple of attempts and as usual had fallen at the crux. Jerry had made one attempt and had cruised the crux, but then fell off higher up. I secretly wondered whether he'd taken the fall deliberately. On the gorge floor

I confessed my feelings, 'I've got a mental block with it, Jerry. I think it's got the better of me, you're looking much stronger, you may as well do it, let's just get it over with.'

Jerry was having none of it, 'No, just relax there's no pressure on, have ten minutes and get focused, you're going to do it next time. I'm not doing it until you've done it first.'

That was what Jerry was like with me. With others he'd be fiercely competitive and show no mercy at all, but with me he was always supportive and encouraging. He was the perfect climbing partner and I respected his wisdom. Next time up, things clicked and I arrived at the belay without incident. Jerry led the route with ease immediately afterwards. The sense of relief was immense. Putting up new routes can sometimes be like that, you can invest a lot of personal effort and emotional energy into their creation. Often you know that they are at the limit of your ability, or even beyond your ability. It can be like creating a paradox. The artist paints the picture, but there's always the risk that someone else will put their signature on it.

The *Revival* of today is a very different route to the one climbed by Jerry and I back in '91. Following our ascent, it became quite popular until the demise of some holds on the crux rendered it unclimbable. A few years later a keen activist called Steve Crowe, in an attempt to bring the route back to life, glued a hold back at what used to be the crux. I think the motivation behind the action was commendable, but the bastard hold ultimately made this section of the climb much easier than it had been previously. Some argue that it is now a more balanced route overall, and better for it.

Opening up new routes has other dimensions to it as well. There's the altruistic motivation of producing something that others will simply enjoy. I bumped into Mick Lovatt at the Harrogate trade show one year. He was there representing one of his sponsors, 'Hey Rad, good to see you,' was his greeting. He then promptly followed this up with, 'I did your new route at Victoria Cave the other week,' he paused, waiting for my inevitable question.

'Oh yeah, what did you think?' I asked.

'Really enjoyed it,' replied Mick and then paused eyeing me, as if trying to gauge my reaction. He then delivered the punch line, 'Just a shame about the bivvy ledge at half height.'

I laughed out loud, 'Bugger off, Mick.'

It was typical Mick, build you up and then put you down, but coming from the *Perfect Man*, I took it as a genuine backhanded compliment. Mick is like that. When I did the second ascent of *Bliss*, I took a long fall from high on the route onto poor rotten gear. Had the gear ripped out, I would have fallen a long way down the wall and probably ended up getting pretty banged up.

Fortunately the gear held and I was able to complete the route on my second go. It was really busy at the crag that day. Amongst others, Ben Moon was repeating a hard route called *Defcon3* and Adam Wainwright was doing *Cave Route Left Hand*. Once I'd finished *Bliss*, I abseiled back down the route to retrieve my gear. Mick had obviously been watching all the proceedings from the entrance to the gorge. Just as I alighted on the ground he strutted into the gorge. I recall that he was carrying his young son on his shoulders and was wearing dark shades that added to his natural air of cool. He walked directly up to me, shook my hand and then in a voice just loud enough for those nearby he said, 'Well done Rad, but that proves it. It can't be E7 can it?' and then he walked off. I wasn't in the least bit offended it was just Mick's sense of humour, but you had to get it.

It's definitely a good feeling when your own bits of climbing history become popular, but sometimes they never do. This doesn't necessarily mean they aren't good routes. This was brought home to me recently when a younger, talented climber called Neil Herbert repeated a route of mine called, *The Skryking*. I was impressed that Neil had made the effort to visit the crag let alone do the climb. This is what he said:

> 'I had to clean it up a bit, but apart from the contrived start it's absolutely brilliant, quite hard and quite committing. I reckon on-sight it's a good E5 6b. If it was on a different crag, or in the Peak, it would be one of the best routes at its grade around.'

It's feedback like that which gives the new router a sense of pride. Not so much as recognition for their ability to climb the route in the first place, but more, that someone appreciates the route and what it stands for. Once again for me it goes back to the altruistic stuff, it's like someone appreciating a piece of art.

A slightly weird element of the new route experience for me is quite personal. It's about occupying a space on the planet where no other human being has been before, the thought of touching a piece of the earth that no one else has ever touched. Doing new routes gets you into these places. It takes a long stretch of the imagination to make this connection with exploration of old, but that's the analogy that I make for myself.

I suppose the last bit in the new route bug for me is down to the sheer challenge. Finding a striking line that looks like it can be climbed, but only just. When you have climbed the hardest routes on a particular crag and then spot a line that is obvious, but still remains unclimbed it usually follows that it's going to be hard. In the late '80s I was keen and fit and was living temporarily with the Cookseys, and my long-term girlfriend Jane, in Cumbria. Naturally, I did a lot of climbing in the Lakes and had done many of the classic hard Extremes on the more popular crags. Looking for new ground I found myself exploring Iron Crag near Thirlmere. For some reason this crag remained a bit of a backwater, but as I worked my way through the routes I realised that it was equal in stature and quality to the neighbouring Raven Crag, whose climbs had received much attention in the climbing press. After a few visits I had virtually ticked the crag and became intrigued by a pretty obvious unclimbed line on the right-hand buttress.

Some talented climbers had been active at Iron Crag over the years, including the phenomenal Dougie Hall, who for my money was one of the best rock climbers around during the '80s. Dougie had climbed the hardest route to date at Iron Crag with his *Western Union*. From below, the unclimbed line that I was visualising followed a vague groove up the right-hand side of the buttress, it looked as though it might only be about HVS and I wondered whether Dougie may have been fooled by this strange optical illusion and dismissed the route as too easy to be bothered with. When I abseiled down the line it became obvious that the route was going to be a tough challenge indeed.

The buttress was so steep I could hardly get into the rock to clean it. The rock was also fused and had little in the way of gear placements. A small roof capped the top of the groove and I managed to place a marginal knife blade peg below it. Just under this I discovered a solitary Thank God nut placement. This would be the only gear to protect the hard moves round the roof. About halfway down the wall there was a niche that might offer some form of rest. I also discovered that a poor Friend could be placed in a flaring crack, but it only held on two of its four cams, there was also a place for a good skyhook. The only really good runner was a bomber peg that I placed in a horizontal quartz vein below the pod. Looking at the route I worked out the maths. From the ledge at the start of the route proper the initial climbing was steep and technical but relatively safe being protected by a couple of pegs. From the niche to the roof would be hard. A fall before the good nut runner would probably rip the Friend and skyhook, but with a bit of luck the good peg in the quartz vein might just stop you short of the ledge. Climbing round the roof would also be hard. A fall at the lip would be scary and would be completely reliant on the security of that solitary nut runner. If that failed I'd be a goner.

On the day of the ascent none of my regular climbing partners were available, so I managed to persuade Jane's mum, Lillian, to hold my ropes. Jane would take photographs. I geared up at the base of the route and reassured Lillian that she'd be fine. I set off up the route and headed for the sanctuary of the niche. I got the skyhook on and placed the Friend, but found that I couldn't really rest. Nervously I set off, heading for the runner near the roof, but the climbing was hard on sloping, insecure holds and the route spat me off. I came to a gentle halt about thirty feet down the wall. I'd fallen further than expected and looking up could see that both the Friend and skyhook miraculously were still in place.

'Are you okay, Lillian?' I shouted down.

'Sorry I didn't stop you sooner, but the ropes ran through the Sticht plate,' she yelled back.

That explained the length of the fall and probably why the Friend hadn't ripped. My fall had been quite a dynamic affair, 'Don't worry about that Lillian, I think it probably helped. Just lower me down to the ledge, I'll have a rest and then give it another bash.'

Next time up I had a bit more faith in the gear at the niche and was a little less nervy. This time I managed to sketch my way up and rightwards to the roof. I got the runner in and clipped the poor peg, took some deep breaths and fought my way over the roof. It felt desperate, but the adrenaline had kicked in and there was no way I was blowing it now. Above the roof I was able to recompose for the final awkward groove that led to the top. It had been the hardest piece of climbing that I'd ever done. I called it *Phoenix in Obsidian* simply because I liked the name.

About five years later, I was at Kilnsey Crag watching an impressive young climber in action. He was obviously very good as he flashed a hard sport route called *The Ashes*. As he lowered off and untied, I congratulated him on a fine ascent and we got talking. His name was Craig Parnaby, and I think he was studying medicine at Edinburgh University. After a while he said, 'Are you, Mark Radtke?'

'Yeah,' I replied

Craig went on, 'I'm glad I've finally bumped into you. I did that route of yours up on Iron Crag, I thought it was desperate. I'd been doing a lot of hard trad at the time and thought I was going to die. I'd done *Conan the Librarian* the week before and it felt at least as hard as that. What style did you do it in?'

'I abbed it, put the pegs in and had a feel of the moves off the rope. When I led, it I took a fall onto a poor Friend and a skyhook in the niche, which held. I then lowered back down to the ledge and yo-yoed it from there. Not the best style I know but I was happy just to get up it, how about you?'

'I flashed it, but I didn't have the skyhook so it felt really scary.'

'Good effort Craig, I'm glad someone finally got round to repeating it. I thought it might be E7 when I did it, but hadn't done any E7s at the time, so I gave it E6. I know you said it was scary, but did you think it was any good?'

'Oh, I thought it was awesome. It's just never going to get popular,' he said, laughing.

It was an interesting comment. The popularity of a route can reflect its quality and popular routes sometimes earn the label of classic. Sometimes, however, popularity, or lack of it, can be down to a route's accessibility. Craig's comment reflected both elements. He'd enjoyed *Phoenix*, or rather the experience of completing it. He was also of the opinion that it was a pretty hazardous affair. In other words it wasn't what might be called a consumer climb. There are climbers around today who use the popularity argument to justify changing the style of routes. Retrobolting comes to mind here, a practice that has been applied to a number of limestone crags throughout the UK. Adding bolts undoubtedly reduces risk of injury and makes routes more accessible to more climbers. This in turn increases the popularity of these crags and creates the notion that developing sport climbing for the masses is a positive and progressive move forward. Yet if we hold the belief that hunger for adventure and dealing with risk are important elements in the human psyche and climbing can go some way to fulfilling these natural urges, we can argue that such actions are indeed short sighted and regressive.

We appear to live in a shrinking world where people have to travel to the wilder extremities of the earth to satisfy their desires to explore and experience adventure. When I was taking my first steps in the world of the vertical, I had a myriad of crags on which to enjoy the voyage into the unknown. Thirty years on and many of these crags have been popularised with the addition of bolts. Many climbers have welcomed this transformation. In a few cases I believe this has been for the benefit of climbers and also sometimes the environment. What I think we need to reflect upon, however, are the consequences of creating a consumer climber mind set, which continues to snowball out of control and denies us the opportunity of discovery forever.

Chapter 8

Lucifer's Hammer

*'To conceal or misrepresent one's true position, potential or intent,
in order to deceive or take advantage of an opponent'.*
The Art of Sandbagging.

Rock types vary tremendously in their morphology. Moorland grit is blasted by wind into sloping and rounded formations. Acidic rain dissolves limestone over the millennia, forming pockets in its skin. As the same rain drips from overhanging walls, calcite is deposited creating flowstone and stalactites that drip like candle wax down the rock. The sandstone boulders in the forest around Fontainebleau sit like petrified primeval beasts. The massive granite walls of Yosemite are riven with uncompromising cracks and corners that soar vertically for thousands of feet. All these unique geologies provide the rock-climber with a vast array of different challenges and a measure of any competent climber is to be able to perform consistently on all of them. There are many rock-climbers who excel on a particular rock type, or gain a reputation for a certain type of climbing, but those that can translate their talent across the global arena are a rarer breed. I think this is one of the reasons why homegrown rock climbers such as Fawcett and Moffatt stood out in the '80s; they travelled and made an impact overseas. Great German climbers, like Gullich, Albert and Glowacs, established hard new routes from their home country to the massive granite walls of Trango Tower in the Himalaya's. The superlative Lynn Hill from America is another example of a globe-trotting rock master who proved that she was one of the best. Not only did these climbers push the standards on their home turf, they travelled and repeated the hardest routes of the period, occasionally showing the locals the way forward. I base this observation on my own personal experiences of rock-climbing throughout Europe, America and Australia.

By 1988 I'd been working in chemical research and development for about five years and had laid the foundations of a solid future career. There was one slight problem. I was also firmly in the grip of the climbing bug. I was managing to climb about five times a week, but still wanted more, and work seemed to be getting in the way. As an escape I decided to have a climbing sabbatical. It wasn't an easy decision, I knew I would be jeopardising a future in agrochemical research, but secretly I hoped that somehow this decision might ultimately allow me to climb full time.

Over the years Frosty had filled my head with tails about the wild outback of Australia, so I formulated plans for an extended visit down under. Frosty hailed from Brisbane in Australia, when I met him in the early '80s he was working as a dentist in Cambridge. He had a relaxed air about him, liked a beer and was generally good craic. He was passionate about his climbing and had slotted into our company with ease. I struck up a strong friendship with Frosty that would see us climbing on and off together for many years. He was a keen rock climber, but I think that mountaineering was always at the centre of his heart and indeed he went on to climb in the Himalayas, making determined attempts on the 8,000m giants, Kangchenjunga and Cho Oyu.

I handed my notice in at the end of November and in January, Jane and I landed at Brisbane airport under the full glare of a Queensland summer sun. Frosty was the perfect host, eager to guide us round his home turf. First port of call was Kangaroo Point, a quarried crag overlooking the river in the heart of Brisbane.

'You'll like the Point,' said Frosty, 'It's our version of West Vale.'

'Won't it be too hot?' I asked sceptically.

'Nah,' replied Frosty, 'we'll go down tonight when it's dark. It'll slot in nicely with your body clock as well.'

Kangaroo Point was floodlit at night and provided the locals with a free outdoor climbing wall. When we arrived the crag was already busy and several parties were working out and top roping routes. One climber stood out as he worked away on what looked to be a desperately thin and technical traverse. Frosty introduced us, 'Can you remember Hos?'

I reached out and shook his hand, 'Aye up Paul, good to see you again.'

It was Paul Hoskins. I'd met him a few years earlier at Millstone Edge in Derbyshire. He'd impressed me on that occasion, with his on-sight flash of the classic route *London Wall*. Like many talented climbers he was a private and rather understated person who just went about quietly doing his stuff.

'What are you going to do tonight?' asked Paul.

Frosty winked and said, 'Put this pommy bastard through his paces.' They both started laughing.

As the evening progressed I certainly felt that I was being put through my paces. The rock was polished and even though it was a couple of hours past sunset, it was still hot as hell. I felt like I was climbing in a greenhouse under the glare of sodium floodlights. As a finale Frosty pointed me at one last route. 'Right, see if you can flash this one, it's only 23, so it's well within your grasp.'

Just to add to the pressure Hos sauntered over to watch the action. I set off up a vertical crack easily enough, but higher up the crack blanked out and I was forced into a thin sequence of face moves. I fought some runners in, with salty sweat stinging my eyes and fingers threatening to slip from the small polished holds. I pressed on for a move or two, but the climb had me on the ropes and next minute I was off.

'Lower me down,' I shouted.

Back on the ground Frosty was triumphant. Hos eased my bruised ego a little, 'I bet he didn't tell you that he only freed that himself last year. You've got to be six foot tall to do it Frosty's way. It's about 25 to do those moves without the massive reach'.

I began to learn that Aussie climbers were masters of the 'sandbag'. Sandbagging is the art of getting you on a climb in the full knowledge that it has some sort of unpleasant surprise up its sleeve. It has different levels of severity in climbing. At one end there's the simple case of one-upmanship: seeing you fail and then stepping in with full prior knowledge of the trick and climbing the route with ease. At the more sadistic end, the sandbagger will manoeuvre you onto a route and watch you climb into a metaphorical cul-de-sac way above runners. The pleasure here comes from the perverse delight in seeing you squirming in extremis, knowing that you're going to take the ultimate screamer.

It's not just the Aussies that derive such pleasure. I remember watching a couple of Japanese climbers at Céüse once. One of the guys had just successfully redpointed a classic route called *Mirage* and next up it was the turn of his mate. He set off up the route and it was obvious he was having a real fight all the way, but he hung in and hung in, until he finally ground to a halt high on the route, just short of the belay. At this point he simply let out a long low moan, and started gibbering out emotive wails. It went something like this, 'Ayeeeeee, nooo, nooo, nooo, Ayeeee, Ayeeee, Ayeeee, nakitoko, nakitoko. Wahawahaha.' The banshee-like wailing went on for about three or four minutes. The lower part of the route was overhanging and meant that the climbers couldn't see each other. Looking across at his belayer, I could see that he was doubled up in uncontrolled belly laughter. It was a funny situation, the noises coming from above sounded like the guy was being tortured on the rack. The guy holding the rope was certainly gaining much amusement from the plight of his mate, but a closer look revealed the real reason for his uncontrolled laughter. Unknown to the leader, he'd paid out a load of slack. Eventually, the guy above succumbed to the inevitable and with a mournful, 'Ayeeeeee', he took flight, probably expecting to fall just a few metres, but as he accelerated down the rock for about fifty feet his mournful ayeeeeee, turned into what sounded like a real death scream. His mate lowered him quickly to the ground and both of them rolled around laughing uncontrollably. Watching that little cameo unfold, gave me an interesting slant on Japanese psychology. Strictly speaking this wasn't a sandbag, but it gives a broader insight into the mentality of the sandbagging climber.

The sandbag can be a devilish weapon and I've seen it used to great effect to counter inappropriate behaviour. Those seen to be taking themselves a bit too seriously can also be at the mercy of the sandbag. An example of this springs to mind from the early '90s. Mick Johnston, Jerry Peel and I made an extended road trip across North America. As we journeyed from Yosemite Valley in California to City of Rocks in Idaho we made an impromptu stop to sample some of the great rock climbing around Lake Tahoe, and by chance, bumped into the great climbing legend that is Jim Bridwell. The instant chemistry between all four of us led to an extended stay which involved hard partying and hard climbing. Mick was keen to try a route called *Warp Factor* a short hard sport route at Donner Pass, so, one afternoon, we wandered up to the cliff and set about working the route. After a couple of hours, the light was fading and so we decided to delay our redpoint attempt until the following day. The following afternoon, having just about recovered from the previous evenings partying, Mick and I toiled up the slopes to Star Walls the home of *Warp Factor* only to be confronted by two serious looking rock athletes and an entourage of loud Americans sporting cameras and videos. We soon deduced that the sultry looking athletes were French rock stars and had their sights set on the hard extension to *Warp Factor* the superbly named *A Steep Climb Named Desire*. They were just waiting for it to cool down a little before trying their on-sight. The Yanks entourage were clearly excited by the whole prospect and made it pretty obvious that our presence at the photo shoot was unwelcome. Mick was in a belligerent mood and suggested to the Yanks that we should try *Warp Factor* while the French guy waited for the temperature to drop. They protested and suggested we take a walk. The ensuing debate seemed to spur the French guy into action. With looks of obvious disdain cast towards us, he put his boots on and stepped up to the mark. He really looked the part, lean of body, angled jaw line, pristine Lycra tights, and so Mick and I sat down to watch the spectacle unfold. As he began to climb the camera shutters started to click. He moved up the rock purposefully enough, but by the third bolt, as he reached up to catch a hold, he failed to latch it properly and fell. The guy was mortified and back on the ground removed his boots and threw them down in disgust, once again casting accusatory looks in our direction. I must admit this riled us a little, after all we had as much right to be here as they did.

'Hard luck, mate.' said Mick in his dry Lancashire accent. 'Don't suppose you'll mind if we have a go now that you've BLOWN your on-sight, will you.' He pressed the point home. Mick isn't known in the climbing fraternity for his Charles Atlas physique and after he'd donned his boots and harness he removed his tee shirt, turned round so the French rocker had the perfect view of his profile and simultaneously pushed his backside and belly out. He looked like the legendary comedian Max Wall, whose character Professor Wallowski, used to prance around the stage in tights doing comedic walks. Mick was deliberately exaggerating that in looks at least, he was the complete antithesis of the French man.

With that, Mick gave me a wink and said audibly. 'Right, Rad, watch me good 'cos I don't want to blow MY on-sight.' The entourage sat back their expressions conveying looks ranging from curiosity to contempt.

Mick pulled onto the rock in full knowledge of what lay ahead, but had hatched a wicked little ruse in his mind. At the point where the French guy had fallen, he reached up for the same hold. From our rehearsals the previous evening we knew that this hold was deceptive and Mick deliberately tried to latch a section where it was hopelessly sloping. After a bit of pretend 'piano playing', his fingers locked onto a small positive section at the far end of the hold. At the next move he feigned a foot slip and, higher up he started to shake deliberately, as if he was about to fall. I shouted up nonsense beta from below to spice things up for our audience. It was a perfect bit of play acting and Mick was loving it. The onlookers were wide eyed as he made what looked like an all out dyno for the finishing jug and completed the route. Back on the ground Mick turned to the French climber. 'Back over to you guys, thanks for your kind hospitality'. It was too much for them, they simply packed up their gear and left. Mick turned to me. 'Serves 'em right, haven't they heard of a bit of climbing etiquette'. He'd used a bit of retro psychological sandbagging to great effect.

Throughout my time in Australia I was often at the mercy of such antics and eventually developed a bit of a skill of out-sandbagging the sandbagger. During the first couple of weeks in Queensland, Frosty had me on the ropes on several occasions. One day he had me strung out dealing with loose rock above poor gear, as I climbed on Tibrogargan, in the Glass House Mountains. On the next he'd be killing himself laughing as I'd take to the air to avoid being bitten by a huge python at Frog Buttress. It should have been rock-climbing as usual, but these crags felt very alien, the nature of the rock, the heat and humidity, and the incessant sandbagging all seemed to be conspiring against me.

I was relieved when we made the decision to move south, to Mount Arapiles. Even though it was still January and the height of the Australian summer we'd be able to escape the sub tropical climate of Queensland by moving further south.

Frosty suggested a stop off at Girraween National Park. 'Even if it's too hot to climb, it's a beautiful spot and it's great hiking and scrambling country. It's also great for the wildlife.'

I didn't need much more convincing, we were on holiday after all. Girraween lived up to Frosty's sales pitch. It is located on the northern extremity of the New England tableland and its scenery is recognised as one of the best examples of granite landscape in Australia. Huge domes of smooth wind-blasted rock rise out of surrounding eucalyptus forest. The word 'Girraween' is aboriginal, and when translated, means 'place of flowers'. It suggests how the national park can look as plants blossom. The forest is brought to life with the rant of kookaburras and the colour of Rosella parrots. Altogether it makes for an interesting and adventurous bush walk.

Although the granite domes do contain some sizeable rock routes, most of the harder climbs have been established on some smaller buttresses dotted randomly throughout the Park. I was surprised to learn that in an area of such outstanding natural beauty, most routes relied on hand-drilled bolts as protection.

On arrival in the Park, we pitched the tents at one of the recognised campsites and waited for one of Frosty's climbing mates. Jonathon Pearson had earned the nickname of Peerless, on account of his unassailable ability to put himself down. He was a rather skinny individual, with a laconic wit and we soon learned that he lived up to his self-deprecating reputation. He was also renowned for his bushcraft and had knowledge of the indigenous natural history that was second to none. I got on well with him from the start.

As soon as Peerless arrived we set about exploring and headed up to a crag called Sphinx Rock. We warmed up there, on a fine slabby wall. The left edge of this wall was defined by an immaculate arête and the presence of telltale bolt heads indicated that it was climbed. It was called *Alex in Wonderland*, was graded 23 and looked superb.

The bolting ethic in Australia differed from most other areas of the world. Here, rather than using purpose designed expansion bolts, standard three inch coach bolts were used. These were normal machine bolts bought from any hardware store. They were modified as climbing protection, by grinding the cylindrical threaded end so it was squared off and slightly tapered. The hole to take the bolt was hand drilled and the bolt was simply knocked in using a hammer until the head remained just proud of the rock. They were known locally as carrot bolts. Clipping carrot bolts became a bit of an art form and was more akin to placing a natural piece of protection like a wire runner than clipping a peg or normal bolt. Purpose designed bolt hangers were manufactured specifically for use with carrot bolts and these were usually carried in your chalk bag. They had to be placed over the protruding head of the bolt and were locked in place when a karabiner was clipped into the hanger. It was a delicate operation, a fumble with the hanger at any point could send it spinning off the bolt head and clattering to the ground below. It could also be a bit of a nerve-racking affair, particularly if a bolt needed clipping from a strenuous or tenuous position. Mastery of this art could sometimes be the difference between success and failure on these routes.

I climbed *Alex in Wonderland*, it was a test of classic laybacking and smearing, but the real challenge was maintaining balance and concentration at each of the bolts. I had to get into a stable position where I could take a hand off; reach into the chalk bag; fish out a bolt hanger; place it over the stud and reach back to the harness for a quickdraw; carefully clip this into the rattly little hanger taking care not to knock it off, then finally clip the rope in and breathe a sigh of relief. It was a new dimension to the climbing repertoire. *Alex in Wonderland*, despite its meagre grade of 23, felt as hard as some gritstone E5s that I'd done back in the UK. It was a superb little route.

The following day we headed up to another huge boulder called Turtle Rock. Our objective was a classic route called *New Paths*. It climbed a steep face covered with granite protrusions known to climbers by the affectionate name of chicken heads. We arrived at the foot of the climb and I turned to Peerless. 'Who's going first?' I asked.

He turned to me and true to form said, 'Well you're the Rock Master. It's graded 25 and I won't stand a chance.'

I tied in and fiddled about for the bolt hangers in my chalk bag. The route was about seventy feet long and looking up the wall, I thought I could spy about five tiny bolt heads. It was going to be a scary lead. I set off in the full heat of the sun and it was hard from the word go. After about forty feet, with sweat pouring into my eyes, I ran out of fight and conceded defeat. Back on the ground I talked Peerless into having a go and racked with self-doubt he clawed his way to the summit of the boulder in fine style. It was typical Peerless, despite his underrated view of himself, he was a fine a rock-climber.

We departed Girraween and made the long drive south to Arapiles. It was a pretty uninspiring journey. I was used to the dramatic landscape changes that you get when travelling through Europe or America, but here you could nod off and wake up an hour later and feel that you were still looking at the same view. We arrived at the famous campground known as The Pines about twenty four hours later.

Mount Arapiles is situated about two hundred and sixty miles west of Australia's capital Melbourne. The crag sits squat and uninspiring in the midst of flat cereal growing plains, known as the Wimmera. From a distance it looks like a jumbled pile of choss. On aesthetics alone you could almost dismiss it as climbing venue and drive on. It's only when you've spent time here that its magnificence as a world-class crag becomes apparent. It's a complex piece of landscape and geology, comprising of buttresses, gullies, bluffs and chasms. The rock is quartzite, a form of richly coloured metamorphosed sandstone that in places looks like gigantic brain tissue. I've never climbed anywhere with such a diverse range of styles thrown together in one area. With over two thousand routes, it felt as if there was a lifetime's worth of climbing. During my first visit to Arapiles I finally started to get to grips with some classic Australian test pieces and at the end of a fortnight I had climbed a number of excellent routes. I'd taken the flight on *Have a Good Flight*, *Spasmed in the Chasm*, managed to find the exit on *No Exit* and avoided the ground on *Hit the Deck*.

After about a month's climbing in Oz, I started to feel that I was beginning to acclimatise to the styles of climbing. I'd left the UK with the mind set that I'd be able to step off the plane and start cruising up grade 24s and 25s. How wrong I'd been. It was almost like stepping back and having to re-learn the craft again. It had been hard and sometimes dispiriting work, it reinforced how good those climbers were, who were able to transfer their talents effortlessly across continents.

We headed back to Queensland with plans to have a couple of weeks sightseeing. Jane wanted to see more of the country and not just cliffs. First port of call was the Great Barrier Reef. Peerless joined us on the trip and we made the short flight to Lady Elliot Island, a small coral cay, sat in an idyllic spot on the reef itself. Peerless supplied some top quality snorkelling gear, including weight belts and depth gauges, and we set about our marine safari. I've always been a good underwater swimmer, but this was a new experience.

'You know with practice, you can learn to hold your breath for five minutes,' Peerless explained and he went on, 'I reckon we could get up to some pretty spectacular free diving out here.'

With that, what had started out as a relaxing, snorkelling holiday turned into the practice of meditation, hyperventilation and a test of nerve.

We started with short dives of ten metres or so. These were spectacular enough, diving down the wall of the reef and navigating underwater tunnels in the company of reef sharks, but as our confidence grew, so did our ambition.

Australia 1988. **Top:** *Language of Desire* Grade 24, Shipley Upper, Blue Mountains. The removable brackets used with carrot bolts can be seen in this picture. *Photo: Glenn Robbins.*

Bottom left: Tenuous smearing and 'carrot bolt' clipping as I climb the immaculate arête of *Alex in Wonderland*, Sphinx Rock. *Photo: Chris Frost.*

Bottom right: Jonathon 'Peerless' Pearson on *New Paths* Turtle Rock. *Photo: Chris Frost.*

Climbing *Leanings*, grade 24, Mount Piddington, Blue Mountains of Australia. *Photo: Glenn Robbins.*

Making the second ascent of *Change Planets*, grade 26 on the
'Dog Face' Blue Mountains. Mike Law enthused about the
unusual nature of his new route. It was a wild position, but a
product of Law in *Michelangelo* mode. Jane can be seen at the
hanging belay near the base of the dark water streak. I'm near
the top. *Photo: Mike Stacey.*

Leading the second pitch of *Lucifer's Hammer,* grade 24, Porters Pass during the first ascent in 1988. *Photo: Fiona Lumsden.*

Making the second ascent of
Greg Rimmer's adventurous
route *Bliss* E7 6b in Gordale.
'It can't be E7 then can it Rad?'
Mick Lovatt's comment after
watching me fall from the crux.

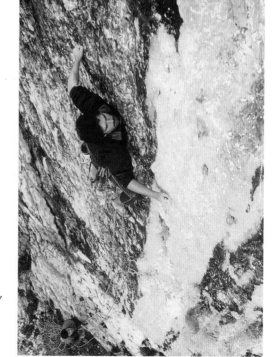

Making the second ascent of
Lovatt's *Introducing the Hardline,*
E5 6b at the obscure White Scar,
Cumbria. Mick Ryan belays.
Both photos: Glenn Robbins.

Jerry, Mick and I enjoyed a great road trip across North America. We hooked up with legend Jim Bridwell and fell into a routine of hard climbing and hard partying.

Top: 'Team Boreal', Peel, Johnston, Bridwell, Radtke. *Photo: Mark Radtke.*

Below: at Donner Summit enjoying après beer with Jim and Winter Olympians Hans and Lynne Stanteiner.

Jerry Peel cruising the superlative *Scirocco* 5.12a. Needles of California.
Photo: Mark Radtke.

The first ascent of *Phoenix in Obsidian*, E7 6b, Iron Crag, Cumbria in 1989.
Photo: Jane Cooksey.

By the end of the trip I was making free dives of up to thirty metres, which were quite freaky affairs. The weight belt made the first ten metres pretty effortless, but starting at this depth your lungs become sufficiently compressed that you start sinking like a stone. This is great because you simply let gravity do all the work for you, the daunting bit is when you hit the bottom and look up. The surface suddenly seems a long, long way away. This is when you've got to keep your nerve and try and enter a meditative state of mind. Getting back to the surface takes work of course, because down here your body is denser than the seawater. Swimming back up requires concentration and pace. I had a couple of scares when I felt the oxygen in my blood stream running out, with the surface still tantalisingly out of reach. On one occasion as I was heading back up from a deep dive, I could see Jane thrashing around above me. When I finally made the surface she was in a bit of a panic, 'Didn't you see it? There was a massive shark and it was heading straight for you. I'm sure it was a Tiger.'

Back on shore we related the tale to Peerless but he was unfazed, 'Yeah there are Tiger sharks around here, but the fact is there's never been a recorded attack. There's simply too much food around.'

The trip to the barrier reef was certainly one of the memorable bits of Australia. The wildlife was simply spectacular. Hovering above Manta Rays with massive twelve-foot wingspans was like having a close encounter with alien beings and diving with huge green turtles was like living a childhood dream.

Back on the mainland we headed north, up to Cairns. Frosty had put us in touch with one of his old mates from Uni, a guy called Jeremy Scrivven.

'You'll like Scrivo, he's sure to have some adventures up his sleeve for you.'

Frosty had made an early ascent of Balls Pyramid, the world's largest sea stack. This huge spire of rock rises out of the ocean for six hundred metres and Jeremy Scrivven had been a member of the team. I remember Frosty recounting tails of the reckless Scrivo, air bedding around the huge stack, surrounded by killer Tiger sharks. He sounded a bit of a character.

When we finally tracked him down he came to the door in his shorts, I couldn't help wondering about a huge red scar on his leg and immediately thought, shark, 'What happened to your leg, Jeremy?' I asked.

'Oh I nearly cut the bloody thing off. Chainsaw backfired on me,' he laughed.

He invited us in for a beer and true to form started hatching a plan. It transpired that a group of local Kayakers were planning the descent of a section of the Johnstone River, located deep in the tropical rainforest. There had been some heavy rains recently and they'd heard that the river sported some fine rapids. The guys needed some help to carry their canoes in and would then need further help to get their boats back up the steep and heavily forested valley, about fifteen miles downstream. Scrivo thought that we'd be able to make the river trip on airbeds. I was a little sceptical, but he reassured us, 'No problem mate. I've done this sort of thing loads of times, it'll be a doddle. Anyway it'll give you a chance to see some real unspoilt tropical rain forest. There's only been a few abbos and bushmen who've explored that area.' I couldn't fault his enthusiasm, so we arranged a rendezvous for the following day.

We met the kayaking team at the designated spot. There were four paddlers and by the look of their kit and tone of their chat, I deduced that we were in for some real white water adventure. We slid into the trees carrying the canoes in pairs. It was a steep descent through thick tropical rainforest and hard going as we circumnavigated large clumps of the notorious Wait a While Vine. The name of the vine had been coined by early explorers and described the plant in a rather understated fashion. It hangs from trees and has long tendrils with vicious hooks that snag clothing and rip at skin. Getting caught up in the vine can lead to long and painful delays.

After about half an hour of bush walking, stumbling and sliding down steep muddy slopes, we could hear the powerful roar of the torrent, rumbling in the valley below. We emerged from beneath the dark forest canopy and arrived at a rocky channel, which contained a fast flowing river, stained brown with freshly eroded sediment. It was about thirty feet wide and maybe fifteen feet deep. We inflated the airbeds, as the paddlers donned helmets and distributed buoyancy aids to everyone. They secured their splash decks and were soon on the water and practising Eskimo rolls. We launched our flimsy crafts, and soon the whole mad flotilla was being carried to an uncertain fate by an unforgiving current.

After about a kilometre the noise of rushing water increased in volume and suddenly we were being pitched helplessly through a narrowing, rocky channel at a true rate of knots. Scrivo clearly loved it as he sat astride his airbed riding the current like a bucking bronco and screaming like someone demented. I was completely gripped and desperately tried to keep on top of my airbed as I spun round and round with no sense of control at all. As soon as it had started, the chaos finished and we were spat out of the channel into a wider length of the river.

One of the paddlers came over, 'Are you lot all okay? that rapid was about grade 2. We've got some fairly fast water for a couple of miles now and then we hit the meat of the trip with some grade 4 rapids, but there's plenty of water, so you should be okay. What you don't want to do is to hit anything.'

The next section of the trip was an exciting test of balance and steering, but it was just about manageable and almost enjoyable. The thunderous roar of the river soon put a stop to any thoughts of enjoyment that I was having though. Sensibly, the paddlers guided us to some rocks on the right bank. We climbed up onto a rocky platform and walked a little way downstream to survey what lay ahead. From an experienced kayaker's perspective it probably looked like a dream, but to me it looked horrific. The river valley narrowed into a gorge and the whole river was funnelled through a channel about twenty feet wide. Large cliffs of red sandstone prevented any form of escape. The torrent raged and foamed for about two hundred metres and then calmed as the river widened. It was like a giant boiling version of the Strid in my native Yorkshire.

One of the paddlers planned the strategy. 'It looks like a good grade 4 rapid. Two of us will go down first and pick out the safest line. We'll wait at the bottom to rescue any of you lot. Scrivo can go first, he's the most experienced, and we'll see how he fares. The rest of you can then follow, and the remaining paddlers will bring up the rear.'

The two paddlers launched their canoes and we observed their progress. They made it look straightforward enough, but we could see they still had to work their boats with skill. Scrivo went next, yelling and hollering as he rode his airbed like a rodeo rider, suddenly he lost balance and inverted. His airbed shot skyward, but we could see his head and his bright red buoyancy vest shooting down the current. The two paddlers rescued him at the bottom and then signalled for the rest of us to make the ride.

Peerless was looking ashen faced with fear, as I suspect I was, but I told him, 'Come on Peerless, it's now or never.'

As soon as I hit the top of the rapid I was pitched upside down and went under, but I kept a vice-like grip with arms and legs wrapped round the airbed. The free diving training on the Barrier Reef was paying dividends as I held my breath, but then the air was forced out of my lungs as I struck a submerged rock. I was dragged to safety by one of the paddlers. All feeling in my right leg had gone. I examined my thigh which was red and bleeding, but it didn't feel broken.

The others had managed to escape unscathed and were in the process of recovering their airbeds, when there was further commotion on the river. One of the remaining paddlers had capsized and was stuck underwater trapped in his canoe. His mates rushed to his side and managed to drag him over to where I was massaging life into a numb leg. He'd hit his head on a rock and was groggy and concussed, but slowly began to pull round. His helmet had saved his life.

We regrouped and talked about the way forward. One of the paddlers described what lay ahead, 'That's definitely the crux of the trip, there's a couple more rapids, but the gorge opens up and I think you'll be able to circumnavigate any tricky sections on foot. The only problem is we'll be travelling faster in the canoes and you'll have to try and keep up. At the end of the rapids we've got about four miles of wide, slow river to paddle before we can climb back up to the rim of the valley.'

He was correct in his evaluation and the remaining technical sections proved uneventful enough. At the end of the rapids the river opened out into a wide flat brown snake about fifty metres across. The current slowed to a snail's pace and paddling the airbeds proved hopelessly inefficient. The day was slipping away and I could sense the kayakers' frustration with our sluggish progress. It was at this point that I noticed the first signs of civilisation, but it wasn't something I'd expected. It was clearly an official hazard warning sign. On it, was a crocodile's head with mouth agape and next to it the picture of a swimmer with a line through it. I shouted over to the others, 'Have you seen that?'

Peerless responded, 'Don't worry about it, they're only freshwater crocs this far up the Johnstone River, and I can't recall any reported attacks by freshwater crocs on humans in this area.'

I respected his knowledge of Australian wildlife, but wasn't convinced. One of the paddlers came to our rescue, 'This is hopeless, we're not going to get out before nightfall at this rate. If you put the front of your airbeds on the sterns of the canoes we'll see if we can tow you,' he said. In this fashion we made slightly better progress, it was desperate work on the part of the paddlers, but eventually we made our escape without further incident or crocodile attack.

Over the coming days my leg from hip to knee turned blue and then black as the severe bruising came out. I've had plenty of adventures in my life, but the Johnstone River epic is one that I'd never want to repeat.

Jane had always intended doing her own thing for a couple of months, knowing that after the holiday bit of the trip I'd be wanting to climb pretty much full time. So when the opportunity arose to combine some work with further sight seeing she took advantage of it. We said our farewells and she left for Thursday Island, an exotic paradise lying in the Torres Strait, just off the Cape York Peninsula, in the very north of Australia.

Peerless and I started the long journey back south under an overcast, black sky. We were headed for the Blue Mountains of New South Wales, but to the east an evil storm was brewing. Cyclone Charlie was gathering momentum and as we travelled south its full force hit us just north of Mackay.

'It's no good this, even with the wiper blades on maximum, I can't see a thing. I'll have to pull over,' said Peerless. I'd never experienced rain and wind like this before. Peerless stopped at the side of the road and we decided to sit the storm out. We'd been parked up for about an hour, when suddenly the car started to move sideways.

'Christ!' shouted Peerless, 'we're being swept away! I've seen stuff like this on the news before, cars left stuck in trees.'

I strained to open the car door and as I did, water gushed into the foot well. Outside the car I could see what the problem was, a nearby river must have burst its banks. The water was about a foot deep and flowing fast. A load of water hyacinths had got lodged under the car and it was the pressure of water on this flotsam that was slowly pushing the car back across the road.

In a panic we set about removing the debris and as soon as the dam beneath the car was breached, the pressure was off and the vehicle stopped its slide. Just at that moment, a police patrol truck arrived. The officer wound down his window and shouted into the wind and lashing rain, 'Follow me, I'll guide you to dry land. This stretch of road will be completely submerged before long.'

We jumped back in the car and tailgated the flashing hazards of the truck to higher ground.

The storm raged for hours and when it finally blew out, we found ourselves stuck near a mosquito-ridden one-horse town waiting for the floodwaters to subside. Several sections of the southern highway had been washed away. I fell ill with a debilitating fever and could hardly leave my tent.

After five days of illness and depressing boredom, we learned that traffic was once again getting through. The oppressive grey sky was finally rent with blue and the malaise I was under started to lift as we made our journey south over newly laid and still steaming tarmac.

We stopped at one of the bridge crossings to assess what the situation must have looked like. The river would normally have been about twenty feet below the bridge, but we could see from the debris littering the branches of the trees that it must have been submerged by about fifteen feet.

'You know, we ought to count our blessings,' said Peerless, 'we were really lucky back there. I wasn't joking when I said I've seen pictures of cars stuck in trees in the aftermath of these cyclones.'

We carried on south, I'd had enough of water, tropical rainforest and cyclones to last a lifetime. I felt the depression lifting at the prospect of getting back to the rock.

I emerged from my tent a few weeks later into a dewy dawn and gazed across the landscape. The sky was blue, there were white mist veiled green pastures and eucalypt forest in the valley below. Sheer cliffs lined the valley walls as far as the eye could see. The sun illuminated the rich colours in the sandstone. Yellows, reds and greys, soft rock, hard crimpy rock, perfect edgy wall climbing. I stretched and savoured the crisp air, I was going to have a good day today. These were the Blue Mountains and I felt at home.

Peerless and I had arrived three weeks earlier. We'd had a slow start after our tropical escapades, once again it had taken time to acclimatise to the rock, the protection, and the style of climbing. Initially, we'd both had our arses kicked on what should have been, judging by the numbers, pretty straightforward climbs, but it had slowly come together.

Peerless had introduced me to local Blueys' aficionado John 'Crunch' Smoothy. Crunch lived in Blackheath in the heart of the Mountains. He was the local Postie, a prolific new router, and possessed a wealth of information. He was a generous guy, but like most Aussie climbers loved to sandbag, and under his soft outward veneer, there lurked a fierce and competitive edge. Crunch provided us with some good knowledge and armed with this gen we'd amassed quite a tick list.

Today we were headed for Cosmic County, one of the Blueys' premiere crags for top quality face climbing. The walls of the County were plumb vertical and were tiger striped with beautiful orange streaks. Routes of varying styles existed side-by-side, fully bolted affairs, traditional routes and those with the occasional carrot bolt. The walls were covered in small edges, so it was crimp and rock-over city. Some people said the climbing was a bit repetitive, but I loved the place. I warmed up on the ironically named *Clip or Die*, a thirty five metre pitch protected by a line of convenient bolts. I then moved on to a steep and athletic 23, called *Walking Wounded* to get the blood pumping, before focusing on to what I had come for - a superlative face climb called *Aesthetic Images*. Assessing the rock from the ground suggested that it might be blank. The only indication that a route climbed it at all, were several widely spaced carrot bolts. The climb lived up to expectations, thin technical wall climbing with holds only revealing themselves at the last moment, or to the feel. A hundred feet of Blue Mountains face climbing at its very best.

For the last few months Peerless had been on extended vacation waiting to see if he'd been accepted into the air force as a pilot. He'd been fine company, but now it was time for him to return home. We'd spent the last month or so wild camping in the bush, cooking on open fires and drinking tinnies. I'd now be without transport, so I decided to move to Blackheath and camp closer to the pub and amenities. Crunch normally finished his post round about one o'clock and said whenever he could, he'd climb with me in the afternoons, which was an excellent arrangement.

The cliffs of Centennial Glen, Shipley and Porters Pass were easily accessible by foot from the campsite in Blackheath, so I'd go exploring in the mornings and meet up with Crunch in the afternoons. Centennial Glen was something of a rarity in the Blue Mountains back in 1988. It was a steep little wall and offered all-weather climbing akin to the Catwalk at Malham. At one end of the main wall an ancient wooden picnic table was carved with graffiti dating back decades and bore witness to a bit of Australian history. Some of this history and the people associated with it had now been immortalised in the cliff. *Bernie Crawley*, *Trix Roughly*, *Nev Loves Trix*, *Pass the Sausages*, *Glad Ingram*, *Nev Herrod* and *Rudy Norry* were all now steep and powerful routes courtesy of Crunch and his friends.

One of these activists was the extremely talented, Sidney-based climber, Mike Law, aka Claw. Claw was a prodigious new router who had really pushed Australian rock-climbing standards. He'd emerged from the underground Sydney punk rock scene and was a bohemian, punk rock mixture. He had a creative imagination and was a bit of a radical thinker. When he applied this to some of his new rock routes the result could be quite controversial. On one of his new routes, on the Sydney sea cliffs, he'd bolted an inertia seat belt mechanism from a car to the rock as the runner to protect the crux. You could just about reach up and clip the seat belt, but if you tried to pull up on it, it just kept extending. If you fell on it, however, it would lock up and hold a fall. It was a practical joke of course, but Claw was making the underlying message, If you're not good enough to flash the route, you shouldn't be on it.

At the Glen, Claw had adopted a Michaelangelo approach to some of his routes and blatantly manufactured them by chipping pockets. These routes were excellent gymnastic affairs and stood the test of time for several years. Claw was viewed as a leading light of Australian rock-climbing and since his actions remained unchallenged, chipping started to proliferate in the Mountains. There was a real risk of it becoming a cultural norm. It took the arrival of young bloods with fresh attitudes, who were prepared to make a stand. These young climbers embraced a different set of values and took the stance of, 'Enough is enough. This is completely against what modern rock-climbing is about.'

They cemented in the chips and in some cases re-climbed the routes, now without the chipped-out pockets. It was a necessary poke in the eye to Claw and his disciples. It was a little microcosm of how local traditions and practices can potentially take hold and shape the direction of a sport. I'm sure Mike Law didn't view his actions as denigrating rock-climbing, or as cheating, since he was completely open, almost proud of what he'd created. In his mind he was simply trying to push the standards of difficulty on a rock type that doesn't naturally lend itself to super hard routes. One of Claws creations at the Glen was graded 31, which in 1988 was close to Australia's hardest grade of 32. I'm sure that Claw thought he was adding something positive to climbing by creating an all-weather training crag. The problem is that Law had been in the media spotlight for many years and by this virtue was viewed as an influential character in the Australian climbing scene. Whether conscious or not, Law's actions communicated a message to the wider climbing community of what he deemed was an acceptable practice.

My own reaction to these chipped routes, like other locals, was not to condemn Laws' actions. On the contrary, I, like them, climbed the routes and professed how much I enjoyed them. In effect, condoning Laws' actions makes me guilty of chipping by association. It is easy to see in this example that what Mike Law was doing was at odds with what climbing should be about, but it still took several years before it was challenged and the balance was restored. This is how things can and do happen in climbing. Sometimes the actions of climbers can be subtle, remain unchallenged, and allow practices to creep in which are at odds with what climbing stands for.

When Crunch was out doing his post round, I'd spend the mornings exploring the crags around Blackheath. There were acres of unclimbed rock and it was a case of trying to identify potential lines that might go without too much effort. The cliffs of Porters Pass attracted me most, big vertical walls up two hundred and fifty feet high. I procured the necessary ironmongery from the local hardware shop and after a short lesson from Crunch, got to work in his garden shed grinding the bolts square. I'd spotted a beautiful pillar down in the pass. It was sixty metres tall and looked pretty blank from below, but from abseil I could see it would definitely go and probably at a reasonable grade. Typical of many of the walls of the Blueys', this pillar had a dearth of natural gear placements. I borrowed Crunch's hand drill and set to work gearing it up. I placed eleven bolts on the forty metre second pitch, but had to place bolts on the lead of the overhanging first pitch. It took me almost a week to equip it.

Crunch met me after work one afternoon and together we climbed *Lucifer's Hammer*, grade 24. Even Crunch, competitive as ever conceded that it was a quality find. I named it in honour of Mike Law.

The Glen was a short walk from Crunch's house on Eveleigh Avenue in Blackheath, and it became a regular hang out as the weather turned unseasonably wet. It was during one of our many sessions at the Glen, that I spotted a new line on the right side of the crag. I seem to recall equipping the route ground up and after a few hours we had it ready to go. It was a bitterly cold day, about seven degrees and Crunch didn't seem overly enthusiastic about taking up the sharp end and after a bit of cat and mouse about who should go first, he talked me into it and I set off. As I got through the crux, Crunch was livid and threatened to pull me off. He later confessed that he was convinced I'd fail in the cold and then he'd be able to steal the first ascent when it was warmer. Unintentionally, I'd out sandbagged him. He cursed me all the way back to his house. The route turned out to be a nice technical wall climb, it wasn't as steep and powerful as its neighbours, so I gave it a grade of 23. Today the description of the route in the modern guidebook reads:

Chase The Lady 14m 23.
Harder than some 24s. A sandbag with a long tradition.
M Radtke, J Smoothy 1988.

The telephone rang in Crunch's house. I'd been staying at the Smoothy - Lumsden household for about two weeks. Fiona was Crunch's long-standing girlfriend and had looked after me very well. She answered the phone, 'It's Mike Law, he wants to speak to you,' she said.

I took the phone and Mike began talking before I could speak. 'Hey Rad, I've got this Yank round at my place and he's looking for a partner for a month or so. His name's Dan, I've told him that you're just the man. He'll call round at Crunch's place tomorrow. Have a good one.'

'Cheers Mike,' I said and I put the phone down. I didn't know what to expect, but I didn't want to overstay my welcome at the Smoothys'.

The following morning, revealed a bear-like character at Crunch's front door. He was about six feet tall and his skimpy shorts and tight vest emphasised a tanned and muscular frame. He looked more like an Olympic sprinter than a rock-climber. He held his hand out and said with a loud Colorado accent, 'Hi I'm Dan Mannix, you must be, Rad. Cool name, please to meet ya.'

'Yeah pleased to meet you too,' I said in a less convincing voice.

After a week in Dan's company, any preconceptions that I had about loud and in-your-face Yanks had evaporated. We'd just had another great day at the County and were relaxing by Dan's pride and joy, a 1967 Ford Falcon.

I knew I'd get on with Dan after our first day. On returning to the car after a good day at the crag he'd opened the boot to reveal an Eski full of ice-cold beers. We fell into a bit of a routine in the days that followed. Wake up and go to the café. Drink coffee and read the newspapers until 11am. Hit the crag about midday and climb until about 6pm. Return to the Falcon and crack open the Eski. So here we were again drinking tinnies by the car.

'Hey Dan, that was a great lead of *Gentleman's Drag* that you did today. I thought you said face climbing wasn't your thing,' I said.

'Well that crack made all the difference. Give me a bit of jamming and I can do a half decent job.'

Dan was from Boulder, Colorado and had grown up on a diet of crack climbing. His observation reinforced how important a climber's local stomping ground was in developing specific skills. Already on this trip, certain rock types and crags had left me witheringly out of my depth.

'Well I don't know about you, Dan, but I'm ready for a change. I think Arapiles will be spot on now, just the right temperature.' I suggested, it was April and the Arapiles would be about perfect right now.

We drove through the night in the 1967 Special. It had a maximum speed of sixty miles per hour, but had bench seats in the front as well as rear, which made excellent beds. We arrived at Araps and made camp in the Pines. It was busier than when I'd been here in January and had a real cosmopolitan village feel about it. There was a Japanese encampment, French, Spaniards, Kiwis, a few Brits and a strong German team headed up by international rock star, Stephan Glowacs.

It was one of the most laid back climbing scenes I've ever experienced. People out on the rock doing their own stuff during the day, then sitting round campfires together, eating, drinking and telling stories long into the night. It was reminiscent of the early days in the Verdon.

Dan was a keen photographer and amateur filmmaker. He was also a great storyteller. He'd filmed the greatly understated British climber, Derek Hersey, soloing the classic *Naked Edge* in Colorado and loved to recall the tale. One evening as we sat by the campfire Dan held court over an audience of eager listeners.

'I was hanging on the rope with my VHS camera round my neck concentrating hard. Derek was cruising up the route in his usual effortless style, straggly black hair blowing in the wind. As he approached me and started some crux moves, a pigeon flew out of hole directly into Derek's face. I nearly dropped my camera with the shock of it. Cool as a cucumber Derek turned and looked directly into the camera and said in his dry Manchester accent, "Did you get that Dan?" and then he cruised on again. Any lesser mortal would have been off, I'm sure.'

After four weeks at Araps, we'd enjoyed some good climbing and had packed a lot in. Personal highlights for me included the scary mind trip of *Ride Like the Wind*. This was a classic signature route of visiting American climber Mike Graham and despite its quality, got very few ascents on account of its scary reputation. I made a rare flash of Mike Laws' technical masterpiece, *Debutantes and Centipedes*, and made a memorable trip up the *Seventh Pillar* on Taipan Wall with the Big Yank.

Dan only had a couple of weeks left in Oz and desperately wanted to climb at Frog Buttress, Queensland's premiere crag. We bade friends goodbye and headed back north. Like Arapiles, Frog isn't the most spectacular crag to look at. Brown rhyolite columns form an edge that rises out of the forest attaining a modest height of about forty metres. The columnar geology means that an aptitude for crack climbing and technical bridging pay dividends. Natural protection is the order of the day, although some fine exposed arêtes and thin faces rely on bolt protection.

It was early May when we arrived back at Frog and the equivalent of autumn in the UK. The temperature was perfect in comparison to the humid and roasting heat that I'd experienced in January. As we got stuck into the climbing, I started to appreciate the quality of the crag and Dan was in his element. He started cranking out 25s and 26s with ease, he was a big guy and had suffered with the steep gymnastic climbing at Araps, but at Frog he demonstrated masterful technique with his feet and was phenomenal when bridging. He could get into positions where he could relax and concentrate on fiddling awkward wires in, in positions where I'd be getting pumped out of my head. It was great to see him excelling and a rewarding conclusion to his trip. We agreed that Frog was probably up there on the world stage, although the huge Pythons that inhabited the cracks could still be unnerving.

We planned a big party for Dan's departure and got together with the rest of the Queensland gang. We were staying with friends of Frosty's, and I got a phone call. 'Where've you been? I've been trying to track you down for ages. I'm coming back, can you meet me tomorrow?' It was my girlfriend Jane.

Dan flew back to the States while Jane and I decided to round our trip off in the Blue Mountains. We called round at Crunch's place and then headed out to Mount Piddington. I'd just set off up a route when there was a kerfuffle nearby.

'Hey, I've heard there's a Pom around here somewhere? Is that you, Crunch? Where's the Pom?'

Crunch replied, 'He's up here on *Leanings*, but you'll have to be quick, looks like he's going to piss it.' He then shouted up to me, 'Just hang fire, Rad, Glenn wants to get some shots.'

Then Jane cut in, 'Come over here, you can get a great angle on it from this position.'

I was getting a little impatient and shouted down to Crunch, 'Right I'm going for it.' I finished the climb under the barrage of the camera auto winder. On the ground Crunch did the introductions, but it wasn't really necessary, I recognised the legendary Australian photographer immediately. He was wearing his signature outfit - black leather peaked cap, black waistcoat, fingerless gloves and black boots. Not the garb you'd expect to see an outdoor photographer wearing. He looked like he'd stepped out of a sadomasochistic film set. It was Glenn Robbins.

In the pub we sat drinking beer and swapping stories. It was no secret that Glenn was gay and I wondered how I'd react to him, but other than his fashion statement and graphic sense of humour, he kept his personal life very much to himself. Over the coming weeks we spent a lot of time with Glenn, he was eager for the shots. Glenn had developed his own unique approach to climbing photography. In an era when posed climbing shots were on the increase, Glenn wanted to buck the trend. In his own words he'd say, 'I want to see the fear in my subject's eyes.' And that's what he tried to capture: the concentration, the strain, the pain, the relief, and all the raw emotion in the climber's face. The true Robbins's photographic signature is instantly recognisable. During the '80s and '90s Glenn's photographs appeared on the covers and pages of climbing magazines the world over. He was the inspiration behind many of today's professional climbing photographers. He liked to get up close and usually ended up suspended from a rope hanging above or close to his models. Typically on our photo shoots, I'd be in mid crux and Glenn would shout down to Jane things like, 'You know what, he's a much better model than some of those skinny specimens I've had, I like his chunky thighs.'

To which Jane would shout back laughing, 'Keep your mind on your photography, that body's mine.'

Glenn would riposte, 'You've got nothing to worry about, any lover of mine has got to be able to lift me above their heads and I don't think Rad's strong enough for that.'

The banter and piss-taking became fierce the more we got to know each other. Glenn was great company, he was generous, considerate and extremely respectful of other people and their views. That's not to say he wouldn't challenge bigots and stand up for his own beliefs. He'd certainly stand his corner and personally I wouldn't like to be on the receiving end of his right hook, but from my experience he was always the real gentleman and will always be welcome in my home.

Our last month in Australia stood out as the best. I completed projects at the County, sampled some of the latest developments in the Wolgan Valley and did my last new route in Porters Pass. It was now winter and the temperatures hovered around freezing. Jane held my ropes as I hooked and engineered my way up through a series of roofs and overhangs and after about six hours I'd got a belay in and had placed a number of carrot bolts. I was exhausted and Jane was completely brassed off. We had to leave in two days, so it was imperative to get the route in the bag. Crunch was working the following day, and Jane had had enough, so Mike Law joined me for the ascent and we both led the route.

'What do you think Mike?' I asked.

'Yeah it's quite good, a little bit like some of my routes on the Sydney Sea Cliffs, not bad for a Pommy.'

I signed off with, *Done Roamin', Done Carin', Done Livin'.*

I flew back to England, racked with the debilitating illness that I'd experienced earlier in the year. I later learned that I'd contracted Ross River Fever, a rare mosquito transmitted disease of the northern territories. It was Australia's final sandbag.

Chapter 9

The Good the Bad and the Ugly

'Danger is always present in rock climbing.
In the final analysis it is an essential ingredient,
but one must realise where the danger lies'.
Royal Robbins
Advanced Rockcraft

During my time in Australia I thought long and hard about how to achieve the right work-life-climbing balance and decided that a career in lecturing might provide a workable compromise. On my return to the UK, I secured a place at Huddersfield Polytechnic, was fortunate to get a grant to finance my studies and completed a Post Graduate Certificate in Further Education. My first job wasn't in lecturing, but as the Manager of a private outdoor education centre in the heart of the Yorkshire Dales. This necessitated a domestic move and I bought a small cottage nestled below what would become one of Yorkshire's premier gritstone bouldering venues, Earl Crag.

After five years together Jane and I decided to marry and life continued pretty much as normal with climbing taking very much centre stage. Any free time was spent hungrily searching out new challenges across the UK, longer breaks would find us heading to Spain, France, or Italy. Most of the time I would be content in pushing myself on classic routes up and down the country, but as ever, I was always on the look out for the elusive unclimbed line. It was during this period that I re-acquainted myself with my old stomping ground of Gordale, and spotted a potential new route. I persuaded Ian Cooksey to join me in the venture, but it was pretty apparent that he wasn't the most willing of partners.

'I hate this fucking place. It's loose and dangerous. I go out climbing to enjoy myself. What the fuck do you want to climb loose rock for?' Ian complained bitterly. He was going through a 'take it or leave it' phase with his climbing and for some reason appeared a bit disillusioned with the whole game. Ian's

116

climbing roots were very much in the adventurous side of the sport, but of late he had been clipping a lot of bolts. His behaviour was uncharacteristic, he was usually really up for some new route action. I thought he'd lost his way a little bit, but deep down I think that he resented the publicity I'd received after our climb at Heptonstall. I speculated on what the result might have been if Ian, rather than I, had been splashed across the pages of the magazine.

'Come on, Ian, it'll be a cracking route. I've abbed down it and it's not loose at all,' I told him.

'Well it can't be up to much otherwise it would already have been done,' he snapped back.

'It's not been done because other people haven't got the vision,' I said firmly.

Hanging on the left wall of the Gorge the fine groove of *Rebel* could be seen clearly. To its left was another groove line which was taken by *Revolt*, the E5 climbed by Ashley Cowell in 1982. To the right of *Rebel* was another groove which remained unclimbed. I figured that the reason this line had been overlooked was that the groove was bottomless and gaining entry would mean breaching a huge ceiling of loose unprotected rock. It looked unclimbable, but I had conceived an alternative start. This would access the groove and would create a pitch of quality equal to that of both *Rebel* and *Revolt*.

We arrived in the Gorge and I talked Ian into leading the first pitch of *Rebel*. This would be a common start for my proposed new route. Ian was still in foul mood and after about fifteen feet was cursing and hurling abuse down, 'It's fucking shit. What the fuck am I doing here? There's no fucking gear!'

I tried to shout up some encouragement, 'There's a peg coming up Ian and then you get a good wire. There's a bit of a runout and then you get to another peg.'

'I can't see any peg,' he shouted back angrily.

'Go on, Ian, it's only HVS,' I encouraged him, but that just seemed to rub salt into an already festering wound.

'That's it. I'm not going to kill myself on a poxy pile of shit like this. If you want to do it you'll have to lead the lot.' With that he climbed back down and handed me the ends of the ropes. I took over and was soon sat in the small cave and bringing Ian up to join me. I started the second pitch by climbing the first bulge of *Rebel*. I then made a delicate traverse right and successfully gained the bottomless unclimbed groove line. Initially the climbing was fairly straightforward, but after about twenty feet it became technical and strenuous. I really had to bite the bullet and just about managed to claw my way up to gain some good holds and the sanctuary of another airy belay ledge. The pitch had felt tough, perhaps harder than the main pitch of *Rebel*. Ian followed, but had no fight in him and after resting on a piece of gear, he arrived at the belay.

'Well done Ian, what do you think?' I asked. I was really chuffed.

'Let's just get the hell out of here,' Ian responded dismissively.

I finished the route by climbing the third pitch of *Rebel*. I should have felt euphoric, but Ian's lack of enthusiasm and negativity had really brought me down. I doubted the quality of the route, maybe it was nothing more than an insignificant eliminate. I decided that *The Cause* seemed to be an appropriate name.

Later that evening, in the company of some fine red wine, I was in a more philosophical mood. I reflected back over some of my Gordale experiences. *Face Route, Jenny Wren, Comedy of Errors, Nothing to Declare, Mossdale Trip.* They had all been fantastic adventures. These were routes that were full of uncertainty. They often followed cryptic lines, climbed dubious rock and had protection that played games with the mind, but above all they endured in your memory. As I slowly drained my wine glass, the self-doubt evaporated, *The Cause* had all these qualities. It was the last new route that I'd climb with Ian for many years.

Jerry Peel and Dave Barton became my regular new route partners on subsequent ventures. My climbing partnership with Jerry had been cemented when we'd unlocked *Orange Crush* at Heptonstall. From that day forward, Jerry and I became firm friends. Although in his forties, Jerry was still masterful on the rock, his bouldering ability was legendary, but what people didn't realize was that he could translate this technical mastery onto routes. Even when the move was way above gear, he could pull it off. He was a true inspiration. The fact that I started mixing in these new climbing circles somehow began to impact on my relationship with Jane. Whether it was the new company that I was keeping, or simply the blind obsession that I had for climbing, after only eighteen months of marriage we'd separated and divorce was firmly on the cards. It was a tough time, but Dave Barton came to my rescue.

I'd first met Dave around 1987, in Pembroke. As I walked along the top of the cliff, with waves crashing in below, I could see a figure walking uncomfortably towards us using a pair of walking sticks to aid his progress. I was with Dave 'Greeny' Green, and he turned to me and said, 'That's Dave Barton.'

He pronounced Dave's name with an air of reverence. As we met on the cliff top path we stopped to pass the time of day.

'What've you been up to, Dave?' Greeny enquired.

A broad grin spread across Barton's face and his steely blue eyes illuminated with a strange fire, 'Oh, I've just done a couple of routes in the Leap, *Headhunter* and *Minotaur*, and I think I'll do *The Great White* tomorrow.'

His words conveyed a matter of fact certainty. He turned and continued to hobble along the path.

'What do you make of that Rad? A year ago they didn't know whether he'd walk again let alone climb and now he's back doing E5s off his walking sticks.' Greeny was clearly impressed.

Over the coming years I bumped into Dave on and off and began to learn not only about how talented a climber he is, but also how honourable a man he is. Dave is an extremely empathetic person, he has an uncanny knack of getting onto a person's emotional wavelength almost immediately. He is able to get the measure of a person within the space of a conversation and ninety percent of the time his intuition is correct. When I started climbing with Dave regularly I think he appreciated the place I was in. During my period of marital turmoil he saw someone that needed support. Looking back, I recognise that I could have carried out some ugly and regrettable deeds during that time, but Dave enabled me to see things from different perspectives and ultimately I retained my dignity.

I think he also connected a little bit with what I was doing on the rock. I was still very much into trad climbing when many other folk who were pioneering in Yorkshire were more focused on sport climbing. Dave has an ingrained thirst for adventure, crack him open like a stick of rock and it would read, Walker Spur, Eiger North Face, Bonatti Pillar, E6s too numerous to count: the list would go on and on. The fact that I was more interested in developing traditional new routes went some way to quenching his adventurous thirst.

Virtually all our first climbs together were doing new routes. During the early '90s Gordale acted as a diversion from some of the domestic strife I was experiencing and I started to channel some of the anger onto the rock. Dave simply loved the adrenaline fix. He made the perfect partner. Our first new route tackled an improbable line on the left wall of Gordale Scar. A number of artificial routes wove their way through some inhospitable territory, but the appearance of the rock and names such as *Manque* and *Grot* suggested unlikely free routes. The description in the guidebook of 'full body armour required by the second to protect against loose rock', provided a tempting challenge for us.

Dave and I shared leads on what became, *The Good The Bad and The Ugly*. Our line linked a series of weaknesses up the left wall and covered two hundred feet of challenging adventure. A bold and committing first pitch, on less than perfect rock, led to a well-protected, but fearsome second pitch which revolved around a wild roof crack. Pitch three followed an exposed bridging groove to horizontal rabbit-mown pastures and the reward of a real summit experience. Neil Foster and Martin Berzins repeated the route and suggested a grade of E7. *Three Wishes* was my next creation, climbed with Jaysen Metcalf, son of the infamous climber 'Matie Metcalf'. Like, *The Good the Bad and the Ugly*, the climbing wasn't pretty, but the position was spectacular, with magnificent rock architecture all around and space below your feet that left you climbing in wild isolation. Once again, Martin Berzins jumped in for the second ascent. Unaware that the route traversed right into a route called *King Rat* towards the top, he found himself climbing tottering rock directly above. Shaking like a half dollar watch, he just managed to complete a direct finish to the route without the whole lot collapsing around him. I suspect that the experience lives in Martin's memory to this day.

In 1994 the ever competitive Berzins began a systematic campaign to fill Gordale's empty spaces. His inquisitive eye revealed, *The Prince of Darkness*, an excellent and long pitch requiring a comprehensive rack of gear. He followed this up with *Redemption*, which climbed the wall immediately right of the Livesey classic, *Deliverance*. Like its neighbour, this delightful climb also employed the controversial minimalist bolt concept. The quality of any climb comes from a number of different characteristics; the moves, the adventure, the exposure and the mental commitment to name a few. The first ascensionist is often faced with dilemmas. It may be that the route is safeguarded with natural protection for eighty five percent of its length, but one section may be devoid of natural gear. It might also transpire that the un-protectable section is the crux of the climb and a fall could result in serious injury.

The paradox that this presents is; does the proposed first ascensionist place a bolt and create a balanced climb? Or do they do it without and produce a route that in all likelihood will never get repeated? Placing one or two bolts on a route that otherwise uses natural pro is termed the minimalist bolt concept. I've been faced with this situation on a number of new routes and personally, I've always tried to be objective about a very subjective judgment call. In these cases I have tried to put myself in the shoes of those who will come after, trying to second guess what sort of experience is best. Others are highly critical of such judgments and offer a range of counter arguments, but these are often black and white views in what is sometimes very grey terrain.

For my own part, the pleasure of climbing comes from enjoying the routes that others have created, and some of the motivation of putting up new routes is creating something that others will hopefully enjoy. This is not just about a physical exercise of getting from A to B. It's about the whole experience. How each climber choreographs the journey. How they deal with the physical demands of the climbing. How they reconcile perceived risks, and how they are left feeling at the end. Climbing can combine mental, physical and emotional elements. It's often the balance of these elements that determine the quality of the climbing experience.

When I abseiled a potential line to the left of *The Good the Bad and the Ugly* I could see that I would be out of my depth on what looked like hard 6b, climbing with no gear, I decided to shelve the idea. After substantial soul searching about the same line, Berzins placed two bolts, stabilized some friable flakes with glue and led the atmospheric, *The Unforgiven* at hard E6. Even with two bolts, the climb still requires a bold and determined approach and is not without considerable risk. The critics will contest that no one has the right to determine the level of risk. Martin Berzins didn't place these bolts naively. He observed local traditions and probably assessed how his actions would sit in the current climbing culture. I'm sure that there was a degree of ego driving his actions, but at the end of the day he was the architect with the vision to create this new route.

When Dave Barton and I climbed, *The Thrivin'*, I was faced with the same dilemma. The route climbed a short wall that I was able to protect with a couple of poor pegs. It then followed a fine groove on natural protection to a ledge at sixty feet. To finish, it tackled an unprotected overhanging section by delightful but short lived moves. The climbing was relatively straightforward, but still required a cautious approach on the lower wall. I placed two bolts to protect the overhanging section. In this state the route went at the amenable grade of E5 6a, and became instantly popular. With increased traffic the rock has settled down considerably and in its solid state it could be argued that the character of the route would be enhanced if these bolts were removed. To date this hasn't happened and rather than removing the two bolts some people advocate the addition of more bolts to turn it into a full sport climb. There are now three options for a route like this. The fully trad option, the fully sport option, or the option in which the route was originally conceived. I would like to quote the great American rock-climbing pioneer, Royal Robbins, at this point, on his propositions about new routes as creations:

'We do not chop or place bolts on an existing route out of respect for other's creations, rather we leave things as they are because we consider the feelings of all the climbers in the future who might want to repeat the route as it was originally done. So we honour the route and the creative effort by leaving it as nearly intact as possible. If this principle is generally adhered to, we can have large numbers of climbers without degrading routes'

In 1995 another Gordale new route boom was still in full swing with several parties, including Dave and me, Jerry Peel and Mick Johnston, and Martin Berzins and Neil Foster all competing for new routes.

It was July when I pulled up in the lay-by at the Scar, Jerry was already packed and waiting. He was excited and anxious to get to grips with a new line in the upper reaches of the gorge. Mick arrived flustered, with his climbing gear in a plastic carrier bag.

'Where's your 'sack Mick? we asked in unison.

'I left it in the hall at home. Told Sue that I'm working late this evening. With a bit of luck it'll fool her.'

He'd been out too many evenings on the run lately and if Sue knew he was out climbing again rather than exercising his husbandly duties she'd throw a wobbler. He once came on a trip to Spain with us, telling his wife he was working in Wales. All week he kept his face covered up to avoid getting sunburn and giving the game away when he returned home. That's Mick for you. Laughing and joking we walked the familiar path into the gorge.

Jerry and Mick were soon ensconced on their route and I began cleaning a loose and shattered wall that I hoped would form an independent start to a new roof pitch climbed a few days before with Dave Barton. I'd already inspected the line and placed two bolts. The first at about twenty feet and the second a further twenty feet above this, I was hoping the climbing in between might take some natural pro or pegs. After much searching for gear placements, I tapped a knife blade peg into a thin crack in the hope that this would protect the first difficult section of the route. After quickly brushing a few holds, I abseiled back to the gorge floor. A quick check on Jerry and Mick revealed that they were making good progress on their climb and I was eager to get my own route in the bag. A stroke of luck saw a young climber and Gordale enthusiast called Matt Troilett arrive. I knew Matt by acquaintance and whilst he was getting ready to climb himself, his mate agreed to belay me on the shattered wall. I put my new belay partner in the picture.

'I've not cleaned this very well, the peg's average, but I think the rock is solid, so I should be okay.'

With an air of infallibility, I set off up the wall and clipped the peg. A couple of moves further and my fingers curled round a large flake. A long stretch off this should bring a jug within reach and from here I'd be able to clip the first bolt. As I began the sequence all I registered was the sound of a loud crack.

Voices like those echoing in some distant tunnel disturb my tranquillity and tug at my subconscious with nagging urgency.

'Rad, Rad, are you all right? Rad, are you all right?'

Matt is calm, but I detect suppressed panic in his voice. The golden glow that's been cocooning my body begins to fade and slowly my dreaming turns to nightmarish reality. Walls of shattered limestone begin to materialise before my eyes. I recognise familiar features carved in the rock. Confused, I try to make sense of the situation. I survey the guilty sliver of steel still clipped to my rope which is strewn chaotically across the boulders beside me.

I knew the knife blade peg was poor, it hadn't given the familiar ringing tone changes normally associated with a good piton placement as I'd hammered it into the thin vertical seam. The rock on the other hand had told me a different story, sounding solid and true to my gentle hammer taps. I had rushed this particular evening, throwing any caution to the wind, eager in my obsession to bag another new route. The rock had failed, the peg had ripped and I'd decked it. So here I was, drifting in and out of consciousness at the bottom of Gordale Scar. My body crumpled and broken, my mind strangely detached from the fear lurking in the background, with thoughts not of animosity, but more of regret, knowing that I will now be deprived of that on which I thrive.

As I was stretchered to the ambulance, another climber approached me, 'I bet you'll think again about placing pegs on your new routes now, won't you?'

His comment appeared to be tinged with a sense of triumph.

My affair with Gordale had been brought to an abrupt end. I didn't fall very far, less than twenty feet, but the landing was pretty appalling. A rubble-strewn floor littered with boulders the size of footballs. I was lucky to escape with the injuries that I did. It could have been far worse. I wasn't wearing a helmet and if my head had hit one of those boulders, who knows what shape I'd be in now. Matt Troilett looked after me that evening. I hardly knew Matt at the time, but it was he who kept talking to me as I slipped in and out of consciousness and I'm very grateful for what he did. Matt probably didn't appreciate at the time just how scared I was.

Jerry and Mick completed their route just as I was arriving at the hospital. It took a line up an overhanging wall, right of a climb called *Darkness*. They christened it *Enlightenment*.

During a four-year period of development a number of climbers had used different tactics and approaches to climbing in Gordale. The approach that each team had used was dictated by personal values and a loose set of unwritten rules. The resulting routes each give the climber a different set of challenges and ultimately different experiences and rewards. Does this matter ? I think it does. The route, *Bliss*, illustrates a case in point. In a period of seven years the route received only three ascents. It was hardly a popular climb, but ask any of those ascensionists to cite some of their memorable rock-climbing experiences and *Bliss* will feature. Before Rimmer climbed *Bliss*, another would-be ascensionist had abseiled the line and drilled bolt holes, preparing it as a sport route. Had Greg not stepped up to the mark to produce this highly satisfying adventurous E7, it would have become a mediocre, modestly graded sport route of questionable quality. Some people will argue that my stance is elitist, but in my opinion a very important aspect of many forms of human endeavour is about raising the bar and giving others something at which to aim. Pushing beyond one's comfort zone can create a new set of possibilities. In this way we develop physically, philosophically, and sometimes spiritually.

A day after the Gordale accident the consultant at Airedale General Hospital informed me of the damage.

'You've had a lucky escape, Mr Radtke, two broken ribs, a broken heel and a cracked pelvis. But there is a complication. I think we're going to have to take you down to theatre. The X-rays appear to show a bone fragment floating around in your groin and if that gets into your blood stream it could prove quite serious. We're going to let you settle down tonight and have another look tomorrow.'

I was wheeled down to radiography for more X-rays and in the afternoon I got another visit from the consultant, 'We've scrutinized the X-Rays and have decided that the initial radiograph picked up something erroneous, we think the risks of operating on you far outweigh the risk posed by blindly hunting around for something that might not even exist.'

I was relieved, but wondered if all potential surgery was as vague as this. I spent five days on Ward Ten and was glad to get home. Much to my relief, the physiotherapists wanted to get me up and active as soon as possible and I started my rehabilitation almost immediately. My hips ached like hell, but using crutches meant that I was independently mobile. The worst injury appeared to be my heel and it took a good six weeks before I could put any weight on it. I discovered that my internal organs must have had a real rattling. I became almost incontinent for about three months, I just couldn't hold a bladder full of pee.

I was determined to get back on the rock as soon as I could, concerned that I'd lose my bottle if I didn't face the fear demons. About three weeks after the accident I drove up to Kilnsey and made the short hobble up to the crag on my crutches. All the lads were there having an evenings workout. They already had a rope down *Déjà Vu*, so I tied in and seconded the route. I felt as though nothing had changed. In the months that followed, however, I started to recognise some very different feelings when I climbed.

When I started to get scared, the fear started winning the psychological battle. I'd always had the knack of keeping the fear in check, but now I was losing the ability to talk it down. It was the end of an era of bold trad climbing for me.

At Gordale Scar *The Chemistry Set* finally got its direct start. *Ward Ten*, was climbed by Jerry Peel, with me in tow. We placed a further three bolts in this tottering pile of choss. Ironically it turned out be the worst new route that I have ever had the misfortune to fall off.

Several months after the accident I got a call from Simon Nadin, 'I've got a bit of spare time on my hands. Do you fancy a trip up to Scotland?'

I didn't really think I could turn the world champ down.

'I'll come Simon, but I'm still a bit fragile.' I'd climbed with Simon on a few occasions over the years and barely knew him, but I also thought that even if I'd spent years in his company I might still be of the same opinion. Simon is your classic introvert. There's a lot going on in his mind, he just prefers to keep it to himself. Conversations with Simon could hardly be described as lively, animated affairs. Basically, Simon is a private person who also happens to be a naturally brilliant climber. When he won the Climbing World Cup, it was a huge ground-breaking achievement. If he'd courted the media spotlight and got the public relations machine into full tilt, it could well have set him up for life. But that's not his way, he'd rather escape the awkward publicity interviews and go climbing.

A couple of days later, with 'sacks loaded full of camping and climbing gear, we made our way up the pleasant walk to Creag an Dubh Loch, in the southern Cairngorms. As we walked a rainbow arched across the loch, Simon captured the moment with his SLR - not only is he a brilliant climber, he's also a very creative person and an exceptional photographer. I found out that he was, in fact a, 'proper' photographer, using his own dark room to develop and print his work.

We made camp near the small lochan, nestling below the huge cliff, and then headed off up to the crag. It looked sombre under a sky the colour of gunmetal. We'd selected a route called, *Voyage of the Beagle* as our initiation climb. The guide's play on words suggested that the route was, a real voyage across the main face. I pictured a bearded Charles Darwin, sat on the deck of a small sailing ship, cast adrift in the vast expanse of the southern seas. The climb takes a diagonal weaving line for five hundred and thirty feet across the main face. Simon led off, but after completing three pitches the leaden sky delivered what it had been promising all day. As the heavens opened and the rock started running with water, we cut our losses, abseiled down to the screes and returned to camp.

We settled into our pits and began exchanging tales of past exploits. Unusually, Simon was in a talkative mood and before long we drifted into the territory of past relationships. Suddenly Simon began chuckling to himself, obviously remembering an amusing incident in the past. He then recalled the tale.

'I went out with this one girl who was great in the sack, but was always moaning on about me doing something exciting. Anyway this one night she was moaning on and on as usual. "The trouble with you Si, is that all you do is just go climbing, it's just so boring, why can't you ever do something that's really exciting?" She just didn't seem to get it,' he said. 'Anyway, on this one occasion something inside of me snapped and I thought, right you bitch, I'll show you. It was about 1am and I said, "come on then let's do something exciting." We got up, and I got my motorbike out, I had a Fireblade at the time and it was damn fast. She got on the back and we were away. I opened up the throttle and soon we were tonning it around the country lanes of Derbyshire. It was inevitable really, I lost it on a bend, and the bike took to the air, crashed through a hedge and ended up as a complete right-off in a field. We were pretty messed up, but not seriously injured. I took my helmet off, threw it to the ground and said, "there, I hope that was fucking exciting enough for you." I walked the ten miles home. Needless to say that was the end of that relationship.'

The thing with Simon, back in the day, is that he was simply so cool on the rock, even if he was in a living end situation, anybody looking on would get the impression that all was perfectly calm. All you'd get from Simon by way of insight into how extreme the situation had been would be, 'Mmm it was quite tasty, that.'

I can appreciate why his girlfriend accused him of being boring.

The next morning dawned fine, but it didn't look like the weather would hold. We were eager to get a classic in the bag, so set our sights on a route called *Naked Ape*. This route had been included in the Wilson/Newman compendium of modern *Extreme Rock* climbs, and from its write up, it sounded superb. I led the first pitch which climbed a steep crack and provided a useful warm up for what was to come. The next pitch was the crux and meat of the climb. Simon led off and after about ten feet he stopped and fiddled about trying to place a runner, eventually he got something in and pressed on.

After about twenty feet he was able to clip a peg. With the peg clipped, Simon moved into cruise mode and traversed delicately across a steep slab to gain the security of another belay. From my belay the climbing looked sensational. As I followed the pitch the climbing was immediately strenuous and awkward. I got to Simon's first piece of gear and it just fell out. It was simply a token piece of reassurance. The climbing above this was desperate, I had to fight every move to stay in contact with the rock, if Simon had blown it here the fall would have been sickening. It was a sobering reminder of the talent of the man. As I stood by the peg, I was able to survey the traverse right across the wall, a fall here would have massive pendulum potential. Simon shouted across words of encouragement, 'Don't worry, it's not as hard as it looks and certainly no harder than what you've already done.'

The climbing looked thin, but it also looked like you could stand on your feet and work the moves out, it was the sort of stuff I relished. I unclipped the peg and made the delicate moves across the wall. The pitch lived up to its reputation.

Pitch three was my lead, it followed a deceptively easy looking groove, which terminated at a capping overhang at about fifty feet. I set off and things went well. At the end of the groove I placed some runners and started to make sense of the overhang. My initial probing suggested that a balancey layaway off a large rounded hold would do the trick, but it would be a committing move quite away above the runners. I reversed back down to a resting place below the overhang and shouted back to Simon, 'I think I can see what to do, it looks like a typical gritstone barn door move. I'll just have a quick shake and I'll give it a go.' I moved back up to the overhang and started the sequence, I reached up and got the big rounded sloper and started to make the move, but as I did, I felt that my feet were starting to slip from beneath me. I reversed with a sense of doubt and panic starting to cloud my judgement. I tried to make the move several times, but each time I did the sense of panic and fear increased. My rational mind was telling me that the move was easy, it was the sort of move that I'd done countless times, the sort of move that was etched in my subconscious. Simon simply looked on patiently from below, but eventually I had to admit defeat.

'I can't do it Simon, it should be a piece of piss, but I just can't commit to the move, I'm scared I'm going to hurt myself.'

With that I reversed the pitch and climbed back to the belay. Fifteen minutes later Simon was at the top of the third pitch. I followed and with the safety of the rope from above, the difficult move through the overhang was a formality. It started to dawn on me that my fall in Gordale had done more damage than I had previously suspected. It wasn't physical damage, something else was at play here. I'd lost my bottle. The last pitch was pretty unimpressive compared to what lay below us, but I was determined to retain a semblance of dignity. 'I'll have a go at leading this last bit, Simon.'

'Okay, but don't fall off, it doesn't look like there's any gear for about fifteen feet and I don't fancy the thought of a lob straight onto the belay.'

The pressure was on, but the pitch was short and proved straightforward enough. As I brought Simon up I reflected on what he'd said. I was unsure whether he could appreciate my mental predicament. Perhaps he'd reappraised my ability, maybe he even thought I was incompetent. I felt that if I tried to explain how I was feeling, tried to justify my ineptitude, it would sound as if I were simply making excuses for an obvious lack of balls. After all, I was climbing with the famous Nads himself, the very man who'd christened one of his routes, *Gonads*. A route that epitomized one of the aspects of climbing that Simon appeared to prize the most. I decided to keep my thoughts to myself.

Rainfall put an end to our plans for any further adventures in Scotland, so we returned to Yorkshire, knowing that we'd be guaranteed some dry limestone. I'd whet Simon's appetite with talk of some of the recent developments.

By his own admission Simon declared that he'd lost much of the form that he'd displayed when he was one of the best in the world, but what he lacked in fitness he made up in raw talent and more importantly, he still held the passion. For the next few days I acted as a tour guide, pointing Simon at some of the new routes put up in the last few years, or recommending routes that he'd simply overlooked during the period, a decade or so earlier, when he'd been on fire.

Nothing seemed to pose much of a challenge, but he reassured me that he was really enjoying himself. On one of the days we found ourselves in Gordale, Simon on-sighted *Pierrepoint*, climbing it in one long pitch complete with the routes original start. Today when people do this route, they usually do it with an alternative easier start and extend runners on the middle section with slings to avoid rope drag on the top bulges. Simon simply used normal length of quick draws and as he climbed through the bulges at the top of the route, the drag on the rope was so great he could hardly pull it up to clip the runners. It was phenomenal and at the time, was probably a first ascent of the route in this style. I was sufficiently inspired by Simon's effort that I suppressed my own self-doubt and led a route called *Hangman*. This route climbed the wall right of *Pierrepoint* and it was common practice to use *Pierrepoint's* alternative easier start for *Hangman*. After I'd lowered back to the ground, Simon asked me about a steep little groove that led directly up to where the main wall of *Hangman* started.

'Oh that's the original start to *Hangman*, it's not been freed yet.'

Simon needed no further tempting. An hour later he'd placed four bolts in the line and had waltzed up *Hangman,* complete with its original start, and made the whole lot look like a path.

'What sort of grade do you think, Simon?'

'Oh about F7c,' was Simon's laconic response.

Two other climbers were present that day who I knew pretty well, I thought I'd better do some introductions.

'Aye up boys. Ian, Gareth, can I introduce you to Simon Nadin, ex-world champ. Simon can I introduce you to Ian Vickers, future world champ.'

After we left, Ian got to grips with Simon's new little addition. He later confessed to me that he'd had a real tussle with it.

'What grade did he give it?' Ian asked me.

'F7c, and he made it look like an absolute path,' I told him.

Ian just shook his head. The grade in the current guide still states *Hangman*, original start F7c. The interesting thing is, that in all the times I've been to Gordale since, I've never seen chalk on it.

Chapter 10

Little Hill Men

Bouldering is the poetry of mountaineering.
It is climbing distilled and requires a different attention span.
As with good poetry, good bouldering comes from within.
It is derived from an inner eye, then refined.
Pat Ament – Master of Rock 1977.

The laughter of children echoes around a cluster of huge boulders and irritatingly disturbs the woodland tranquillity. The rock formations sit like primeval beasts grazing in the forest glade. Dappled sunlight illuminates their sandstone skins and suggests that the rocks have an organic rather than mineral origin. I step up to the mark, determined to climb the meagre fifteen feet of rock that will land me at the top of this frustrating lump. Shock waves run through the stone as my palms slap its smooth hide and my fingertips vainly search for something positive on which to pull. With belly floundering, knees shoving and power fading I begin the inevitable slide earthward and land with a thud in soft sand eight feet below. This is the Bleau, it's 1981, it is the same trip as our Eiger fiasco and I owe my present state of frustration to Pete Livesey and his little guidebook *French Rock Climbs*.

When I first climbed on the boulders in the forests of Fontainebleau, I came away with mixed emotions. I enjoyed the experience but I was by no means hooked. Over the coming years I came to appreciate bouldering more and more and eventually, I became as passionate about it as my trad climbing. A number of factors combined to develop my love of the sport. Jerry Peel was a pivotal influence, he revealed a unique insight into the whole concept of bouldering and this had a profound influence on my own attitude. When I moved from Halifax I bought a small cottage below Earl Crag. Earl is an excellent bouldering venue in its own right, but I was also closer than ever before to a whole range of class gritstone crags that possess some of the best bouldering in the UK. In 1990, Ledge and his girlfriend, Sharon, moved and set up permanent residence in Fontainebleau, so naturally Font became a frequent destination. The bouldering revolution that had yet to take hold was in its infancy, unclimbed problems existed in abundance and this provided another natural avenue to satisfy my interest in new routing. Finally, following my accident in Gordale, bouldering seemed safe.

From the early days, I always appreciated bouldering as a way of training. At the beginning, I like everyone else, just followed tradition when climbing on the diminutive gritstone crags of Yorkshire. It seemed more hassle to get a rope out for routes that were only fifteen to twenty feet high, so we developed soloing circuits at crags such as Shipley Glen and Halifax Rocks. Many of these micro routes had been conceived in this fashion. Crash pads had yet to be invented and part of the appeal of this form of climbing was dealing with the psyche. Avoiding falling tended to stimulate mental clarity and focus. These elements were at the core of the wider climbing experience and since they were retained in bouldering of yesteryear, it felt like proper climbing.

In the UK the origins of bouldering can be traced back to the Victorian era, but I think modern bouldering probably had its genesis in the early '70s. Jerry Peel, a self-confessed boulderer, cites Al Manson as one of the early originals.

As Jerry observed:

Al was doing some pretty impressive stuff in the '70s, but I think he was the first person from the UK who went to America with the sole aim of repeating some of John Gill's test pieces. He went to America purely to boulder when others were going to climb big walls in Yosemite.

John Gill was an American phenomenon. He was immensely strong and powerful and could perform extraordinary gymnastic feats. In the 1960s he was able to do a one-arm, one-finger pull up and developed the ability to do the one-arm front lever. He transferred his gymnastic talent to the short sandstone walls and boulders of Fort Collins in Colorado and here he left his signature with some visionary boulder problems.

Another great American rock-climber called Henry Barber once said of Gill:

'If bouldering is considered to be the purest form of climbing, then Gill would be at the highest peak.'

Manson must have been pretty inspired by Gill to make such a long trip with the sole aim of bouldering. For me, it demonstrates that he had grasped the concept of this sub sport as an end in its own right. During the 1970s, Manson wasn't the only solitary boulderer in the north of England. Whether by luck or design, Leeds University, and its crude red-brick climbing wall, became a focal point for a group of extremely talented rock-climbers. Most of these lads left their mark on the rock with some fine boulder problems. Even now, some still hold their own against modern day test pieces. Mike Hammil's *Red Baron* at Shipley Glen commands respect. Its grade of V8 gives an indication of the power and technique that is required to climb it. Pete Kitson's problems, *The Gypsy* and *The Virgin* at Almscliff, require mental commitment as well as technique and are not for the fainthearted. Climbing them today gives an insight into what the climbing scene probably felt like back in 1973, without the luxury of crash pads and modern rock shoes. Manson's own problems from this period were prolific and many are regarded as classics. *Pebble Wall*, a V8 highball problem at Caley Crag, is a masterpiece of precise footwork and pebble pulling.

Other climbers were equally active on the Yorkshire bouldering front during the '70s, '80s and into the '90s, and although they weren't quite pushing the standards like the Leeds wall boys, they were beavering away behind the scenes. Tony Barley was a driven explorer and had established some excellent rock-climbs throughout the UK. Barley was constantly on the look out for unclimbed rock and had a massive appetite and enthusiasm for developing whole crags. Tony would clean and climb most of what he could and if he found something that was beyond him, he'd import a secret weapon, often in the form of his good friend, Jerry Peel, who'd climb the remaining plumbs. Many of today's wilder bouldering venues are down to the dedication and efforts of Tony Barley. I'd put myself in Tony's category, never a great boulderer, but I loved roaming the wild moorland seeking out unclimbed problems. My own romance with bouldering was really inspired by Jerry Peel. Jerry is a masterful rock-climber and in his day he was equal amongst his peers. He was in his early forties when I first started climbing with him and perhaps past his best, but still revealed true flashes of brilliance. I remember one time, after struggling a little on a desperate boulder problem, he said to me:

'Rad, there was once a time when I could have levitated up that!'

It wasn't arrogance on Jerry's part, it was simply that in his prime he'd been very, very, good indeed. Ian Cooksey isn't someone who hands out compliments, but he once said to me:

'I think Jerry is the best technical climber I've ever seen, he must have been awesome at his peak.'

Jerry had grown up on a diet of technical gritstone. His local crag was The Bridestones, and it was here that he'd cut his teeth, climbing with his early sparring partner, Barry Rawlinson. Barry was another highly talented climber, and both were fiercely competitive, pushing each other and bouldering standards sky high at The Bridestones. Rawlinson's, *Horror Arête*, is still regarded as a modern classic, Whilst Peel's own, *Jerry's Arête*, at a grade of V9 was probably the hardest boulder problem in the country when it was climbed in the early '80s. Like Al Manson, Jerry embraced bouldering as a sport in its own right early in his climbing career. He started making regular trips to Fontainebleau in the late '70s with like-minded enthusiasts, Will Simm and the Healey brothers. Their sole aim was to boulder in an era when other Brits were simply using the Bleau as a stopover as they travelled to the Alps. They developed friendships with local Bleausards like Jo Montchausse, who gave extra insight into the art form and in turn they imported some of this philosophy back into the UK to produce some outstanding problems. Lakes climber, Dave Birkett, on a recent visit to The Bridestones, climbed *Jerry's Arête* three times in a row, because in his own words:

'It's got to be in the top ten best boulder problems in the country.'

High praise indeed. By climbing with Jerry it was inevitable that my own, bouldering-as-training philosophy would be transformed. I now recognise that this discipline, other than extreme soloing, is perhaps the purist form of rock-climbing that there is. Particularly the version of the game that we played in the pre-crash pad says of the '80s and early '90s. The memories I have from this period are amongst some of my best. I spent fierce weekends sampling the subtle delights of Northumberland sandstone and the not so subtle Wooller Disco, receiving the Peel master class at Widdop or The Bridestones. Exciting mileage days at Almscliff, climbing problems all day and then finishing with solo ascents of, *Black Wall Eliminate*, *The Dolphinian*, and *Western Front*.

Jerry had made some impressive ascents over the years at Earl Crag. His wittily named, *Desert Island Arête*, is a great route, but Jerry is most proud of its boulder problem start. *The Flakes*, is another testament to Jerry's bouldering vision. Earl is an impressive edge commanding a fine position above the village of Cowling. It offers fine views into the Yorkshire Dales, and, on clear days, the summits of Pendle Hill to the West, and Pen-y-Ghent and Ingleborough to the North, are easily recognisable. Even wealthy Victorian mill owners thought its elevated position worthy of their follies, and Lund Tower and Wainsman's Pinnacle stand like guardian sentinels at each end of the edge. The crag is extensive, a series of superb buttresses and boulders run westward for about a kilometre. It contains routes of all grades up to twenty metres high, but what makes Earl so special is bouldering, which in my view is some of the best to be found in Yorkshire. I was fortunate indeed to find myself living below Earl in 1990.

Earl faces mainly north and from a distance can have a dark and brooding appearance, but on sunny spring evenings when the sun illuminates the rock and the air temperature remains cool, Earl rock feels like no other. This is when the expression 'Gods own rock' takes on the meaning for which it was coined. It was an evening such as this that saw Chris Gibb, Jerry and I, meeting up for an evening's session.

'Aye up, Crozzley, I hope you're ready to get your arse kicked,' was Jerry's opening gambit to Gibby.

'I hope you've got your comb in your back pocket, cos you'll need it when I've ruffled your feathers,' Gibby's riposte was a strike at Jerry's vanity.

'Aye, Ron, and at least me and Barry never used to give each other Yorkshire tight.'

Jerry was inferring the use of dubious climbing tactics. Jerry still uses the 'Aye Ron' phrase today, when he's talking to himself. He was of course referring to Ron Fawcett, Gibby's long time climbing partner.

'Yeah well at least me and Ron got on with the climbing, unlike you and Barry, who were more interested in tending your coiffeurs,' Gibby continued with the needle.

It was always like that with Gibby and Jerry. Gibby often got a bit of stick for his role as Fawcett's eternal second, but when it came down to bouldering, he could hold his own, even against Jerry. He was light and immensely strong, and we would often joke that Gibby didn't need to use his feet. Gibby could campus, before the campus board was even invented.

The competition and banter was always fierce and it was great fun. We started at the east end and after a few warm ups got stuck in.

'Who did this first, Jerry?' Gibby was making a deliberate footless ascent of an overhang known as the *Kipper Roof.*

'Aye, go on then Gibb, you got this one before me,' Jerry conceded and so the evening progressed with problems falling thick and fast, constantly interspersed with razor sharp jibes and needles. As we arrived at the main buttress, in the middle of the crag, the setting sun was illuminating the rock with an orange glow. Jerry turned to me, 'Come on we'll do a bit of soloing.'

Gibby looked us up and down. 'I'll bow out here I think,' he said.

First up was *Earl Crack*, a nice VS. Then came *Earl Buttress*, one of Yorkshire's best gritstone E2s.

Jerry peered down from the top. 'Don't use that pocket, it throws you wrong. Use the one in the crack it makes it much easier.'

There was no room for error here, as I didn't think you'd survive a fifty-foot

The first ascent of *The Warriors of Hanuman*, E5 6b Guisecliff,
Yorkshire in 1997. *Photo: Greg Rimmer.*

Top: Los Mallos de Riglos. The Fire Tower is on the left with the Pison Central and the overhanging face of the Visera on the right.
Photo: Mark Radtke.

View of *Fiesta de los Biceps*.
Left: Looking down at Dave Barton on the lower section of the route.
Photo: Mark Radtke.

Another view of *Fiesta de los Biceps*.
Looking across at Mick Johnston and Greg Rimmer from
neighbouring route, *Zulu Demente. Photo: Mark Radtke.*

The Dolomites.

Top: the north faces of the Tre Cima di Laveredo, Cima Ovest in the foreground, Cima Grande central. *Photo: Mark Radtke.*

Bottom: Photo of Dave Barton in action on the *North Face Direct (Hasse)*. His sixtieth birthday present from us. *Photo: Mark Radtke.*

Dave Barton again in action on the *North Face Direct (Hasse)*.
Photo: Mark Radtke.

The Tofana. The Apollonio/Constantini route the *South Face Direct*, takes a direct route up the Pilastro di Rózes, the obvious and well-defined pillar towards the right. *Photo: Mark Radtke.*

Cima Piccola. *The South Arête (Yellow Edge)* roughly follows the illuminated arête of the spire. *Photo: Mark Radtke.*

Multi pitch Swiss rock.

Left: Ian Cooksey on pitch twelve of *Motorhead*, grade 7, Eldorado near the Grimsel Pass.
Photo: Mark Radtke

Right: Super Alpinists Dave Hesleden and Andy Cave completing pitch one of *Traumschiff (Dreamboat)* on the Hohenberg in the Goscheneralp. Not particularly long at 200m, but 'as good as it gets' hard and sustained with four grade 8, two grade 7 and just one grade 5 pitch, to break up the difficulties. Jerry Peel and I followed the boys up the route. 'You're not bad at this game you two are you?' Dave Hesleden's appraisal of our ability as we shared a few beers together after the route.
Photo: Mark Radtke

ground fall. I was grateful for the beta as I pulled over the top. Not quite an on-sight solo, but not far off. Next it was *Trite Rib*, a nice E3.

Jerry set off up the arête, 'Just watch what I do, it's only 5c and the holds are good.' He waited for me at the top. It was another first for me and I was well and truly buzzing.

'Have you done *Sour Grapes*?' Jerry asked.

'Yeah a few years ago, I had a tough time on it, I might have even yo-yoed it,' I confessed.

'Come on, we'll go and have a look, it's like the old days this.' Jerry made the route look like a VS. He peered over the edge, 'Just use a determined approach,' he encouraged. Climbing terminology for, don't falter and don't hesitate.

I arrived at the top of the buttress just as the sun sank behind Pendle Hill. For the last half an hour or so we'd been existing in the moment, no memories of the past, no thoughts of the future. It was a pointless activity, but subliminally it allowed a little journey into the realms of possibility. It set risk and self-belief in juxtaposition and in turn this acted as a mind cleanser. Pure focus and clarity of thinking, mind and body working as one.

As we sat drinking fine ale in the pub below the crag, Gibby looked at me and said, 'Well Rad, you were certainly on fire this evening.'

'Thanks Chris,' I replied. What a fine compliment, I thought, and coming from such a legend.

'I told you I'd convert him,' Jerry said. It was like they'd had some sort of secret bet.

It had been a magical evening, an evening that no amount of material riches could ever replace.

Throughout the '80s the concept of climbing competitions had grown and had taken a firm hold in the form of international Grand Prix events. Early competitions in mainland Europe were held on outdoor crags often on manufactured routes, but these quickly gave way to competitions that were held on purpose built climbing walls. Jerry had even held podium places in the veterans, over forties, events that had been held in the UK. In the late '80s the Americans introduced the idea of outdoor bouldering competitions. It seemed an ideal way of letting climbers compete against the rock and each other. There was no need to manufacture routes, since boulder problems could easily be created with a bit of imagination. One boulder problem might utilise everything on a bit of rock, but by simply eliminating holds, essentially barring their use, an entirely different problem could be created. All the climbers had to do was honour the rules. Jerry had spoken with one or two Brits, who'd competed in such events in the States, and was fired up by the whole idea.

'I'd have given my right arm to have competed in a bouldering competition when I was in my levitating days,' he'd say enviably.

In 1991 Jerry announced that he was going to hold the UK's first outdoor bouldering competition. It would be a low-key affair open to all comers. At the time, Mick Ryan was contributing editor at the domestic climbing magazine *On The Edge*, or *OTE*. He loved anything a bit radical and used the pages of the magazine to raise the profile of the event. Jerry and his friends beavered away behind the scenes developing new problems at Crag X, the secret location for the competition. Meanwhile, informal invitations were issued to canvass the level of interest. As a possible date arrived, the weather forecast was checked and when the portents looked good, formal invitations were dispatched, advising people where and when to assemble.

It proved a good turn-out as climbers assembled in the car park behind Skipton Town Hall. Strong climbers like Ben Moon, Mick Lovatt and Dave Pegg, mingled with old stagers, Pete Gomersall and Graham Desroy. In all there were about seventy entrants from all over the UK. We even had an international representative, with Frenchman Olivier Marc, and official photographer in the form of Glenn Robbins who'd come over from Australia. As everyone assembled, Jerry signed them in, took their entry fee and revealed Crag X as Crookrise. He informed everyone that the rules of the competition would be explained at a crag briefing just before kick off. People drove round to the reservoir car park and then made their way excitedly up the hill to the crag. Crookrise occupies an elevated moorland setting with fine views south, towards Pendle Hill. On the day of the competition, the crag was bathed in sun and Jerry, together with Mick Johnston, held their briefing below End Slab, at the right end of the edge. The rules were simple. Climbers were randomly assigned into teams of three. Problems were marked on a topo overview and each problem was numbered with a piece of card at its base. Every climber was issued with a score card, if a problem was flashed the climber was awarded ten points, success on the second attempt scored seven points, third go received three points. It was the responsibility of each team to marshal the scoring.

The circuit consisted of thirty problems ranging in difficulty from V0 to V8, including a number of top rope problems. Once the rules had been explained, each team was at liberty to decide which problems and in what order they were attempted. Crookrise is an extensive edge, about a mile long with boulders littered up and down the hillside. As the teams dispersed the initial throng was soon absorbed by the vastness of the crag. It could have been just another busy day at any normal crag. For all participants, the competition was a resounding success as they handed in their scorecards with bleeding fingertips, aching limbs, personal triumphs, and some newly formed friendships.

Next on the agenda was the evening's entertainment and prize giving. The podium places were calculated. Ben Moon took gold, Dave Pegg silver with veteran dark horse and former Clean Hand Gang member, Graham 'Streaky Bacon' Desroy, stealing bronze. Micky Johnston and Mick Ryan provided entertainment with a pub climbing quiz and brawling on the dance floor, whilst everyone else partied long into the night.

The following Monday I was back at work. As I sat in the office in Grassington, a fax spewed out of the machine. It read:

British Mountaineering Council (BMC) outraged at move by local climbers to contravene BMC policy on outdoor climbing competitions. They are considering what steps and action should now be taken against both organisers and participants.

It was from Graham Desroy, a competitor and climbing wall builder. Over the following days, faxes and phone calls were exchanged between various parties, including Jerry Peel, *OTE*, the BMC, and some of the more high profile participants.

The BMC had a number of views on competition climbing and most of them were unfavourable. Their main concern was that competitions could set precedents that might erode the very essence of what climbing in the UK was about. Their fears centred on commercial and environmental issues and they argued that outdoor bouldering competitions could jeopardise access and accelerate erosion. The BMC were in a bit of a cleft stick, however. They did recognise that indoor climbing competitions were here to stay and that potentially, they could play an important role in supporting British climbers. At the time of the Boulder Bash, Ben Moon was active on the international competition circuit and as a high profile semi-professional climber, he had a reputation to protect.

Things came to head when the BMC started sabre rattling and threatened that any climber who'd participated in the Burnley Boulder Bash, or any future outdoor competition would be black listed, and any potential promotion, support or funding would be withheld. I think they even went as far as saying that they would endeavour to prevent these climbers from participating in all future national indoor competitions. It was strong stuff and certainly got the back up of a lot of those who were close to the event. Some of what we valued in climbing seemed to be under threat. It felt like freedom of choice was being violated. In the end sense prevailed. Derek Walker from the BMC sat down with Jerry Peel and after exploring differing perspectives, the BMC's arguments won the day. The Burnley Boulder Bash was a one-off and no further, formally organised, outdoor competitions on this scale have since been held in the UK.

Today bouldering is immensely popular and is an international phenomenon. The introduction of the crash pad was undoubtedly one of the catalysts in popularising the sport, as was the development of indoor bouldering walls. Unlike other forms of climbing, you don't need lots of equipment and the risks are far less. The apprenticeship of the traditional climber and all that goes with it becomes redundant, making bouldering instantly accessible to the newcomer. It can be done as a solitary pastime, or as a fiercely competitive contest between several individuals. As for me bouldering is about unlocking the mystery of the move and gaining the elusive summit, but ultimately I guess it's just down to the pleasure of moving over rock, unencumbered by the paraphernalia of everyday life. The wild moorland grit of Yorkshire and Lancashire still hold their special magnetism for me, as does the forest of Fontainebleau.

I sometimes worry that Fontainebleau may become a victim of its own success. These days, at certain crags, it can be like walking through a busy children's playground. I count myself as a sociable person, but I draw the line when it turns into a circus. Fortunately there are always crags in the forest in which to escape the masses. Malesherbes is one such area. Initial impressions can be a little alarming, especially to the boulderer seeking the ultimate move, without the diversion of worrying landings. I remember my first visit to Buthiers, where we were shown round the gargantuan rocks by Ledge, who was now a local Bleausard, and our regular host. Furtive glances and painful grimaces were exchanged as our local guide enthusiastically extolled the virtues of this thirty odd foot high arête with an awkward rockover, and then a twenty foot high crack with the evil-looking mantel at the top. On that occasion we thanked the heavens for the light drizzle that was falling and politely ran away.

A year or so later, Ledge's infectious enthusiasm for the place, and our own desire for some new bouldering, had our team of Fontainebleau veterans gearing up in a sandy glade surrounded by towering blocks of calcite-encrusted sandstone. As the day progressed the pace increased. Dave Barton laid down the gauntlet with a blurring ascent of a highball wall, with an evil landing. Jerry and Gibby entertained us with their verbal swordplay. Roger Hindle dispatched a thin crimpy wall that no one else could touch. Micky J's persistence paid off on a complicated traverse, while everyone else gave up. Eventually we gathered at a problem that had been in my mind's eye for over a year. I began the process of psyching up. The perfume of pine resin permeated my nostrils, inducing an evocative sense of déjà vu. The minuscule footholds at the base of the arête were given the ritualistic smack with the Poff.

Ledge reassures us all that the move at fifteen feet is okay, but looking up at the disconcertingly high crux suggests this problem is definitely not one to jump off. I know there's no retreat. I step off the doormat, and the squeaky-clean rubber of my slippers sticks to the resin-dusted footholds. Arms ache as I palm the arête and make a long reach to gain good pockets. Placing my right foot on a high smear I commit myself to the rock over. The fingers of my right hand threaten to burst from the tiny pocket that they are tenuously undercutting. My left hand creeps spider-like towards an invisible edge and instinctively I drop my left foot to counterbalance my body. Fingers lock on to the small flat hold that they have been desperately seeking and the previous microseconds of dilated time are compressed back into reality. I gibber from the top of the rock and watch with relish as the next suitor casts himself into this addictive ritual that we call bouldering.

In the auberge that evening we quaffed pitchers of warm red wine beside the fire. As the alcohol took effect we relived the day's exploits with amplified gusto. We calculated that the twenty or so Black problems climbed that day had amounted to about three hundred vertical feet of constantly exciting climbing at a sustained grade of British 5c-6a. Nature had dictated the rules of the game and the result was one of the most memorable days of banter and exhilarating bouldering that any of us could remember. All we had been doing was climbing rocks, but it seemed to me in that moment, these rocks could have been fashioned by some power with a foreknowledge, that having left the trees, we might one day need to fulfil some ancient memory of the past.

Chapter 11

The Warriors of Hanuman

He flew fast towards the Himalayas,
But unable to find the herb picked up the whole mountain
and flew back with it on his hand.
Sandara Kanda

It was a crisp autumn evening in November and Jerry Peel and I descended down the moor after an eventful day's bouldering at Crookrise.

'My hip's still giving me a bit of gyp you know, Jerry,' I said.

'Well it doesn't seem to be affecting you on the rock,' Jerry replied.

'No, I feel okay bouldering, but look what happened at the top of *The Shelf*, it's a good job you were there to rescue me.'

I'd frozen near the top of a classic Allan Austin E2. Jerry had dangled his leg over the top and I'd used his ankle to complete the solo. It was five months since I'd had my accident in Gordale.

'Don't worry about it you'll be back. Anyway let's get down to more serious matters. One of Jeanette's mates is looking for a man. She's got her own house, likes dogs, has got no ties, and she's a right little fit 'un.' Jerry wasn't born of the politically correct generation.

'Jeanette thinks that you'd be the perfect match and has asked me to fix you up on a blind date, what do you think?' he added.

'Thanks, Jerry, but blind dates are not really my cup of tea, I'll pass.' I didn't think too much more about Jerry's offer.

I worked hard over the winter trying to regain fitness and get my head back into gear. A trip to the impressive conglomerate walls of Los Mallos de Riglos with Dave Barton, Greg Rimmer and Micky J did great things for my confidence.

By the spring of '96 I was feeling good and was out bouldering again with Jerry.

'You know it's my birthday in a couple of weeks,' Jerry said.

'Yeah,' I replied.

'Well I'm going to have a bit of a do at Nino's in Rawtenstall. Jeanette's coming and I think she's going to invite Dawn, you know the girl who's looking for a man. Have I to tell her that you're going to come. It won't be like a blind date will it?'

'No I guess not,' I agreed. And no pressure on, I secretly thought to myself.

'I'd love to come, Jerry,' I said, after a brief pause.

Dawn was a feisty individual, ten years my junior with beautiful brown eyes and a mischievous sense of humour. We hit it off.

Jerry later jokingly said to her, 'I just wanted Rad to have a fling. Not fall in love with you.'

My mother summed her up, giving me a bit of cautionary advice in the process, 'Dawn's really pretty and what's more, I can tell that she's a homemaker, not a home breaker. You'd better look after her.'

Despite the ten year age gap, we seemed to have a lot in common. Dawn wasn't into climbing but she was sporty and as driven as I was. She'd been into bodybuilding and had been crowned Miss United Kingdom a couple of years before I met her. She also loved to travel, which seemed to give us enough common ground to make a go of things.

After a couple of years working in outdoor education, I'd moved into the field of corporate management training. I gained my experience working with a Cumbrian-based management training company, but after a few years I left the business to work as freelance trainer. It was another convenient excuse to get more climbing in, which had worked well until the Gordale incident put a bit of a temporary dampener on things. When I met Dawn in the spring of '96, I was pursuing my own professional development by fitting in further study at Bradford University with freelance management development work. My time was mine to manage and I was eager to recapture some of the form I'd had before the accident. It was around this time that I was making one of many regular trips along the Aire Valley bypass between Crosshills and Keighley, when I noticed what looked like fine-looking gritstone peeping out from behind some trees. I made a quick detour, parked up and walked up through woodland to investigate. It became apparent why I hadn't noticed the crag until now. A recent spate of heavy logging had really opened up the buttresses. Hawkcliffe had been climbed on before of course, I even recalled Mick Ryan telling me that he'd done some new routes there with

Paul Jenkinson, but it had become heavily overgrown. A large boulder had been spray painted with the words, Climbing Strictly Forbidden, suggesting access problems. I walked past the boulder and continued my investigations. The crag was a mixture of quarried rock and natural outcrop. As I wandered around my excitement grew. I could see that there was loads of potential, and it was literally on my doorstep. I felt as though I'd rediscovered a little gritstone gold mine.

The following evening I was back with ropes and abseiled and cleaned a steep slab of quarried grit. It had a couple of small wire placements at half height. The crux looked like it would be at the top of the route and a fall from there might leave you on the ground, I shuddered at the prospect of leading it. I phoned Jerry that evening, 'I've found a new crag. I might be getting a bit excited, but I think it might be as good as Wilton.'

The following day Jerry joined me at Hawkcliffe and I asked him, 'What do you think then, am I getting a bit over excited?'

'Not at all, look at that arête, that's just crying out to be climbed. Come on let's get to work!'

I could see that Jerry was well and truly fired up. By the end of the day we'd added two routes. *Jerry's arête* turned into *The Blood on the Shamrock*, a fine E6 and the steep wall that I'd cleaned proved to be a committing E5. Dave Barton often used to tell me about one of his childhood terrors, a horrible creature that used to lurk at the top of the stairs before bedtime. It was called, *Ginny Greenteeth*. It seemed an appropriate name for my route.

Over the coming weeks Hawkcliffe became a hive of activity for our team and between us we added another ten routes between E4 and E6. This find had been just what the doctor ordered, it had fired up my passion for creativity and subtly, Hawkcliffe acted as the catalyst through which I recaptured a bit of my old spirit for trad climbing. It also coincided with another significant event. Dawn and I had only been dating for five months when she announced that she was pregnant.

It was around this time that Dave Barton proclaimed that I was ready to test myself on some real stuff. 'I think we need a couple of trips to Gogarth,' he announced. 'We've both got a bit of free time midweek and the chances are we'll have The Main Cliff to ourselves.'

Mention Gogarth to some climbers and you can almost see the blood draining from their faces, but my experiences and memories of the great sea cliffs of Anglesey were all of romantic adventure. I'd first climbed at South Stack with Dave Green in 1989 and since then I'd been rewarded with some truly awesome climbs. My first acquaintance with the main cliff had been the classic *Positron*, climbed with Ian Cooksey, and over the following years I'd ticked my way through many of the hard classics, but there were still numerous challenging lines to add to my climbing CV.

I picked Dave up in Great Harwood in Lancashire one early spring morning in 1997, and by 10am we were enjoying a coffee in the café at South Stack. It was a pleasant sunny day as we made our way across the island towards The Main Cliff. Dawn's bump was quite pronounced, so we ambled across the island, deliberately suppressing the temptation to sprint along the footpath.

We arrived at the familiar spot high above the main cliff and Dawn settled down in the grassy hollow with a good book.

'Looks like we haven't got the cliff to ourselves after all,' said Dave. A couple of rucksacks stuffed beneath a boulder indicated that another party were also at work.

Dave and I went through the ritual of sorting the rack: two sets of wires numbers one to seven; some of Dave's big lucky stoppers threaded on Kevlar; a full set of cams numbers half to three, including Bev and Ian, two affectionately named *Camalots*; a few slings and plenty of quick draws. It amounted to quite a weight. We each shouldered a 9mm rope and said our goodbyes to Dawn.

'We'll probably be about three hours, so hopefully you won't get too bored.' I told her. We then disappeared from view as we scrambled down the steep gully that led to a narrow path giving access to The Upper Tier.

The Upper Tier is a substantial cliff in its own right and hosts many fine climbs. It occupies an atmospheric position overlooking the Irish Sea, with the ground tumbling precipitously down to wave-washed boulders about a hundred feet below. The narrow path that gives access to The Upper Tier, also winds its way steeply down to sea level where a short rock scramble leads to The Main Cliff. Negotiating this exposed path was always the most unnerving part of any Gogarth visit for me, as the exposure usually threatened to trigger an attack of vertigo. Perhaps because I was so relieved when I got to the base of the routes, is the reason I always felt so relaxed when I actually climbed on the main cliff. I don't think any of my climbing partners really appreciated that I was more terrified on the approach than on any of the routes.

As Dave and I arrived at the base of the rocky scramble, two other climbers were sat on rocks with the sea gently lapping at their feet.

They turned to look at us and said in unison, 'Bloody hell it's Dave and Rad.'

'Aye up boys, I bet you thought you'd have it to yourselves, didn't you?' I said.

The two climbers were old friends and accomplished Gogarth pioneers, George Smith and Adam Wainwright. Both had a string of hard new routes under their belts and we soon learned that they were down here today prospecting another new climb.

'What about you guys?' Adam enquired.

'*Wall of Fossils,*' Dave informed them casually.

Quick as flash, George cut in completely straight-faced, 'Perfectly named route for you that Dave.' There was a silent pause and then we all cracked out laughing as the joke dawned on us. It was typical George using his razor like wit to disarm the unwary.

'Anyway what you doing sat here?' we asked.

'Well that's what's called perfect timing,' George replied as he peered round the arête guarding access to the cliff, 'The tide has just about gone out far enough, I think we can traverse in now.' And with that he set off crabwise across the steep traverse line, occasionally making a move upwards to avoid getting soaked by an incoming wave. It was then that I noticed a big bunch of bananas hanging from his harness.

'What's with all the bananas, Adam?' I asked.

'Oh George reckons they make you climb better. See you later boys have a good one,' Adam danced effortlessly across the rock, following George.

Dave turned to me and said, 'Let's give it another fifteen minutes, I don't want to get a soaking and it'll be a lot easier then.' It sounded like good advice to me, particularly as we suddenly heard shouts and cursing coming from George.

'What's up?' I called out.

Adam informed us of the tragedy, 'He's dropped all his bananas in the sea.'

'That'll teach him,' said Dave, laughing loudly.

We made the traverse ourselves and were soon enjoying the unique atmosphere and isolation of one of the country's finest sea cliffs. Hundreds of feet of pale quartzite soared skyward. Grooves, cracks and corners defined enticing lines, whilst steep overhangs and roofs stood out as blatant and daunting challenges. Our intended route took in some impressive ground, ascending the cliff in three long pitches. If we were going to triumph today we'd have to demonstrate considerable form. Neither of us knew of anyone who'd climbed *Wall of Fossils,* but both of us knew of at least one good team who'd tried and failed.

I led off up the first pitch, easily at first, but then stalled at a roof that barred the way ahead. After placing some gear I tested the next moves, they felt hard and after a tentative foray I retreated back to a resting position where I could stand and gather the necessary composure. I surveyed the way ahead and mentally rehearsed what I was going to do. I could see that once I'd started through the steep section the stamina clock would be ticking. I shouted down to Dave, 'I'll just have a few minutes and then I'll go for it. It'll be up or off.'

I started a sequence of undercutting moves right. I felt under pressure but managed to win through and get some more gear in. The climbing above was steep, but some long reaches gained good holds and I arrived at the first belay with a sense of triumph and relief. Dave joined me at the small hanging stance.

'Well done, those undercuts felt really damp,' he said.

We eyed the overhanging wall above. It looked forbidding. It was situations like this that always gave The Main Cliff such appeal. In the back of your mind there was the nagging thought that retreat might be made impossible by the rising tide. In addition, we'd picked a route that was at the upper end of our ability. This meant there was a possibility of taking falls, or worse, not being able to get up the damn thing at all. All in all this created a mental cocktail of uncertainty and excitement. Any fear had to be kept under control and Dave was a master at it.

'Give us the gear,' Dave said, and then set of with determined purpose. I paid the rope out at a steady pace for about ten minutes and then it stopped.

'How's it looking?' I shouted up.

'I can't make out where it goes and it doesn't look like there's any gear,' came the reply.

There was a moment of silence and then, 'Get ready.' With that the rope started moving again. I could see Dave blasting straight up a steep wall climbing quickly, just pulling on anything that his fingers touched. After about fifteen feet he stopped and I could see that he was fiddling some gear in.

'Thank fuck for that,' was Dave's stark appraisal of the climbing.

I followed the pitch and when I got to the crux section, I could see Dave's dilemma. The way forward appeared really improbable from below. It looked like you might be climbing into a cul-de-sac. The moves were tough, it had been given a grade of 6b by Fawcett, who'd done the first ascent seventeen years earlier. When I got to the gear at the top of the steep section, I looked down. A fall would have been heart stopping, unthinkable really.

'Great lead, Dave.' It was an understatement. It had been inspirational. The third pitch was now a formality, pure pleasure to be space walking above the void with the smell of the sea and the cackle of gulls for company. We were suitably chuffed as we emerged from the steep heathery slopes and coiled the ropes above one of the best sea cliffs in the UK.

'You've got to take your hat off to Ron for doing that in 1980, haven't you Dave?' I said.

'Aye he was definitely The Man. That's when rock climbers were rock climbers.' Dave acknowledged.

Spurred on by our success on *Wall of Fossils*, we were back the following week and this time our prize was another fine E6, called *Eraser Head*. I felt re-connected with my climbing roots.

Personally, I think the late '70s and early to mid '80s represented the zenith of traditional climbing in the UK. It was a period when the true on-sight approach to hard traditional climbing was the benchmark by which climbers measured themselves and others. Grades continued to rise after this period of course, but the way climbers approached routes particularly those that combined boldness with extreme technical difficulty, also began to change.

The genius that is Johnny Dawes, held the torch for adventure aloft in the '80s. His *Indian Face* at E9 on Clogwyn Du'r Arddu stands out. It is an iconic example of Dawes as a rock pioneer and explorer of his inner self. Ironically, I think it's also a useful illustration of why the mainstream pursuit of The Holy Grail of traditional climbing began to dwindle for a while. Dawes had talent and self-belief that set him apart. Time would be required for others to develop that ability of mind and body, which Dawes clearly possessed in order to cope with such extreme risk. Dave Birkett's *If 6 was 9* on Iron Crag in Cumbria climbed in 1992 is another E9, which illustrates that the flame for adventure was still burning in the hearts and minds of certain individuals. Routes of this stature and beyond are still being produced today and, although relatively rare, show us that the fascination for extreme adventure is alive and well in the consciousness of British rock-climbers. This said, I still maintain that the true on-sight approach to hard traditional climbing that became the norm in the late '70s and early '80s, for those at least who were true to themselves, was exceptional. Take a climber like Dougie Hall from the early '80s, with his huge catalogue of flashed 'second ascents' of E6's. This is someone who, in my opinion, demonstrates the meaning of rock-climbing standards. Controversially, I don't think the big numbers attributed to some of the modern contemporary traditional routes, always reflect the advance in standards that they might suggest. I think there are climbers around today who might succeed on an E8, E9 or even E10 after practice and rehearsal, yet, might still fail to on-sight E6 or E7. I'm not denigrating the achievement of the 'Head pointer', they still have to put their neck on the line and make that dangerous voyage. Sometimes, the biggest challenge with an activity is deliberately stepping into the unknown, in the full knowledge that it is fraught with hazards. Coupled with this, is perhaps the biggest reward; managing your emotions and thinking intelligently, so you emerge from the journey safely. Perhaps in this way we acquire wisdom.

'Rad, you better get home she's having it,' It was Chris Gibb, shouting from the road. I was halfway up a route at Kilnsey Crag, it was the 27th April 1997.

'You better let me down Jerry.'

Back home I found Dawn having regular contractions.

'Thank goodness you're back. I was getting into a real panic, I couldn't get through on your mobile and it was pure luck that I managed to get through to Gibby. Any later and he'd have been out of signal as well,' Dawn said.

Lauren was born four hours later in Burnley General Hospital. It was Dawn's birthday. What a birthday present.

In the weeks before the birth of my daughter, I'd started investigating one of Yorkshire's esoteric crags, the lost world of Guisecliff. By gritstone standards Guisecliff is a big crag, up to thirty metres high in parts. It is also extensive and is comprised of both quarried faces, and natural outcrops. Despite its impressive proportions the crag faces north and receives little warming sunlight. The base of the cliff is overgrown, making access along the bottom an arduous affair and all these factors conspire to deter all but the keenest pioneers. The crag has had a chequered history, but the names of some of the prospectors who pioneered here suggested that they thought it worthy of their efforts.

My old hero, Arthur Birtwistle, had climbed new routes on the crag in 1937, just a year before he added the bold and classic, *Diagonal* to Dinas Mot, in the Llanberis Pass. The great Allan Austin had been active in the '50s doing numerous first ascents, and then Robin and Tony Barley stepped in and dominated new developments over the next fifteen years. By 1975, the Barley brothers had climbed 64 new routes. Some surprising names appeared in the first ascent lists, like the late great Alpinist Joe Tasker, and the super talented John Syrett.

Mick Ryan instigated my first visit to the crag and in 1993 he persuaded Jerry Peel and I to take a look.

'You ought to go and have a look at Jenky's route, *On the Edge*, it's right up your street, Jerry, a perfect arête. It's quite bold, but I seem to remember that there's gear on it, so you're not going to die.'

Mick had been present when Paul Jenkinson had climbed the crag's first E6 three years earlier and his description of a perfect arête was too great a temptation for Jerry to resist. Jerry was no stranger to Guisecliff as he'd partnered Tony Barley on new routes himself in the '70s, but hadn't been back for some years.

'Let's do it,' Jerry said.

Jerry abseiled the line of *On the Edge* to check out gear placements, while Mick and I recced the crag. The rock architecture was steep and angular and had an uncompromising look. Our own goal took the striking right arête of a big blank quarried wall, about seventy feet high. The featureless wall enhanced the aesthetics of the arête. It looked compelling. Jenky's route was in good company. At the left side of the blank wall was an overhanging, evil-looking chimney, which was a formidable route, called *Barleycorn*. It looked horrific. Left again was a Barley brothers' masterpiece, a route called *Creation*, a striking off width crack which was deemed to be the hardest climb in Yorkshire when it was done in 1965. It too looked daunting.

'You know, Rad, there's still got to be stacks of potential for new routes,' Mick declared, after wandering around the base of one or two buttresses. I suspected he was right.

Back below the arête Jerry was pulling the ropes down.

'What do you think, JP?' I asked.

'The start looks like it'll be the crux, this lower wall is quite thin and it'll feel quite bold. Once you get to the arête there's a slot that takes a good Friend, and you can get a bit of a blow. The upper arête looks technical but it's protected by a peg.' Jerry tied on and breezed the second ascent in his inimitable smooth, foot perfect style. Back on the ground he handed the ropes to me.

'Your turn,' he said.

I led the route in what felt like a slightly more stuttering style, but got to the top without incident. *On The Edge* was a class route, slightly marred by the fact that you could stray off line part way up, but nevertheless good climbing. I thought that if this represented what the crag had to offer then I could appreciate the interest expressed in the place by the great pioneers of yesteryear. Despite the obvious potential for new routes at Guisecliff I didn't return immediately, my attention was taken up by competition for new lines on Yorkshire limestone.

However, over the winter of 1996 I did return and spent several wet weekends stumbling, falling and sliding around in the undergrowth at the base of The Lost World of Guisecliff, searching for a last great, unclimbed problem. By the end of my labours I thought that I might have found a couple, but they'd have to wait for drier weather, which eventually coincided with the birth of Lauren in the spring of 1997.

In the centre of Guisecliff a magnificent prow of natural grit about thirty metres high juts out like the bow of a huge ship. It was known appropriately, as Comet Buttress and contained some fine climbs including a route by Tony Barley called *Mastermind. Mastermind* was a great route - airy, bold and on excellent rock. It traversed the huge prow from left-to-right providing exposed and exhilarating climbing. Tony had done the route in 1975 and at E4 it represented quite an achievement. Fortunately for me, Tony had finished his route up the right wall of the buttress leaving the magnificent ship's prow, virgin territory.

When I told Dave Barton about the route he was fired up for it. I told him that it would be a five star classic if it were in the Peak District. After cleaning the line, I sorted my rack and set off to do battle. I thought it would be a formality after pre-inspecting the moves from the abseil rope, but as soon as I started up the arête, everything seemed to change. It was a fight all the way. I was really blowing when my fingers finally curled round the finishing holds. I abseiled back down the route and removed the gear. Dave wanted to climb the route placing gear on the lead, to get a proper feel for it. He powered his way up the route making it look like a path.

Back on the ground he gave his verdict, 'Mmm it's not E6, more like a soft touch E5, but you were right, if it was in the Peak it would be a classic.'

The *Skryking* was named in honour of the sleepless nights I was now experiencing.

Further along the edge on one of the quarried sections, I'd spotted a superb aesthetic feature that was just crying out to be climbed. It was like a huge demonic head with a parrot-like beak sticking out from the top of the crag. A fine lower arête looked like it could be climbed to a large ledge below the beak. If there were holds on the wall above, then it might just be possible to make sense of this most unusual feature. I abseiled the line and found that I was in luck. There were holds, but it looked like it would certainly provide a technical challenge. To my amazement there were also some slots that would take a peg. I returned with Jerry, Greg Rimmer, Dawn and the baby. It was a warm sunny June day.

'You'll love this one, Jerry. It's like a classic boulder problem in the sky.'

I abseiled back down the line and tapped a peg into a shallow pocket. The tell-tale tone changes, as it was hammered home, suggested it was good. The lower arête provided a good introduction to the technicalities to come. From the ledge I arranged some protection below the huge roof, clipped the peg and retreated to rest and compose. It looked like it was going to be a wild piece of climbing. I set off with heart rate elevated; a long span gained a large jug on the edge of nowhere. I matched on this with both hands and cut loose hanging from the jug with my feet in space. A heel hook back right gave just enough purchase to make a slap right to gain the beak. I now had to drop my right foot off and try and stand on the jug with my left and make a dynamic slap for a sloping layaway with my left hand.

'Watch me, Jerry,' I grunted.

SLAP, I was airborne.

Back on the ledge, I re-psyched and tried to figure out what had gone wrong. 'It was self doubt, you didn't believe you'd hold the sloper,' I told myself. I tried again and the same thing happened. I tried again and the same thing happened again. I sensed despondency creeping in. Jerry shouted up some words of wisdom.

'Have a good rest this time, you're rushing. I'm quite happy down here. You'll get it next time, just relax.'

I took his words on board. Greg was taking photographs from across the way and shouted encouragement, 'It looks fantastic, you looked really close on that last attempt.'

'Cheers, Greg,' I shouted back.

Dawn was less supportive, 'Come on you old git, get your arse up it, I'm starting to get thirsty.'

I rehearsed the moves in my head.

'Okay I'm ready.'

SLAP, and this time I latched the sloper. Concentrating hard, I began udging my right hand up the fine arête that was the bird's beak. Udge, udge, udge, udge, and suddenly I was able to release the sloper and inch up to gain a thin break. It was tenuous, but as soon as my fingertips touched that break I knew I was in. The break took a Friend runner. I clipped the rope in and made the final pull. Success.

'Nice one, Rad,' floated up from below.

Thank God for that, I thought to myself.

Then Jerry tied on, and led the pitch as fluidly as ever. First go. Still the master, even at fifty, it was good to see. He did give it the courtesy of a whoop when he got to the top.

'What you going to call it?' Jerry asked.

'*The Warriors of Hanuman*,' I told him.

'The Warriors of what?'

'I'll tell you a little story. In Hindu mythology, Hanuman was the Monkey God and king of the monkeys on earth. He had a bit of a chequered history, but in short he fought many epic battles against the Demons. During these battles he would call on his warriors who were Langur monkeys. Hanuman's Langurs still inhabit ruined temples in India today and legend has it that they can rise up at any time if they're called upon by Hanuman. When I was climbing that feature up there, I'll tell you I felt like one of Hanuman's monkey

150

warriors, doing battle with a Demon's head, and at one point I thought it had me on the ropes. I must admit though, the way you climbed it you could have been bloody Hanuman himself.'

'Aye there's always a little tale behind a Radtke route name,' Jerry said, laughing.

Chapter 12

Climbing With Vultures

*To repeat a route, especially a classic route
always gives me great satisfaction.*
Riccardo Cassin

As I clip into the belay, a Griffon Vulture erupts from a nearby cave and allows
its huge prehistoric form to fall into the abyss. Its wings unfold to capture the
air and the feathers at each wing tip spread like outstretched fingers to catch
the early morning thermal. The bird wheels out across the wall in an effortless
display of gravity, defying grace. This is Los Mallos de Riglos, a series of
precipitous towers in northern Spain. Looking down at Dave Barton, one
hundred and fifty feet below, creates a strange illusion, the dangling ropes
are swinging way out from the rock face, and the three hundred feet of rock
below him now looks like a slab rather than an overhanging wall.

Dave arrives at the belay and clips himself to a bolt that has been drilled
into a large pebble. The pebble itself is one of millions grouted into the face
by what appears to be red dirt and even now, after several days of climbing on
the stuff, I still touch the mortar to reassure myself that it is solid.

Above us is a further four hundred feet of impending rock that on closer
acquaintance has taken on roof-like dimensions and looks more like a petrified
field of unearthed potatoes than a climbable rock face. Here, however, rather
than creating an atmosphere of oppression, the surreal-like world which we are
leapfrogging our way up is providing us with a space walk of truly exhilarating
proportions. Eager for more spud bashing, Dave leaves the belay, swinging
from potato to potato like a gibbon, barely using his feet and only interrupting
his flow to clip an occasional, widely spaced bolt. He hangs from one arm off
the tip of a huge rugby ball shaped pebble and laughs loudly, 'This is what
it's all about!' Miraculously the huge pebble remains in place and soon Dave
arrives at the next belay. The rope tugs at my waist urging me upwards and
once again I'm engrossed in the potato fields, pulling on a myriad of bizarre

features that protrude from the face. Three pitches later sees us reluctantly standing at the top of the Visera, an outrageously overhanging wall of red conglomerate. Our route, *Fiesta de los Biceps*, wears its name well, overhanging over a hundred feet in its thousand feet of ascent. It must rate as one of the finest multi-pitch routes in Europe. Overhead, vultures use their massive eight-foot wingspans to ride the thermals in their quest for carrion. Below, the whitewashed village of Riglos sits sleepily, dwarfed by the spectacular backdrop of walls and towers. Now, as the noonday sun cast its red glow over Los Mallos and our burning bodies, cold beers are calling. Dave gives me a nod, 'Those vultures will not be dining on climbers today'.

'Come on, Dave I'm ready for a beer. Let's head down and see how Greg and Mick have got on.' Greg Rimmer and Mick Johnston had joined us on this flying visit to northern Spain and today had opted for an equally spectacular route on a neighbouring tower called the Pison.

That afternoon, as we lazed in the tiny street outside Antonio's, the old gentleman, who'd been stood at the bar since our arrival, peered suspiciously out of the door into the bright afternoon sunlight. He may have been thinking that we might do a runner, but I suspect it was just to cast an eye over what were probably all too familiar proceedings. Dave gazed dreamily back up at the Visera reliving some memory of the past. A few other climbers chatted excitedly, pointing up at tiny figures on the face high above us.

Greg shared the remains of his beer with Lotto, an old moth-eaten boarhound and guardian of the street, whilst Mick engaged another group of locals in lively banter. As I caught the old man's gaze, what I had taken for his look of doubt evaporated, and wicked wrinkles formed at the corners of his bright blue eyes. He gripped his bicep in a gesture that might be construed as improper in certain company and said in a language that was neither Spanish nor English yet which I understood better than either, 'You must return'.

The conglomerate walls and towers of Los Mallos are by no means the biggest cliffs to be found and would be dwarfed if they were placed alongside some of the world's giants. That said, they still form an awe inspiring and unique backdrop to the medieval village of Riglos as they rise for over a thousand feet, seemingly straight out of the tiny streets of the village itself. *Fiesta de los Biceps* is an unusual route. It's fully bolted and as such can be described as a sport climb, yet it still retains a real adventurous feel. I think this comes from its tremendous exposure and the unusual nature of the rock itself. As you prepare to embark on the climb and crane your neck upwards your mind is still in denial that the route goes where it does. In reality, if you fell off this route you wouldn't come to too much harm, yet the prospect of a fall is still gripping. A sport climb it may be, but climbing the *Biceps* is still an adventure. The fact that this route has been soloed is remarkable, but also understandable, such is its beauty.

Not all the routes at Riglos are bolted, some were conceived with more traditional tactics. One of these was established by two of Spain's climbing heroes, Alberto Rabada and Ernesto Navarro in 1961. They climbed ground up, to produce a classic twelve pitch route on the South East face of the Fire Tower, a huge spire that frames the northern end of the cliffs. On the climb they used natural protection and only placed a minimal amount of fixed gear in the way of a few pegs and small rivets at some of the belays. Ian Cooksey and I climbed this route and were impressed with the ground it covered. It was an intricate line requiring some instinctive route finding. Since its first ascent, some bolts have been added reducing the seriousness of certain pitches. Despite this, the whole route retained what some climbers describe as, a bit of feel. The climbing wasn't as strenuous and exposed as that to be found on the *Biceps*, it would probably equate to a British traditional grade of about E3 5c, but in my opinion, the sense of satisfaction in climbing it was equal to that of the *Biceps* experience. I would imagine that back in 1961, when the lads topped out on the route, their feelings of satisfaction and accomplishment would have been immense.

I felt that climbing the Fire Tower gave an insight into the character of these two pioneers. They were certainly pushing the frontiers of climbing at the time. People sometimes romanticise climbing with talk about courage and bravery. Others try and denigrate risk taking by clouding the issue with talk about macho egos. Personally, I think what Rabada and Navarro were doing at the time gives us a clear insight into what climbing was about back then, human endeavour and the pure spirit of adventure. Those who came after and placed extra bolts, in my view, were not up to the challenge. People argue that climbing should be about individual choices. Were the retro bolters justified in placing bolts where Rabada and Navarro had done without? I don't think they were. I agree that climbing should embrace personal choices and freedoms, but climbing is also another way of expressing human achievement and, in my opinion, we should respect what our forebears have achieved and strive for greater things. When Ian and I climbed the Fire Tower, did we clip the new bolts? Of course we did. If these bolts hadn't been present, would we have had the wherewithall to continue forward like Rabada and Navarro did? Perhaps, but there would certainly have been some deep breaths as we battled with the fear and uncertainty. What then would the feelings have been like had we topped out successfully, you ask? Probably magical, I hear people saying, and then adding, well you didn't have to clip those bolts did you?

But it boils down to the Serpent in the Garden of Eden metaphor. Two years after climbing the Fire Tower the two young Spanish climbers died on an attempt to climb the North Face of the Eiger. I'm sure that these guys didn't have a death wish. I suspect that they were simply searching for that often-elusive Holy Grail, a sense of achievement.

Over the years I have enjoyed all forms of climbing. Bouldering, sport climbing, ice-climbing and even the odd bit of Alpine mountaineering. I've done hundreds of great sport routes around the world, but can only really recall a handful in meaningful detail. I've also done a fair share of big multi-pitch rock routes and interestingly enough the memory of all these climbs remains fresh in my memory. What I conclude from this is that the big multi-pitch experience has most meaning for me. I think this in part has been down to the way I have approached these routes, which has usually followed a formulae something like this:

Step one – lull myself int ） a feeling that I'm fit by climbing a lot of domestic rock.
Step two – read some books and pick out some big route or other that I'll be able to get some of the mates fired up about. Make sure that the route has got several pitches on it that are as hard as anything that any of the team have climbed that year.
Step three – go and do it and hope that everything comes together.

When I look back at some of these climbs, it is clear that the outcome was often in the balance. The objectives we chose often meant that we would be climbing at our limit, but when we did win through the taste of success was all the more sweet.

Sometimes the seed of a new challenge is sown by a bit of story telling:
'Hey Rad, it's absolutely awesome. The lower wall leads you gently in for two hundred metres and then the overhanging diedres are like climbing five Malham *Yosemite Walls* one on top of the other. You've just got to go and do it. Jenky's drawn a topo. I'll get him to post it to you.'

Andy Cave was waxing lyrical, he'd just returned home after a fantastic six weeks in the Alps. One of the highlights that he was just relating to me was the first British free ascent of a route that he'd made with Paul Jenkinson on the North Face of the Cima Grande in the Italian Dolomites. The route Andy was describing had been first climbed by Dieter Hasse, Lothar Brandler, Jorge Lehne and Sigi Lowe over six days in July 1958. Andy and Paul had done it in one.

The North Face of the Cima Grande is five hundred and fifty metres high and is gently overhanging in its entirety. In 1958 free climbing such a line seemed impossible. In making their ascent the climbers placed a hundred and eighty pitons and eighteen bolts on the route using mainly artificial technique to make their way to the summit of the spire. Even back then, the amount of fixed gear that was used attracted considerable criticism. The achievement was described more as a feat of engineering than as a step forward in climbing. Despite this, the route became recognised as a tough undertaking and gained a reputation as a challenging aid climb that persisted well into the '70s. As free climbing standards rose, many of the aid points on the lower face were eliminated, but the central section of the route, known as the overhanging diedres, follows steep and overhanging terrain for about a hundred metres. Looking up at this section from below makes the prospect of free climbing it appear remote. It wasn't until 1987 that the German free climbing pioneer, Kurt Albert, together with Gerold Sprachmann, managed to eliminate all the aid on this section and climbed the route using the redpoint style. In so doing, they created what must rank as one of the great free rock-climbs in Europe.

Cavey's enthusiasm had sown the seed for my own ambition to make a free ascent of the route. In 1997 my old mate Chris Frost was over from Australia and this provided sufficient justification to wangle a month off work. Dawn appreciated the situation and was kind enough to let me go. 'Just don't go doing anything stupid, you're a dad now,' were her parting words.

Our daughter Lauren was fourteen months old and Dawn was heavily pregnant with our second child. It was with mixed emotions that I embarked on the trip. Frosty was a keen Alpinist and good rock-climber and I'd fired him up about the *North Face Direct*, also known as *The Hasse*. Unusually, I'd put together a pretty robust sports plan for the trip. We'd start out at Céüse in France, go down to Chamonix to do some multi-pitch routes on the Aiguilles, we'd then move on to the Englehorner group in Switzerland and finally onto the Dolomites via some cragging around Arco. The trip started off well enough. Céüse is a magnificent crag perched high on a hillside above the town of Gap. As a rule, I generally don't find sport climbs particularly memorable, but Céüse is an exception. Some of the routes I have climbed there are amongst the best I have done. The steep pockety rock certainly got us pulling hard, but the weather turned and we had to move on.

We managed a couple of good long routes in Switzerland before being driven out by unrelenting rain and it wasn't until we got to Arco in Italy that the impending ceiling of black and grey was finally pierced by welcome shafts of sunlight. The hot Italian sun soon burned the wet streaks from the cliffs and we were able to get into a bit of rhythm as we climbed some of the fine multi-pitch sport routes in the Sarca Valley. After a few days we both felt like we were moving well and decided we were ready for something bigger. A phone call home revealed an excited wife on the other end of the line, 'Guess what, Lauren has just taken her first steps. She's walking!' I'd missed a milestone in my daughter's development, such was the draw of the rock.

As we drove down the Falzarego Pass towards Cortina, it was apparent that unlike Arco, these mountains hadn't escaped the ravages of the storms. The orange and yellow rocks of the huge, Dolomitic walls were draped with long black water streaks. Not to worry, we could still relax in the town. I liked Cortina. Even though it was a sizeable town, it was spread out with a neat compact centre and had an uncluttered feel to me. In the immediate surrounds there was an abundance of wooden farm buildings and ski chalets dotted across green pastures and beyond these, your eyes were drawn to precipitous cliffs of Dolomite limestone. Not quite chocolate box stuff, but not far off - if you were able to blot out ski lifts and electricity cables. After a day drinking beer and eating pizza, the weather brightened and the forecast looked good for the next three or four days. We made plans. We'd do a warm up route on a south face which would hopefully be drying out, have a rest day, and then go and try the *Hasse* on the Cima Grande.

For our warm up climb we chose the Constantini/Apollonio, which tackled the *Pilastro di Rózes* on the South Face of the Tofana. We'd been informed that it went free at about E3 6a. At five hundred metres it was a sizeable route, but with a quick forty minute walk in, and what the guidebook described as a relatively easy descent from the summit, it looked like a good choice.

Six o'clock the following morning saw Frosty and I gearing up at the base of the pillar. We packed training shoes into our rucksacks and started the voyage. The line of the route was pretty obvious as it followed a well-defined diagonal crack system up the pillar. The rock was good solid limestone and although the crack oozed water in places, after only a couple of hours, two hundred metres of climbing lay behind us. The middle of the climb was reputed to be the crux of the route. Here a couple of short-lived, but strenuous overhangs, had to be surmounted. Despite rucksacks tugging on tired arms, the small roofs went free and we arrived at the second terrace. The way above looked evil and uninviting. An overhanging black chimney oozed green slime and dripped a steady stream of water. This pitch was known as the *Mule's Back* and looked like it was going to be more akin to potholing than climbing. A desperate struggle ensued for both of us. Feet slipped and slid on the slick wet walls of the chimney and pulling on old rope slings hanging from wooden wedges sent cold water running down into our armpits. After about forty minutes of undignified thrutching, grunting and squirming, we eventually won through to drier ground and more conventional climbing.

The upper part of the route proved fairly straightforward and eventually we traversed left across the wall to gain a series of narrow gullies that led up to the summit. Ordinarily this part of the climb should have been a simple formality, but today rather than being an easy rock scramble, the chimney system was choked with ice and snow and we had to deal with some exacting conditions. Ironically what was supposed to be the easiest bit of the route was probably the crux of the whole climb. Once at the top, we made a cautious decent in training shoes over treacherous snow-covered slopes that dropped into the abyss. It wasn't until we were back on a proper path in fading light that we started to relax. Climbing is a funny game. I've learned that it's about striking a mental balance. If you let yourself get wound up, tense and stressed, you can become over cautious and risk failure, yet if you take things for granted and become complacent you can get yourself killed. In climbing, getting to the top often means that you're only half way through the voyage.

A couple of days later and we drove round to the Tre Cima di Laverado, the famous mountain group which was the home to the main objective of our trip, the *Hasse*. We parked the car at the Auronzo Hut and set off to recce the North Face and check the route out. It was a peculiar feeling as we walked along the track in the company of young mums with push chairs, grandparents with families, and couples dressed in their Sunday best out for a stroll. It seemed incongruous to see such folk in what should have been an inhospitable mountain environment, but that's Italian culture for you. As we walked along the track the south side of the Tre Cima looked like a huge pile of rubble, but as we contoured round below the east flank the scenery began to transform. The Cima Piccola and Piccolissima came into view. Two handsome-looking spires of yellow limestone, each home to historic routes from the golden age of Dolomite exploration in the 1930s. We continued along the path and eventually arrived at a small col. The view across the north face of the Cima Grande and Cima Ovest was breathtaking. These two gigantic monoliths stood side by side like guardian sentinels, their scale exaggerated by the solitary position perched above the screes. I visualised myself as a dot, at sea amidst the vastness of the wall and I must admit the feeling was scary. I turned to Frosty, 'What do you reckon?'

'Awesome, but we're not going to be setting foot on it on this trip.'

Frosty was right. It was mid-June but heavy compacted snow was still in abundance at the base of the wall. The summit was also covered in snow and black streaks stretched like long dark fingers all the way down the face. The upper chimneys would be running with water. The following day we packed up and headed home. Despite being thwarted by frustrating weather we'd still managed to get some good climbing done, but whether it was worth missing my daughter's first steps, I was unsure.

Eight years later and I was back in the Dolomites with a small team of trusted comrades intent on the *Hasse*. I was the architect of the trip and had formulated the plan as a birthday treat for Dave Barton. It was Dave's sixtieth year and he'd swallowed the bait that it would be good to get another Alpine north face under his belt. He'd climbed the classic Walker Spur on his first visit to the Alps forty years earlier, when I was just five. He'd followed this with the North Face's of the Dru and Piz Badile, but the icing on the cake had been a storm-strafed ascent of the Eiger North Face in 1971 with Martin Burrows Smith.

'The *Hasse* will be a walk in the park, Dave. Think of it as a road-side crag,' I'd encouraged him.

The rest of the team consisted of Jerry Peel, who qualified on the basis of his Yosemite Valley experience, and Terry Holmes, who was in because, he'd always wanted to do a biggish Alpine wall. We had a week to pull the stunt off, but already things weren't looking good.

A walk round to recce the North Face revealed a steady stream of water pouring out of the base of the overhanging diedres and spattering the screes. It had been raining for several days prior to our arrival, but the forecast looked fine for the week ahead. It was Monday and optimistically we agreed that if it stayed dry and sunny we might have a stab at the route later in the week. We pencilled in Thursday and walked back to the Laverado Hut for a beer. As we sat on the verandah we surveyed the Yellow Edge of the Cima Piccola. From a distance the route looked to follow a beautiful and impressive line up the left arête of the slender spire, but in reality we knew that it meandered its way up the wall right of the arête and the pitches themselves were reputed to be somewhat disappointing. Nevertheless, it was still regarded as a classic product of the golden age of Dolomite development. Comici, Varale and Zanutti had climbed it in 1933, and as such it represented a piece of climbing history. We decided to do it as a warm up the following day.

We enjoyed a laidback ascent. The route was a bit loose and broken in places, but one or two pitches left us paying respect to the early pioneers who'd first climbed here. After a few hours we were back on the verandah of the hut quaffing cold beer. We decided to take a quick walk under the North Face of the Cima Grande to reassess conditions. Things were looking up, water was now dripping rather than pouring from the face and the whole lower section looked dry, and that was after just a day.

We returned to Cortina and spent the following day sport climbing at the Crepe de Oucera. On our return to camp we prepared our gear for an attempt on the *Hasse* the following day. After the prep we walked up into town for an early meal. After a litre of wine each, washed down with several beers, our war council had concluded that we would go for it no matter what conditions we found on the face. Midnight saw us back at our tents with the alarm set for 4am.

The 'beep beep' of my mobile phone signalled the start of our adventure. I struggled out of the tent into a cool and dark September morning, the universe was studded with a billion white diamonds and huge peaks could just be discerned against the blackness. We parked the car at the Auronzo Hut and made the familiar walk round to the North Face, each of us isolated in our own pool of headtorch light, content to keep our thoughts to ourselves. As I walked I drank from my bottle, I'd made the decision not to carry water on the climb, so I wanted to imbibe at least two litres before I started the ascent. The others had adapted CamelBaks in their rucksacks and would drink on route.

As the four of us waited at the base of the mountain for first light, two young Slovenian climbers arrived and asked us, 'You will do the *Hasse*?' We nodded our intentions.

'Will you try to climb free?' they continued with a degree of scepticism.

'We'll try,' we informed them. We were going to climb as two independent pairs, I would partner Dave and Terry would partner Jerry.

After weighing us up they declared, 'We will go first, we know the face. We will climb much faster than you.'

Ordinarily Dave would have said something to the tune of, 'On yer bike', but on this occasion he stood aside and let the young guns take the lead.

I pulled onto the belay ledge at the top of pitch twelve and was greeted by one of the Slovenian lads, he asked, 'Did you manage the steep section free?'

'No, it was too wet. How about you?' I enquired.

'The same, I gave it everything but the holds were too slippery,' he said in a disappointed tone.

'C'est la vie, but the rest of the route has been superb?' I suggested.

'Yes,' he agreed and then continued, 'Anyway, you climb clean and very fast for old men. In England your friend must be very famous, no?'

With this somewhat backhanded compliment, he left the belay and disappeared around another overhang on his way to the summit. More like infamous, I thought with a chuckle to myself, if only he knew the half of it. The Slovenian hotshot was, of course, referring to Dave Barton. Much to the surprise of the Slovenian team, we'd been hot on their heels all the way up the face. As we exchanged pleasantries at the belays, we'd learned that the two lads were both F8a climbers. It was their second attempt at free climbing the route. The face is home to several hard routes, sometimes waymarked with old bits of ironmongery and tat.

The year before, the lads had strayed off the *Hasse* onto the *Via del Sassoni* route and had then been stormed off. It was good to be following a couple of handy pace setters. In turn, they had gathered the celebratory nature of our ascent. I think this had prompted the comment about Dave's fame. We ploughed on up the face and eventually gained the exit chimneys by about 6pm, one of these proved quite awkward.

It was oozing water and the green algae which coated the walls made the rock as slick as ice. I inched my way cautiously up the chimney, only finding one peg on the whole pitch. Dave arrived at the belay and suggested that it might speed things up if we threw a rope down to our compadres, suggesting that the leader would climb much faster with the security of a rope from above.

I was carrying a bright yellow rucksack, when I'd finished in the chimney it was dark green. By the time Dave and I had finished the pitch the other guys were feeling the cold. Below, Jerry had watched me grovelling up the chimney, slowly getting myself covered in muck and slime. He had bought a smart looking thermal top for the trip. As he prepared to climb he removed his top and packed it in his rucksack. A shivering Terry turned to him, 'What are you doing, aren't you cold?'

To which Jerry replied, 'Of course I am, but you don't think I'm going to get my new top dirty do you?'

As all four of us gathered at the top of the pitch, we realised the light was fading fast. We'd lost count of where we were on the face. I thought we had perhaps two pitches to go to reach the summit band. We mounted our headtorches and tried to press on in the dark, but the chimney terrain ahead was not easy to read and a mistake here could have proved serious. Other than the guidebook description, we didn't know the way off the mountain either, so we decided to bivouac where we were and finish the climb in the safety of daylight. We cleared as much rubble from the sloping ledges as possible and settled down for a long uncomfortable night. Jerry and Dave occupied the most palatial bit of the bedroom, a ledge about three feet long and two feet deep. I had a bucket seat at the back of the gully, whilst Terry slumped in slings on a sloping ledge with both feet dangling over the abyss. It was a fitful night, drifting into sleep, and then waking up shivering.

'What time is it?' someone would ask.

'Ten o'clock?' another would answer.

'What time is it now?'

'Twenty past ten.'

'How're we doing?' I asked.

'Nearly eleven… '

And so the time crept past.

Later a low growling rumble echoed round the mountains, 'What's that?' I asked.

'Thunder,' said Dave.

A few minutes later the mountains were illuminated with a yellow flash. This time the rumble was louder.

'What time is it?' I asked

'One o'clock,' someone answered.

Dave spoke up, 'I think the storm is quite distant at the moment, but it's definitely creeping this way. If it hits us here, this gully will turn into a death trap. We'll have to climb on in the dark and risk it. If we get to the summit band, we'll have a better chance.'

With that we sat and waited in tense silence. For the next twenty minutes the lightning flashes grew brighter and the thunder louder. I was resigned to the inevitable. Being caught up here, in an Alpine storm with only a thermal T-shirt and lightweight thermal top to stave off the elements was an unsavoury prospect. To our relief the intensity of the lightning flashes and volume of the bangs began to fade. After about an hour the occasional weak yellow flash signalled that somewhere in the massif some unfortunate souls might not be sharing the luck that we'd had on this night.

A weak grey light signalled the arrival of dawn. .

'Did you enjoy that lads?' Dave was having the crack, it was Jerry and Terry's first proper bivouac. 'It took me back to my days with Bivouac Bill.' Dave was referring to his formative years climbing with his Alpine mentor Bill Bowker. Bill was notorious for his views, he'd often say, 'You haven't done a proper Alpine route unless you've had a bivvy.'

In the growing light we eased stiff and aching limbs into life.

'Whose lead is it?' someone asked. Furtive glances suggested how everyone was feeling.

Terry, ever the stalwart, stepped up, 'I think it's my turn to do a bit.'

He led off up through the overhang above us and after about two minutes we heard, 'Safe.'

We found Terry belayed on a wide ledge that led off round the mountain to his left. We'd bivouacked a mere twenty metres below the summit band.

As we descended the South Face we met a guide and his client. The guide interrupted the song he was whistling to himself, and asked, 'Where have you come from?'

'The *Hasse*,' we informed him.

He gave Dave a slap on the back and turned to his client, 'See these men. These are hard men.' He turned back to us and said, 'Arrivederci!' Then he laughed and continued on upwards, whistling his song as he went.

Terry turned towards us, 'Did you hear that lads? It's official, we're hard men.' We all cracked out laughing.

Three hours later we were at the foot of the South Face, it was 10am and it had been a thirty hour round trip. I hadn't had a drink since starting the climb at 6am the previous day. That first beer was going to taste very good.

That evening we were back in Cortina enjoying a fine meal in our favourite pizzeria and we sat out on the terrace, eating and enjoying fine views of the surrounding mountains. It had been fine all day, but now the skies began to darken and the wind began to howl. Suddenly a ragged fork of blinding electricity sprang from one of the summits. Seconds later an ear shattering crack shook the buildings and rain hit the canvas awnings above us with waterfall force. The storm raged long into the night.

Some people approach aspects of their climbing in a very systemized fashion. Detailed planning, careful research, gathering all available beta in an attempt to guarantee a successful outcome. A sensible approach I must admit. In sport climbing I've seen climbers practising routes to the stage where it's pretty clear that they are capable of doing the route, yet they resist their redpoint attempt until they are completely sure that they'll succeed. Their primary goal is to get the route in the bag and so all uncertainty is removed first.

I've tried this myself, but have found it to be a soulless experience. For me an integral part of climbing is dealing with risk and uncertainty. Sometimes I fail, but when things do work out okay, the sense of achievement is magnified.

Big routes can amplify this further and the sense of satisfaction and self-fulfilment is consequently greater. It's a little bit like life in general. In today's society some people seem to hold the belief that somehow hazards and risk shouldn't exist. You turn the TV on and advertisements from law firms suggest that if you have some mishap or other, then someone else is to blame. We are in danger of developing a litigious culture where personal responsibility for managing risk is removed. In doing so, I believe that we are in danger of damaging a fundamental part of our human instinct, something that is a part of our evolutionary biology and supports our survival, safety, and well-being. My seven year old daughter once asked me, after a disturbing nightmare, why in her dream she'd been chased through the forest by wolves and monsters. I told her that thousands of years ago, we had a real need to fear the likes of wolves and bears and that her dream was probably caused by some instinctive memory from that time.

Through climbing, we are able to hone our ability to process risk and perhaps this ability might stand us in good stead when, out of the blue, it really counts.

Chapter 13

Jack of All Trades

It is the consequences of the act rather than the act itself that is the ego's priority.
Freud ca 1923

Climbing has many disciplines. Over the years I have dabbled with ice and snow and even done a little bit of Alpine mountaineering, yet deep down I would describe myself as a rock-climber. Whilst winter climbing has generally taken a back seat to my preference for rock, some of my memories on the 'white stuff' are amongst the most sharply etched on my mind. Having some first-hand experience, which extends beyond the genre of rock-climbing, can be helpful in gaining some insight into the mind of the climber. Without doubt, climbers who take their chosen pursuit seriously, connect strongly with their emotions, personal motives and drives. Climbing not only occupies daily thoughts, it becomes part of our subconscious and I think, over time, it feeds our desires and deeper values. In short, we become passionate about it. I have met people where climbing clearly plays an important part in their whole belief systems and from my experience, I would say that most climbers will, at some point, use climbing as the basis on which they judge themselves and others.

Climbers who excel tend to do so in one or two disciplines. It makes sense, it's easier to specialise than to generalise. A dedicated one hundred metre sprinter will achieve better times than the decathlete in the same discipline. Occasionally, however, someone comes along who performs exceptionally well in all aspects. Andy Cave is a man, who I believe, fits this category. Andy has climbed 8,000m peaks, pushed the boat out on hard new Himalayan routes like the North Face of Changabang, regularly on-sighted traditional E6 and E7, has climbed F8b sport routes, and has succeeded on some of the hardest Alpine routes in the world. He's a strong boulderer and has a catalogue of hard new Scottish ice routes under his belt. What's more, he turned his early career as a coal miner around through self study and went on to obtain a PhD, whilst simultaneously qualifying as a UIAA Mountain Guide. Despite all this, Andy once confessed to me that one well-known climbing pundit described him thus, 'A jack of all trades, but master of none'.

The context for this comment is important. Andy wouldn't have been bothered if the person had simply been expressing a matter of personal opinion, but the comment had been made at a well-known outdoor trade show, where climbers have professional interests at stake. I knew the person to whom Andy was referring. He is an extremely accomplished rock-climber who has made many significant climbs over the years. Why had this person made such a comment then? Was it that he simply had a hyped up view of himself and judged others by his own personal rock-climbing benchmark, or was it a veiled but deliberate professional put down. As to the motive behind the comment I can only speculate, but it suggested that in climbing circles big egos and competitive jealousy could certainly exist beneath a veneer of polite climbing etiquette.

Climbs are given grades and numbers to help other climbers understand the level of difficulty. This is useful information and enables the climber to choose the sort of experience they want from a climb. If the climber is set on stretching himself, then he can select a climb with a grade at his own personal limit, if he wants a stress-free affair, then he can choose climbs well within his top grade. I think most climbers use the grading system to set personal objectives and benchmark their own performance, but ego can also manipulate a climber's thinking. Rather than using grades to measure one's own personal performance, some people use the numbers to judge themselves against others and I think, when climbing becomes a consuming obsession, there is a danger that this can be corrupted into feelings of superiority, not just on the playing field, but in the broader context of holding higher moral values, or being a better person.

I don't think this is restricted to climbing, far from it. It probably spans many activities. I was staying with friends in Provence recently. Vicky and Craig (aka Enty) Entwistle have a guest house near Buis les Baronies, from which they run a cycle tour business. One of the big cycling challenges of the area is the classic Tour de France stage that incorporates Mont Ventoux. We were out on a family holiday, primarily climbing, but also doing a bit of biking. My wife, Dawn, was keen to ride up Mont Ventoux. Enty is a keen amateur racer who has stood on the champion's podium on several occasions, he knows his cycling stuff and attracts clients who value his knowledge and experience. On the occasion of our visit we happened to have dinner together with some of Enty's clients. It was obvious from our conversations that one particular husband and wife couple were experienced and competitive cyclists.

The first ascent of *The Skryking*, E5 6a, Guisecliff, Yorkshire in 1997.
Photo: Greg Rimmer.

Top: Climbers returning from a winter's day bouldering. The introduction of the crash pad is an example of how a simple bit of safety equipment can impact on the popularity of climbing.

Bottom left: Joe Healey technical genius and inspirational talent in the early '80s.

Bottom right: Roy Healey making the first ascent of *Roy's Arête* during our development of the rediscovered bouldering area of Crookstones. *All Photos: Mark Radtke.*

Top left: Neil Herbert repeating
my route *Ginny Greenteeth,* E5 6a, at
Hawkcliffe in Yorkshire.
Photo: Mark Radtke.

Bottom left: Mick Johnston on a 5.11
in the Californian Needles.
Photo: Mark Radtke.

Top right: Convalescing after my
Gordale accident on *Voyage of the
Beagle,* Creagh An Dubh Loch.
Photo: Simon Nadin.

Bottom right: Jerry Peel making
the second ascent of *Lost in Thought
and Lost in Time* F7b+, Victoria Cave
Buttress, Attermire Scar, Yorkshire 1994.
Photo: Mark Radtke.

Top: Jerry Peel doing what he enjoys most bouldering on the wild moorland where he started climbing. *Photo: Mark Radtke.*

Bottom photos: Mid '80s Scottish ice-climbing.
Left: Steep ice at the start of *Smith's Route*, Creag Meaghaidh. *Photo: Chris Frost.*

Right: Ian Cooksey belayed in the ice cave on *Smith's Route*, Gardyloo Buttress, Ben Nevis. Soon after I took this photograph, I found myself in extremis on the steep ice ramp above. *Photo: Mark Radtke*

Jerry Peel spotted by Roger Hindle, soloing his own route the 'highball'
Yarn Spinner, V5, Thruscross, Yorkshire. *Photo: Mark Radtke*

Fontainebleau bouldering.
Top Left: Jerry Peel giving a master class on the classic *La Liberte*, Font 6b.

Top Right: Pete Robbins on the highball *Super Prestat*, Font 7b. The nonchalant spotting style of Ledge and Dave Hesleden give an indication of the faith they have in Pete's talent. *Photos: Mark Radtke.*

Bottom: Dave Barton competing in the veterans' event staged as part of the International Grand Prix climbing series. National Indoor Arena, Birmingham 1991. *Photo: Glenn Robbins.*

Terry Holmes enjoying the delights of Italian ice in 2011, *Patri Right-Hand*, Cogne.
Photo: Mark Radtke.

Above: The next generation The Ledgways, The Radtkes, The Johnstons and little Miss Rimmer. Where will they take us?

Left: Dawn, Lauren, Bryony and Molly in the Dauphiné. As parents we try and introduce the children to the pleasures of our natural environment, but they're still up against the desire to possess 'stuff'.

Carefree days, Mick Johnston, Chris Riley, Chris Gibb and Roger Hindle taking a relaxing break from intense bouldering at Buthieres in Font early '90s.
Photos: Mark Radtke.

A day or so later, Dawn and I did our ride up Mont Ventoux and back at Enty's place I happened to bump into the wife of the couple we'd had dinner with. A brief passing conversation ensued:

'Have you been out climbing?' the lady enquired.

'No we've been out for a ride,' I said.

'Oh… where did you get to?' she asked.

'Just up Ventoux,' I answered.

She paused appearing a bit taken a back and then pressed further, 'Did you do it from the Bedoin side or from Malaucene?'

'Malaucene,' I said.

She seemed relieved, and I added, 'Enty advised us to take it from the easier side since it was our first time. We were on borrowed bikes and Dawn's only been out on a road bike four times before.'

She seemed a bit rattled by this, so she went straight for the jugular, 'How long did it take you?'

'A couple of hours,' I admitted.

'Mmm not bad,' she conceded and then wandered off.

Her questioning had been incision precise. There had been no enquiry about how we'd found the ride, or whether we'd enjoyed the experience. I got the impression that all she wanted were the numbers, so she could make some form of measurement. I don't know what she concluded from the data, but I'm certain that she would have made some sort of judgement similar to, 'I'm better than you'. I've met many climbers who display the exact same behaviour. The conversation is often peppered with questions such as:

'What have you done today?'

'Did you flash it?'

'Was it on-sight?'

'How long did it take you?'

This sort of language has the sole purpose of massaging personal egos, or to make judgements about others.

I'm not attempting to absolve myself from egomania. Chris Gibb once gave me a reality check many years after we had climbed a lot together:

'Do you know what me and Roger used to call you and Jerry?' he asked me one day, while we were enjoying a pint

'Go on then Gibby,' I said, feeling slightly intrigued.

'The Back Slappers. Whenever either of you did anything even remotely good, you'd fawn over each other, massaging each other's egos. It was as though you were constantly slapping each other on the back.' He went on, 'then, there was that occasion when we'd been to Wilton and I'd held your ropes all day. In the car on the way home, you turned to me and said, "You know Chris, you can't call yourself a real climber if you never lead anything." What you said probably has some truth in it. But it really hurt at the time.'

I was appalled at the revelation. I couldn't remember ever saying such a thing. What's more, I couldn't believe that I'd even think such a thing. I didn't recognise the person that Gibby was describing, but it gave an indication of where my head probably was at the time. Stuck firmly up my proverbial.

Anyone who believes that someone like Andy Cave is a 'Jack of all trades, but master of none' is, in my opinion, clearly deluded. Andy himself would never assert that he is a master, but his achievements speak for themselves. Personally I could wear the 'Jack of all trades' badge with a degree of pride. Whether the badge would be an accurate description is open to question.

During the mid '80s we had some cold winters in the UK and Ian Cooksey and I got quite addicted to Scottish ice. As was typical then, we'd leave Yorkshire after work on Friday evening and make the arduous journey to Scotland. If we were Ben bound, we'd get a couple of hours kip on the golf course at Fort William, wake up at about 5am and then slog up to the mountain. Our first ever, real, ice route was *Point Five Gully* on Ben Nevis, we got it in perfect conditions and topped out onto the summit plateau under a brilliant blue sky with views for miles around. I still remember it as one of the most enjoyable climbs that I've ever done.

During the winters of '85 and '86 we managed to tick many of the hard classics of the day. It didn't always go like clockwork however. On one visit Ian and I set our sights on *Smiths Route* on Ben Nevis. The route is fairly short by Scottish standards, only five hundred feet in length, but it had the reputation of being steep and sustained. It is situated on Gardyloo Buttress, and the route itself starts high up on the mountain at an altitude of nearly four thousand feet. As usual, Ian and I had slept at the golf course car park the night before our climb. Ian opted for the cramped but relatively warm comfort of my white Mini for his bedroom, whilst I chose the ground for my bed, which at least allowed a couple of hours of horizontal relaxation. At 5am we'd woken and forced some cold Ambrosia creamed rice pudding down our gullets. Daybreak revealed a flat grey sky, light snow tickled our glowing faces as we toiled upwards, through steep avalanche-prone snow, towards Gardyloo Buttress. Just getting to the start of the route felt harrowing enough and we eagerly fastened ourselves to the ice and carved a platform into the steep névé. Ian led the first pitch and belayed in a neat ice cave fringed with huge icicles. The next pitch was technical to start and I tentatively picked my way through the overhanging icicles and gained a steep ramp. It was really cold, the ice was iron hard and getting good axe placements took real effort. Sometimes when it's a bit warmer, the ice has plasticity to it, and in these conditions you can really motor, but today I had to fight for every placement. I was thirty feet above Ian and decided to place some gear. Tubular ice screws, called Snargs, were state of the art in the mid '80s and I proceeded to bash one of these into the ice. After about four inches, it bottomed out hitting the rock below the veneer of ice, it was only half in, so I tied it off with a piece of line. It amounted to what could be described as a morale-boosting piece of protection. I pressed on up the steep ramp. At the time, I was climbing with curved axes made by a company called Snowdon Mouldings and as I swung my Curver at the ice, the whole head snapped off the fibreglass shaft and was left dangling from my wrist. I was fifteen feet above a marginal ice screw, on steep terrain with one ice hammer and no axe. I had some serious thinking to do. I tried to use the axe head as an ice dagger, but I couldn't even scratch the ice with it, so I threw it into the abyss. I couldn't place any screws because my hammer was my third and very necessary point of contact with the ice. Falling from here was not an option. If I tried to press on I felt sure that I'd lose my balance and fall. I decided that retreat to the tied-off screw might be a possibility, it only required fifteen feet of balancey down climbing and I might be able to hook my ice hammer into some of the holes that I'd already made on the way up. I informed Ian of my predicament and started a very cautious retreat. Luckily it worked out and I arrived at the tied-off screw. There was no way I could back climb through the overhanging icicles below, so I had to trust my weight to the screw whilst Ian lowered me back to his belay on the rope. I can't remember why we decided not to bail out from here, it may have been concern about being avalanched trying to descend the steep snow below, but in any event, Ian decided to lead on with me in tow, using my hammer in one hand and pulling on the ropes with the other and in this fashion we completed a superb route. It's interesting how things turn out, had I not placed that marginal ice screw I doubt that I'd be here to relate the tale today.

Despite my early foolish foray on the Eiger, I was drawn back to the Alps time and time again and had some successful adventures. It was on an early visit to Chamonix, that I met Australian climber Chris Frost. Although he loved his rock climbing, Chris's feet were always firmly planted in the mountains. Ice and snow were integral part of the whole experience for him.

One January, I got a call from Frosty:

'Gidday, Rad, fancy a skiing and climbing trip to Cham?'

I was a self-taught skier, with one trip under my belt, but the prospect of some winter climbing action appealed and I agreed.

After a couple of days on the pistes we decided on an attempt at the North Face of the Grand Charmoz. Frosty had climbed the mountain previously in summer and felt that his prior knowledge would prove useful in getting back down. Our attempt was an abortive affair, wallowing through chest deep powder snow beneath the foot of the face brought back memories of my Eiger fiasco. Just trying to get to the start of the route was epic enough and bailing out was the sensible option. We eventually made it back down to Chamonix by about 2am, it had been a long and tiring day to achieve nothing. We reappraised our trip and decided to put the climbing gear aside and enjoy some skiing. The memories of previous hardships soon fade, however, and Frosty broke the news of a new cunning plan, 'What about the North Face of the Tour Ronde? It's only a thousand feet long and it'll be a doddle compared to those Scottish grade fives that you've been doing. We can ski in, leave the skis near the base of the mountain, solo the route, and then ski out down the Vallée Blanche. We'll be travelling light and fast. It'll be a great day out.'

To just ski the Valley Blanche would be a good day out I thought, so I agreed. Starting near the summit of the Aiguille du Midi, at an altitude of around 3,700m, the classic ski tour descends for over twenty kilometres back down to Chamonix, and passes through some of the most spectacular Alpine scenery in the world. To throw a climb in as well would be a real bonus. I couldn't refuse. The night before our proposed climb excited exuberance saw us partying into the small hours. The alarm woke us from an alcohol-induced narcosis. A dishevelled pair of un-cool skier climbers shared the téléphérique cabin with the smart looking guides and their glamorous clients, as it made its journey skywards towards the summit of the Midi.

We exited the cable car station and made our way down the sensationally exposed summit ridge to a place where we could clip into our skis. The day was perfect, clear blue skies and hardly a breath of wind, and in minutes we were flying through pristine snow, dwarfed by spires of rich red granite. I'd walked and climbed up here on several occasions in summer, but it was great to be up here and travelling at such speed. At first we followed the route of the ski tours, comfortable in the knowledge that most of the crevasses that the route crossed had been made safe with boards placed over them earlier in the season, but eventually we had to break away from the main track and head off towards our objective. It was hard going as the angle of the slope changed and we had to start a gentle climb. After an hour or so of uphill work we decided on a spot that would be close enough to our descent down the east side of the mountain to make the recovery of our skis most convenient and changed into our climbing gear. Up to now I'd been wearing a thin pair of Damart thermal gloves, but I'd need something more substantial for climbing in. I rummaged through my rucksack trying to locate my Dachstein mittens. 'You stupid bugger', I thought to myself, as I realised I'd left them back in the apartment.

'Well I've come this far and I'm not turning back now,' I announced, and with that we started up the face, climbing unroped.

The Tour Ronde is a modest little mountain by Chamonix standards, but it is a perfectly formed triangular-shaped peak and its North Face holds a permanent sheet of ice. The angle of the face never exceeds sixty degrees and has even been descended on skis. The icefield has the appearance of an egg timer, wide in its lower half narrowing to a slender couloir midway up and then opening up again in its upper half. Despite its modest proportions it can still generate feelings of great exposure. The lower part of the face had a liberal coating of frozen snow and proved straightforward enough, but the higher we climbed the more the texture of the ice changed, in places it was hard and green and in others it was black and rotten and trying to get a good purchase with axes became more problematic, as whole sections would shatter, peel off and go exploding down the face. We had to climb obliquely to one another to avoid the firing line. As we entered the upper part of the face the dinner-plating ice worsened and the sense of exposure increased. I really had to slam my axes into the ice to get decent purchase and each time I did, I could see that my knuckles were leaving blood on the ice. Looking down the face, I was hit with a horrible recurrence of my vertigo. I cursed my luck and stopped to close my eyes in an effort to suppress the panic attacks that were welling up in the pit of my stomach.

Frosty had made good progress and was now about two hundred feet above me. He shouted encouragement, 'Move out right across the face, the ice improves and the angle eases back.'

I followed his advice and was mightily relieved when I clawed my way onto the summit ridge. The light was starting to fade when we reclaimed our skis at the base of the East Face and we still had to negotiate the Geant Icefall. The icefall was a chaotic jumble of massive seracs and crevasses formed as the glacier flowed over a huge cliff hundreds of feet below its icy depths. It would prove a challenge for a competent skier in daylight, let alone a novice attempting it at night with a headtorch.

After the psychological ordeal of the climb, I actually enjoyed skiing the icefall, and soon we were sliding effortlessly down the Mer de Glace Glacier towards the twinkling lights of Argentière in the valley below. The moon was up and cast an eerie light across the glacier as we slid beneath the huge mass of the Grandes Jorrasses and then the majestic spire of the Petite Dru. I felt an inner sense of wellbeing.

We arrived back in Chamonix before midnight and headed for the bar. As I picked up my first beer and raised it to my lips, Frosty gasped, 'Christ, have you seen the state of your hands!'

Huge pink blisters were forming on the middle knuckle of each of my fingers. They were swollen and filled with fluid, it looked as if each finger had been scalded with boiling water. In the morning the blisters had turned dark blue. The doctor in the Chamonix hospital examined my hands and told me, 'It's lucky for you that you've come to one of the best hospitals in the world for treating frostbite.'

I was prescribed two different types of drug and advised that I had to bathe my hands in lukewarm water every three hours for several days. Slowly the blisters subsided and by the end of February each knuckle was covered in a leathery black callus about the size of a two pence piece. I'd been informed by the Chamonix doctors that these would eventually slough off to reveal regenerated and perfectly formed skin, provided I completed the medication and was diligent with my hand bathing.

Frosty was due to return home to Oz having completed his dental locum and was keen to get one last Scottish ice route in before his departure. It was now early March and I happened to bump into my old mate Dave Green at the Dickie Dunn. He'd just come back from Scotland and was raving about the classic gully climb, *Smith's Route* on Creag Meaghaidh.

'It was pretty thin and bits of it were falling down, but if you get up there in the next few days you might be in luck,' he told me.

I was still concerned about damaging my fingers, but I could tap quite hard on the black calluses and there was no tenderness. I got on the phone to Frosty and the following day we were Scotland bound.

The walk into Meaghaidh can be quite a pleasant affair if the path is free from snow, it climbs gently from the roadside car park, and the impressive cliffs can be reached after about four miles. On the occasion of our visit the path was covered in patches of slushy snow indicating that the thaw had well and truly set in and we kept our fingers crossed, hoping there would still be enough ice clinging to the gully to make it climbable. We arrived at the small lochan nestled beneath the cliffs and were encouraged by what we saw. The cliffs of Creag Meaghaidh are extensive, over three kilometres in length and up to five hundred metres high, and offer some of the finest ice climbing in

Scotland. Our route was partially hidden on Pinnacle Buttress, on the west side of the mountain. As we looked on from our vantage point, we couldn't really assess the condition of *Smith's Route*, but over on the right we could see plenty of blue ice still clinging to the cliffs above Central Gully, and this gave us a degree of optimism. Looking around we couldn't see any other climbers at all and reckoned that we had this remote wilderness completely to ourselves. It was a great feeling.

We made our way round the lochan and started the steep assault up *Raeburn's Gully*, eventually gaining a comfortable little platform that had been cut into the compacted snow. It provided us with a neat little camp in which we could rope up and sort the climbing gear. We began to assess the route. Steep ice, which looked to be near vertical, gave access to a narrow gully that snaked its way up the cliff. The back of the gully looked like it had variable amounts of ice interspersed with protruding rock. We could see for about a hundred feet or so, but above that the route went out of view. Higher still, it looked like there was abundant ice. Dripping melt water was forming little pits in the snow and it gurgled behind the icicles of the initial steep pitch.

The portents weren't good, but we decided to give it a go and I set off up the first pitch. Despite its steepness the ice was of the plastic variety and my axe placements sank into it with satisfying thuds. I found a belay and Frosty was soon out on the sharp end. I paid the rope out and it slid off up above me soaking up melt water as it went. I informed Frosty that he was about to run out of rope, but he shouted back down that he couldn't get a belay and that we'd have to move together. Reluctantly I dismantled my belay and started to follow. After climbing together for some time, I got the reassuring news from above, that he'd found an adequate belay and I relaxed a little knowing I was now protected with a secure rope from above. I emerged from the confines of the gully to find Frosty grinning from ear to ear and ensconced on a spacious ledge of snow.

He loved this sort of stuff and was completely in his element. I was never so relaxed on such climbs, rather than simply enjoying the moment my thoughts were often preoccupied with what was coming up next. Looking up revealed a steep ice-filled gully that appeared to culminate in a series of ice bulges. It looked hard. It was my lead and with a brief, 'Good luck,' from Frosty I ventured upwards, all the time hunting here and there for some form of protection. I tried to place a Snarg, but it was useless, the ice had started to take on a mush-like texture and I could simply pull the screw back out with my fingers, there was nothing for it but to press on. The ice above reared. Lower down I'd been able to keep most of my weight on my feet, but I could see that to overcome the next section I'd really be hanging from my axes. I assessed the difficulties. It looked like there were some ice mushrooms on the left that would offer more in the way of footholds.

After a further fifteen feet, a few moves right looked like they would lead to easier ground. All that existed between me and Frosty and seventy feet below was rope and air. To all intents and purposes I would be soloing the next section.

As I embarked up the steep barrier of decaying ice, I could feel my palms sweating inside my gloves and had no spit to spit. The climbing was insecure and the ice was rotten. If I tried to swing my axes into it, they simply knocked lumps off. I had to place them with care and gently tug on them until they felt they would hold under my weight. More often than not they'd just rip right through the thawing mush. I made slow progress, but eventually arrived at the point where I had to make a delicate series of pulls rightwards. My assessment from below had been correct and I could see that above me the angle eased. Success was a flea's jump away. I hunted around, trying to get a couple of decent axe placements, but each time I tried to weight them, they pulled through the ice. Eventually I got them to stick. I brought my feet up and kicked the front points of my crampons into the ice, but as I did, the whole plate of ice that my feet were trying to gain purchase in collapsed. At the same time my right axe ripped. I was left hanging from one arm. Instinct kicked in and somehow I managed to get back on the ice, but I was utterly gripped. I felt that I was sitting on a ticking time bomb. My heart was pounding in my chest and the internal dialogue in my head was bouncing around like a deranged lunatic in a straight jacket:

'Retreat... out of the question, press on... you'll fall off and die, you're going to fall off anyway!'

I tried to suppress the panic and get some rationality back into the situation, and then a minor miracle happened. At least it was a minor miracle in my mind. As I looked around, I spied something over to my left, it was a piece of red tat, winking at me from below a small rocky overhang. I recognised it instantly, it was climbing tape and by the position of it I knew that it was attached to a peg. That peg suddenly became the sole and whole focus of my life. Meticulously my body obeyed as I inched my way left. Slowly, I removed a karabiner from my harness and then I reached across and carefully clipped it to the tape.

Nearly there!

I was immersed in complete silence with just the thud of my own heartbeat drumming in my head. I eased one of my ropes upwards and clipped it through the karabiner and then the church bells rang out and I felt like I was capering around like a mad thing. I couldn't assess how good the peg was, but I didn't care because to me, at that moment, it was bombproof and it had saved my life. I finished the pitch and ran up the steep névé above to where it met a rock wall. I found a crack in the rock, selected a rock peg from my rack and pounded it home. I slumped onto the belay. It was perhaps the most terrified I've ever been whilst climbing. Frosty joined me at the belay.

'Jeeze, Rad, that was desperate, it was a good job that you had that peg clipped!'

'Aye, it was pretty tough,' I agreed.

In 2010 I returned to Meaghaidh, I hadn't been back since I'd climbed *Smith's Route*, twenty-four years earlier. This time I was with Ian Cooksey, it was a clear cold day in February. Internet reports told us that conditions on the mountain were excellent. We'd also got good gen about avalanche danger and which routes were in nick. As we stood at the lochan we could see chains of climbers all over the mountain. They looked like ants at work on a giant wedding cake. It was going to be a busy day. As we approached our chosen route, a classic called *The Pumpkin*, we could see two parties already at work and another party waiting to start.

'I don't like the look of this,' I confessed to Ian.

'Don't worry, they're bound to be quick,' he reassured me.

Two hours later and we were still sat in the queue. Eventually the party in front of us were able to start and Ian and I followed on their heels. They were a competent pair and as we shared belays with them, we shook off our mutual frustrations and struck up some banter.

'What's your name?' I asked

'Susan,' replied the lady. Her face was partially covered by a balaclava, she had an endearing smile and the glint from her sparkly blue eyes suggested a zest for life. I warmed to her as soon as we started talking.

'You look nice and relaxed on the ice, have you been doing it long?' I asked.

'Thank you. Not that long, about five years now,' she replied.

'Do you like rock-climbing?' I continued.

'No not really, I find it a bit too technical and I'm not that strong.'

I was curious, 'How did you start ice climbing?'

'Oh some friends just invited me. They said, "We're going ice-climbing in Norway, why don't you come along." So I thought that sounds interesting, what have I got to lose? I was 62 at the time and my grand-kids said, "what do you think you're doing grandma?" I just tell them that life is for living.'

We followed Susan up the climb. At a couple of the belays her partner had placed rock pegs. As she left, she asked, 'Do you think, you could get those out for me? I'm struggling a bit, I'm not strong enough really.' How could we refuse? As we overtook the ageing couple on the path back down the mountain we were able to return their gear.

'We'll just take our time,' they informed us, 'these old legs don't move quite as well as they once did, we'll be a few hours yet, but we'll get back down okay. Thanks and see you around boys.'

Boys! What a nice touch, I thought to myself. I'd be fifty in June and here she was calling me a boy. Age is such a relative thing, just like climbing. It doesn't matter about the number. It's about what shape you're in at the time, one person's E6 can be the same as another person's HVS. That's part of climbing's appeal.

I turned to Ian, 'A sixty-eight year old grandmother climbing a Scottish grade five, what an inspiration! There's hope for us yet.'

'Yeah and I'd have liked to have seen how those legs moved when she was in her prime,' Ian said laughing.

Susan was a breath of fresh air. She was sixty-eight yet it seemed that she had the vitality of an eighteen year old. She reminded me of what it felt like when I was starting out. No ego, no bullshit, nothing to prove. Just a simple desire to taste what climbing brings.

The joy of life itself.

Chapter 14

Sixth Sense

Knowing something without knowing how we know it,
or, perception via the unconscious.
C G Jung on intuition

Dave sat patiently belaying as Jerry methodically climbed the bulging wall of orange granite. We were nestled on a broad ledge covered in green turf and the sea crashed onto rocks below us sending spray hurtling skywards. This was Bosigran, one of the jewels of Cornish climbing, overlooking the Atlantic and bristling with quality climbs. I chatted to Dave, idly reminiscing about more serious days spent in the nearby Great Zawn. We were in holiday mode, soaking up the sun, listening to the crashing waves and enjoying the banter. We'd already had our turn on the sharp end and were happy relaxing as our respective leaders tested themselves above. Jerry continued his journey to the top of the crag and my own climbing partner, Ledge, made steady progress up an immaculate crack that went by the name of *Kafoozalem*. Dave and I continued our banter and while we were talking two other climbers encroached into our territory. I recognised the strangers and it soon became apparent that they recognised us, or at least one of them did. They closed in and Jerry shouted down that he was safe so Dave began to ready himself for the climb. As he did one of the strangers walked directly up to him. He was a tall guy and towered over Dave.

His introduction was less than courteous, 'So I was right, you're Dave Barton aren't you?' There was menace in his voice.

'Whose asking?' replied Dave.

'Mike Raine,' said the stranger, and then he continued, 'I've been waiting years for this moment. I don't know whether I should be talking to you, or simply knock you off this ledge right here and now.'

I looked on in amazement. Big, big mistake, I thought.

Dave fixed Raine with eyes of steel. 'Listen pal and listen good, there's only one bloke going off this ledge and it ain't me.'

Dave took a step forward and Raine took two steps back.

Dave turned to me and gave me a knowing look. He was deathly serious. He then looked up and shouted, 'Take in Jerry, before something really ugly happens down here and take in fast.'

With that Dave sprinted up the rock like a baboon, climbing faster than Jerry could take the rope in. It had taken Jerry about thirty minutes to lead the pitch, Dave got to the belay in about three.

I looked across at Raine, 'I think you've made a big mistake here Mike, I know what your beef is about, but I think you've got the wrong end of the stick. Nobody threatens Dave like that, if I were you I'd do some quick thinking, or clear off.'

It was too late, Jerry and Dave returned to the base of the crag. Jerry greeted the other stranger, 'Now then, Mike Hammill, long time no see.' The pair shook hands like the old mates they were. Jerry appeared to be diplomatically attempting to keep the peace.

But Dave was having none of it. He turned to Raine, 'Right pal if we're having it, come on we'll sort it out right here and now.'

I knew that Raine was making a point of principle. I'd read his various rants on the Internet. What he didn't really appreciate was that he was dealing with a battle-hardened warrior, someone who'd climbed the Eiger's North Face in the early days, someone who'd got countless E6s under his belt, but most importantly of all, someone who could throw well-aimed punches in the thick of it. Dave was ready for a fight and I think Raine realised that his confrontational bluff had backfired.

'No no, I don't want to get into a scrap, I was just trying to make my point. I wasn't happy about you retro bolting my route at *Troller's Gill.*'

It was well known that Raine was angry about bolts being placed on his route, *The Jim Grin*, a classic E5 in Yorkshire. He'd spoken out publicly on the matter on many occasions.

Dave relented a little, 'Listen, let's get the facts straight. I didn't turn *The Jim Grin* into a sport route. All we did was replace the fixed gear with like for like. We simply put four staples in. One where the thread was and then others where the pegs were and that's how we left it. You still had to carry a rack and in my view it was still E5.'

Raine replied, 'Yeah, but as far as I'm aware more bolts have gone in since and so in a way you were responsible for starting the trend.'

Dave doesn't have an intransigent mindset and as the argument went to and fro, the tension between the adversaries dissipated. As they argued their personal and ethical perspectives, I think there was a grudging recognition that in actual fact they held some similar values about climbing. Everyone heaved a big sigh of relief when the incident ended peacefully, but once again it was a stark reminder that certain individuals like Mike Raine were prepared to stand up for what they valued and believed in, even threatening violence in the process.

It's interesting how fate can play its hand. Many years after the Bosigran incident, *The Jim Grin* dealt me a blow that nearly put an end to my climbing for good. It was the May Bank Holiday of 2007, the weather had been good and the crags were dry. The weekend started off well enough as Terry Homes and I made an early Friday dash up to Scafell in Cumbria.

'We need to get some traddin' done,' declared Terry. 'If we get off early we can get two or three routes in.'

By 10.30am we were ready for action below our proposed route underneath the magnificent East Buttress of the mountain. Blue skies stretched for miles overhead and the rock was powder dry. As we sat sorting gear another couple of climbers toiled up the slopes towards us. I recognised the lead climber as Lakes activist and new router Keith Phizacklea. Keith is a complete climbing enthusiast, living and breathing it as much as anyone I know. He was also a real character and comic. Secretly I thought he originated from the same gene pool as the legendary comedian Stan Laurel. He had a similar look and hailed from the same part of Cumbria and I thought this was too much of a coincidence to be down to chance.

Keith greeted us loudly, 'Bloomin' eck, it's Terry and Rad, I thought you lads never got out of Yorkshire these days, what brings you up to the best crag in the world?'

Terry shouted a quick retort, 'What do you mean best crag in the world?' It was well-known that for some strange reason Keith didn't have a passport and in his thirty-odd year climbing career he'd never climbed outside the UK. He arrived at our stance below the cliff. 'Well I suppose it's the best crag in MY world,' he observed dryly.

We cracked out laughing. Our plan was to climb *Roaring Silence* and then drop over to the Central Buttress and climb *Saxon*. I'd climbed quite a few of the harder Extremes on Scafell over the years, but these two classics had eluded me. Keith assured us that we were in for a real treat. I led off up the first pitch of *Roaring Silence* and was somewhat relieved when I arrived at the belay. It had been my first trad lead of the year and I calculated that it had been fifteen years since I'd last climbed on Scafell. The pitch had been superb, intricate and technical, the sort of climbing that you had to study before making the moves. It had felt quite bold, I'm glad I didn't jump on anything harder, I thought to myself. Terry arrived at the belay and then led off up the second pitch making short work of a tough looking roof.

At the summit we coiled the ropes enjoying uninterrupted views of the Cumbrian fells bathed in spring sunshine, 'This is what it's about Terry, fantastic weather, mountain virtually to ourselves, and superb climbing. You know Keith might be right. It could be the best crag in the world.'

We made our way cautiously down the mountain to where a broad rocky slab looks like it leads down to the col. Terry stopped and said, 'I'm sure we go down here you know.' He pointed down the slab.

'I think you're right, but I don't like the look of it myself. I seem to remember last time I was here, I made a little abseil, just have a look over there.' Sure enough a load of slings indicated an abseil point and after a few minutes we were at the base of the cliff.

As we approached our stashed rucksacks we could hear someone shouting for help. About fifty yards away we could see someone hunched over another person lying on the scree. Terry and I looked at each other and no words needed to be exchanged. We hurried over and appraised the situation. The casualty was lying on his side on steep scree below the notorious rocky step called Broad Stand, the very slab that we'd avoided fifteen minutes earlier. A young man was cradling the poor guy's head and offering words of encouragement. The casualty was breathing but was unconscious. He was wearing a rucksack that provided some support and his feet were elevated. 'What happened?' we enquired.

'I'm not sure, we'd just got up here to do some climbing when we heard a yell. I came over and found him lying here with his mate in a panic. They were trying to get down Broad Stand, he must have slipped and fallen. My girlfriend has gone off with his mate to try and get a signal so they can call the emergency services. I'm staying here. I'm doing my best to stem the bleeding. I've not moved him cos as near as dammit he's in the recovery position.'

'Good thinking,' Terry reassured, 'We'll check and see if a call has gone through to the emergency services, otherwise one of us might have to leg it down to alert them. We'll then nip over to the mountain rescue box and see if there's anything there that might help, even though it's quite mild he's going to chill down rapidly.' The casualty was only wearing shorts and a thin shirt.

We established that the emergency services had been contacted and the air ambulance had been deployed. We retrieved a thermal sleeping bag and collapsible aluminium stretcher from the mountain rescue box. As we made our way back to the casualty I confessed my fears to Terry, 'He must have fallen thirty or forty feet head first into the scree. I saw the precise rock that his head hit. Even if he makes it, he's going to have permanent brain damage.'

On our return we could see that the injured man was in exactly the same position and was still breathing.

'How's his head?' I asked.

'It's still bleeding, but I think I'm stemming the loss,' the young man replied.

'Good. As far as we know the air ambulance and mountain rescue are on their way all we can do know is wait and keep our fingers crossed,' I told him.

We did our best to insulate the injured man from the cold with the thermal bag and figured out how to assemble the stretcher in preparation for the evacuation. I nipped back up to the col to check on the injured man's friend. He was sat on the scree with his head in his hands, a crumpled figure.

'How is he?' the man asked me. I got the impression that the question had already been answered before it was asked.

'Difficult to say, the guy down there is doing a sterling job looking after him. We've made him as comfortable as we can and with a bit of luck, he'll be getting some medical help and be on his way to hospital soon,' I assured him.

The friend continued, 'We were just out for a walk that's all. What am I going to tell his wife? What about his kids?' He was an image of absolute despair.

After about an hour the air ambulance buzzed into view and after assessing the situation from above disappeared over Mickeldore to find a suitable landing spot. Twenty minutes later a paramedic arrived. He was lathered in sweat and his chest was heaving, he'd almost sprinted up the steep gully from where the helicopter had dropped him. A few moments later a doctor arrived in a similar state of exhaustion. The pair quickly took command of the situation, asking questions of the attendees whilst simultaneously working on the injured man. The mountain rescue team arrived next and the doctor co-ordinated operations with precise and calculated orders. He'd quickly established that the casualty needed to be airlifted out. The air ambulance wasn't equipped for this operation and before long we could hear the throbbing engines of a Sea King droning its way up Eskdale. Another thirty minutes of hazardous flying, superb leadership and focused team work followed and the big yellow bird with casualty and doctor on board departed Scafell. Three hours had elapsed.

'Come on, Terry, let's go for a pint, I haven't really got the stomach for another climb.' We made our way down the mountain in reflective mood.

'Poor bugger, he must have started out this morning just like us. Looking at the weather and thinking, "what a cracking day I'm going to have."' Terry said.

The following morning the local news broadcast, informed me of what I'd feared. Despite the efforts of the medics the man had died in the helicopter. I thought about those he'd left behind.

I'd arranged to climb that afternoon and met up with Terry and Greg Rimmer at one of Lancashire's premier gritstone quarries, Wilton One. After doing a couple of warm ups I followed Greg up the classic and bold, *Isle of White*. It was a superb route, but my heart wasn't in it. It was another beautiful day, the rock was in great condition, but I didn't want to be there. It was an irrational feeling and I put it down to the experience of the previous day.

The following morning I awoke to clear blue skies. It looked like it was going to be another good crag day. Jerry Peel confirmed that the team were going to *Troller's Gill*.

'We can clip some bolts and have a relaxed mileage day,' Jerry encouraged me. I agreed to go and put the phone down. I met Dave and Pam Barton in the car park and we began a leisurely walk up to the crag. The scenery on the approach walk is idyllic, the spectacular gritstone moorland of Simon's Seat dominates verdant rolling valleys, Yorkshire Dales geography at its best.

Troller's Gill is a modest limestone gorge, but one wall has some excellent little climbs, which were great early season testers. It was here that Mike Raine had climbed *The Jim Grin* in 1983. It was perhaps the classic route of the crag and a creation that Raine was justifiably proud of. He'd been aggrieved and angered when Mick Ryan and Dave had taken it upon themselves to replace fixed gear with resin staples. Dave's motivation was simply pragmatic. The pegs and slings were past their sell-by dates, so instead of replacing them with similar gear that would also fall into decay, it made more sense to replace them with something that would last. It seemed to make perfect sense.

Raine, on the other hand, held the view that placing the staples completely altered the character of the challenge. In a way it was another example of the *Frankie* and *Supercool* scenarios.

Mick Ryan might have had slightly different motivations however. At the time he was the creative driving force behind Vertical Brain Publishing and was revolutionising the shape of climbing guidebooks. Shortly after the bolting of *Troller's Gill*, Mick published a topo guide to update his first publication, *Yorkshire Limestone*. He included *Trollers Gill* in his new topo, even renaming it as the trendy and slightly continental, *Secteur Barguest*. Perhaps Mick's motive behind the bolting had a deliberate controversial twist to it. The old adage, any publicity is good publicity, springs to mind.

When we arrived at *Trollers Gill* on the Monday of that ill-fated May Bank Holiday in 2007, the crag was pretty busy, most of our team were already geared up and ready for action and other teams were hard at it. The crag has a limited number of what might be described as warm up routes and all of these were occupied. The only route that appeared to be free was *The Jim Grin*. It wasn't really a true sport climb, with its spaced bolts, and hardly an early season warm up, but I'd done it many times and so Dave and I opted for this as our first route. It was definitely a great little climb, but was also a product of its own success. A consequence of its popularity meant that the passage of countless hands and feet had polished the rock. In places it had the look and feel of glass.

Dave handed me the end of the rope and I prepared myself for the first fifteen feet of slippery insecure climbing that would gain the first staple bolt. As soon as I pulled onto the rock an imperceptible feeling triggered in my brain. It wasn't a conscious thought, it was more of a gut feel, but something appeared to be telling me that things weren't right. I clipped the bolt and pressed on upward trying to ignore the internal dialogue, but I couldn't shake the negative feelings. I knew the crux of the climb was making the moves to gain the belay, but there was also a tricky section to surmount an overhang at two-thirds height. This involved a powerful pull and rock over to gain a standing position above the overhang. I knew the sequence well enough, so I threw myself into it, eager to get the climb over with. I reached up with my right hand and my fingertips crimped the familiar positive edge. Big move now, throw the left foot up and crank on the edge. As I made the move the finger edge snapped off. My body had been in full tension against the rock and rather than falling down I exploded backwards almost horizontally. The last staple was about eight feet below and as the rope took the tension the velocity of my falling body was accelerated. I could feel the rate of the acceleration, I knew I was on my side and I was perfectly aware that I was going to hit the rock at a phenomenal speed. I threw my right arm out to take the impact. Whack, I was whipped into the rock like a ball on a piece of string. The fall had taken seconds yet it felt that I'd had time to think through a survival strategy. I was vividly aware of what was happening, knew what the consequences would be and acted accordingly. If my head had hit the rock at that speed, I'm sure I'd have been in the same position as the guy who we'd tried to save a few days earlier. People sometimes say that your whole life flashes before your eyes before you die. I think your brain simply recognises the danger and kicks into overdrive creating some sort of perceived time differential.

I came to halt about ten feet above the ground. It had been a good thirty foot fall. Dave lowered me to the deck, 'How are you?'

'I think I've bust my arm, but I can walk and I'm still alive. You know Dave, as soon as I set off something was telling me, that I shouldn't be climbing, but I didn't listen.'

'Well it's not been your weekend has it? You'd better have someone look at that arm.'

Pam drove me to hospital. Rock fragments were removed from my elbow and the X-ray revealed a fractured ulna, but from the pain and lack of mobility, my shoulder seemed to have suffered the most trauma.

The doctor offered an explanation, 'There are no broken bones in the shoulder, but it's a complex joint and you've probably strained some tendons or ligaments. Your arm will need to be immobilised for two weeks and then you might be able to start some physio.'

What a weekend, I thought. I cast my mind back to *Roaring Silence*. Something then was telling me to take it steady. It was almost like a little alarm bell ringing. Then there was the poor bugger who'd died and now this. I'm not a superstitious person, I'd been in situations like this before when climbing, not necessarily in a position of extremis, but subliminally when things just didn't feel right. More often than not in these situations I'd backed off. I now believe that intuition might be underpinned by something more than simple luck and coincidence, it may even have elements of cognition to support it.

As the weeks went by, I recovered some mobility and strength in my arm and even started climbing again albeit at a modest level, but it was clear from the pain and lack of movement that there was some underlying tendon damage. I couldn't lift my arm above my head. My physiotherapist finally suggested that I should have a scan on my shoulder.

'I don't think there's any more I can do, I'm afraid you might need surgery,' she looked at me thoughtfully, 'Mm,' she mused, 'there are two consultants that I can recommend, but which one?' she asked herself aloud. Then, as if the penny had dropped, she looked at me and said, 'Mr Funk, he's the one for you. Some people say he's a little arrogant, but his work is the best in the business. The scan won't be cheap but you'll get an accurate diagnosis.'

'I'm not bothered about arrogance, Sarah, I just want someone who can get me back on the rock,' I told her and then thanked her. It was now September. What had started as a promising trad climbing comeback had deteriorated into a year of pain and frustration. I was desperate to get things fixed. I had no medical insurance but decided to go private.

I sat in the waiting room of Euxton Hall private hospital near Chorley. It was more like a hotel reception room than a doctor's surgery. A young woman sat opposite me in a high backed comfy chair. Her arm was held in a cumbersome abdication sling. I wanted to ask her what had happened, but felt it would be impolite to enquire. I'd been waiting about ten minutes when a gentleman entered the room and announced, 'Mark Radtke? Would you like to follow me.'

I followed him down a short, carpeted corridor and into a small consulting room. He stood before me, slim built, wearing a casual open-necked shirt and beige slacks. He had a pair of thin-framed glasses and a welcoming smile. I'd have put him at around forty years old.

'Hi, I'm Len and I'm pleased to meet you.' He held his hand out and I responded with a courteous handshake.

'Have a seat,' he gestured to a nearby chair.

I thought I detected a South African accent, but I couldn't be sure. Len Funk wasn't what I'd been expecting. From the word go he was polite and professional and immediately empathetic. We got down to business and he quickly built up a thorough case study about my professional life, sporting career and my expectations. He had me in the palm of his hand, not only did he command instant respect, I liked him as well. It was clear that he was passionate about his work, but I also detected that he was a bit of a medical explorer, a pioneer in his chosen field and I liked that.

'OK take off your shirt, I'd like to do some physical tests first.' He got me to do a range of pulls and presses and then he did a whole batch of range of motion evaluations on the shoulder. After making a number of notes, he sat me down next to a laptop computer with a small scanner attached and proceeded to examine my shoulder. An image appeared on the computer screen that reminded me of the pregnancy scans that my wife had undergone.

'Yes just as I suspected, look here,' Len pointed to the image on the screen. 'That's a massive cuff tear.'

I tried to make sense of the image, but to my untrained eye it could have been anything. 'I'll take your word for it Len.' I told him, slipping my shirt back on and listened to the prognosis.

Len proceeded in a calm unwavering manner, totally confident in his craft, 'It's a massive tear that definitely needs repairing. Even if you were just doing a sedentary desk job I'd still recommend you had it repaired. At your age you've got lots of active life ahead of you and you'll need the full mobility of your arm. I'm confident that I can give you that back. Now the bad news, you can't drive for six weeks following the operation and you'll only be able to do light exercise after three months, but if you follow all my rehabilitation protocols you'll be back climbing in six to eight months.'

I did some quick calculations. If I got the operation done before Christmas I could be back climbing by next summer.

'When can you do it?' I asked.

I was booked in for the 30th November. Len Funk is a pioneer of arthroscopic, or keyhole shoulder surgery. All his work is done through minor incisions. The shoulder is inflated using liquid and then cameras are inserted to observe proceedings. Then he would make necessary repairs using precision instruments. Even though the ultrasound scan highlights the damage, it isn't until the cameras are inserted that the true extent of the trauma is established. Many shoulder specialists still advocated open surgery, but Mr Funk argued that his techniques were far less invasive and allowed speedier recovery. His rehabilitation protocols also challenged the thinking of the traditionalists. My view was that the arthroscopic methods required far more skill than the butchery of open surgery and I had total confidence that Len had both the skill and the wisdom. It was ground-breaking stuff. I also knew that he'd been well-mentored. He'd worked with Professor Angus Wallace. I knew of the professor since he'd been the specialist consultant who'd repaired John Dunne's' shoulders many years earlier. John always gave Angus Wallace the highest praise. I knew I was in good company.

My operation sheet following surgery gave a clear indication of the findings. It read:

> The biceps tendon was greater than fifty percent deficient. When the rotator cuff was viewed from within the shoulder, a full thickness tear was identified. The tendon involved was the supraspinatus and the infraspinatus and the cuff tendon was poor and thinned. The cuff tear appears to have been caused by trauma, impingement and degeneration. This was a large 5cm x 3cm wide C-shaped tear that had retracted to expose the articulated surface but not as far as the glenoid. The subscapularis tendon had a full thickness tear. The tear was large 5cm x 2.5cm wide and had retracted less than 5cm.

The treatment summary gives an indication of the techniques used and the skill of the surgeon.

> A tenodesis was performed on the biceps tendon. The tenodesis was carried out as a dynamic tenodesis as part of the cuff repair. This was performed arthroscopically. The acromion was resected laterally and anterior to the ACJ. It was then bevelled posteriorly to create a flat acromion. The CA ligament was not resected. The supraspinatus was released and infraspinatus was advanced. The rotator cuff was repaired through the arthroscope. Mobilisation of the tendon was fairly extensive to allow non-tensioned relocation to its insertion. The repair was performed with the shoulder in neutral abduction and under minimal tension and produced a watertight repair. This was carried out by excising the degenerative tissue then secured laterally, using an end to bone repair. The bony trench created for

attachment of the cuff was created at the original cuff insertion. The tendon was secured laterally by two bony anchors. The anchors used were 5mm Mitek Fastin anchors double loaded with Orthocord suture. The subscapularis tendon was repaired. Access was through the arthroscope. Mobilisation of the subscapularis tendon was fairly extensive to allow non-tensioned relocation to its insertion. The repair was performed using an end to bone repair under minimal tension. The repair was carried out with the shoulder in neutral abduction and under minimal tension. The subscapularis tendon was secured laterally by two bony anchors. The anchors used were 5mm Mitek Fastin anchors with Orthocord suture. The portals were closed with single sutures using a subcuticular 3-0 monocryl.

Mr Funk made his post operative visit the following day. He checked out how I was feeling and then said in a rather understated and modest fashion, 'You were under for a long time, we found that we had a lot more work to do than we anticipated.' I thought his words were touched with a sense of achievement. What a man, I thought myself.

During the following months I followed the rehabilitation protocols and bit by bit regained the use of my arm until the stage where I started climbing again. Initially taking it easy top roping on the indoor climbing wall, but then graduating to routes outside. It was around May when Jerry suggested a trip to Dorset. It was an appealing proposition. Lots of vertical and steady sport routes to go at. It would be good to do a bit of leading, nothing too taxing, just get my arm working and my head back into being on the sharp end. That's what went through my head at any rate.

We chose Dancing Ledge quarry as our first venue. The last time I'd visited this crag was on my first climbing trip to Dorset with Mick Johnston and Mick Ryan. At that time Mick Ryan was working with Dorset aficionado Pete Oxley on the first *Rockfax* climbing guide to the area. I reckoned it must have been about fifteen years previously.

I followed Jerry up an easy F6a. My arm felt good, so I opted to lead a slightly harder route. It was graded F6b+ and gave me quite a fight. I'd lost a lot of fitness. Jerry led a F6c and suggested that I'd be better off following it, 'There's a couple of tricky moves and they're on your right arm. If you feel as though you're pulling too hard, just weight the rope.' It was sound advice. I set off up the route and sure enough got into difficulty. Just as I was trying to execute one of the difficult moves that Jerry had described I pulled a hold off with my right hand, instinctively I lunged for a jug with my left hand and as I latched it I felt something snap in my left shoulder. Searing pain followed.

Back on the deck I examined the range of motion I had in my left arm. It was severely restricted. I couldn't raise it above my head.

'Perhaps you've just strained it,' Jerry tried to reassure me.

'Let's hope so,' I agreed sceptically. Rather than easing off, the injury got worse over the weekend. That evening in the pub I couldn't lift a pint to my mouth, and in the morning, I could only wash my face using my right hand. I was familiar with the symptoms. A visit to Len Funk confirmed my worst fears and almost a year to the day after the operation on my right shoulder, my left arm was in an abdication sling following post operative surgery. Only this time I wasn't alone, my old mate Terry Holmes was in the same boat. He'd been carrying a long term shoulder injury following a nasty fall off *Adrenaline Rush* at Caley. After seeing the success of my first operation he'd taken the plunge and seen Mr Funk.

I followed the rehabilitation protocols and by March 2009 I was back on the climbing wall. By the summer I was on-sighting proper F6cs in France. It had been a testing three years.

None of the injuries that I'd suffered had been life threatening and compared to what many people go through, could even be described as trivial. Some might argue that they were even self-inflicted, the result of pursuing a selfish and pointless activity. This may be, but I have decided to include this case study for the benefit of anyone unfortunate to suffer physical injury. There are people out there with levels of talent, dedication and pioneering spirit similar to that of Len Funk and his team. With a bit of determination, luck and the support of brilliant medical professionals there is always possibility. Never say never.

I've talked about risk and adventure at length in this book. People of less adventurous dispositions often look at extreme sports and say, 'How can they do such a thing? They must be crazy.' When I reflect on some of the scary situations I've been in, or mishaps that have befallen me, I think that in reality, when you're aware of the hazards, you're probably at your safest. In these situations you're tuned in, your senses are heightened and your reactions are quicker. The unfortunate guy who fell from Broad Stand on Scafell was not the first to do so, it's a well-known death trap, but I doubt he had knowledge of it. He was probably ambling down the mountain blissfully unaware of the danger, all it took was a trip or a stumble and it was all over. When *The Jim Grin* spat me off, I wasn't expecting it at all, doing the route should have been a formality, like driving the car. I wouldn't have said that I was complacent, in fact I've suggested that my intuition was at work, but I chose to override it and nearly curtailed my climbing for good. Perhaps there are some lessons to take from this. Sometimes the safer we think we are, the reality can be that we are actually more at risk. .

If things don't feel right, they're probably not.

The Nature of Reflection

During the months that I worked on this book it had a working title of 'Climbing Through The Looking Glass'. This seemed entirely appropriate as I found myself reliving and reflecting on a life not just spent in the vertical, but also considering what led me to pursue a passion that continues to this day.

Having worked professionally in the field of experiential learning and personal development for over twenty years I recognise that reflection is a powerful and dynamic stage in the whole learning and development cycle. The important word here is development which implies change, action or progression. Reflection is not just thinking about and musing on the past. To do this in isolation is to ignore the very things that give reflection its character and significance; the ability to re-frame thought and take action.

Stephen Kemmis is an eminent professor of educational research. When I read his thoughts on the nature of reflection published in 1985 in a book entitled; *Reflection: Turning Experience into Learning*, his words held a certain resonance with my own thinking.

I present a short paragraph from Professor Kemmis below in the hope that his words will provide context for the last chapter of this book , which is entitled *Climbing Through The Looking Glass* .

'We do not pause to reflect in a vacuum. We pause to reflect because some issue arises which demands that we stop and take stock or consider before we act. We do so because the situation we are in requires consideration: how we act in it is a matter of some significance. We become aware of ourselves, in some small or large way, as agents of history: we become aware that how we act will influence the course of events, at least for ourselves and usually for others too'.

Reflection: Turning Experience into Learning: Edited by D. Bout, R. Keogh, D. Walker, Publisher: Routledge; 1st edition (April 1985).

Chapter 15

Climbing Through the Looking Glass

Miraculous you call it babe
You ain't seen nothing yet'
They've got Pepsi in the Andes
McDonalds in Tibet
Yosemite's been turned into a golf course for the Japs
And the dead sea is alive with rap. It's a miracle.
Roger Waters, Amused to death.

Climbing has been a spiritual journey for me. Not spiritual in the religious sense, I use the word because climbing has taken me into places that seem to transcend normal interactions. I'm not suggesting that everyday life is mundane. I appreciate that for many, simply living from day to day is challenging enough. The fact I have spent such a large percentage of my waking life climbing rock was in part the stimulus behind this book. I was curious to see if the pursuit of a rather pointless pastime has taught me anything.

On the face of it, the reason I got hooked on climbing might seem the result of chance, but in reality my destiny to climb was shaped by childhood experiences. From an early age I had the freedom to play, roam and get up to mischief, unbound by some of the fetters that seem to define the society I find myself in today. Back in the '60s the adventure started as soon as you stepped over the threshold of your home. These early experiences shaped my inner values and discovering climbing later in my life reconnected me to something that was a fundamental part of my psyche. It seems to make sense to me now. If we find something that is harmonious with our deep-seated values, then we are more likely to be self-fulfilled.

We learn in many different ways and some are more powerful than others. As a kid growing up in and around Hemsworth, some of my childhood experiences left me under no illusions that the world was a dangerous place. I deemed that risks associated with climbing pylons or trees were worth taking and indeed were part of my childhood culture. I had near misses and scares during these escapades, but I was learning through experience and I think it had a powerful impact on my development. I also learned that bad people existed in the world, men who would prey on others like the man who attacked me as a young child. There were others who seemed to have a scant regard for the life, like those who drowned their dogs in Sally Walsh's Dam. This didn't make me paranoid, or make me a prisoner of imposed fear, it simply raised my awareness of dangers and stripped away innocent naivety. With the guidance of my parents and family, some of these lessons instilled in me a sense of right and wrong, good and bad. But above all, I think these early experiences gave me a bit of 'nous'.

I have met people purportedly possessing good intelligence. People adept at analysis and theorising, good at calculus, with heads full of facts, yet when given a simple practical problem, these same individuals can often demonstrate a stark lack of common sense. Others, on the other hand, will openly confess their inability to intellectualize, yet, approach life, relationships and environment in a naturally intelligent way. They possess common sense, show respect where respect is due and demonstrate wisdom. These in my book are some of the hallmarks associated with survival and harmony.

I don't think education and teaching in the classroom can teach us common sense, it can't be learned from books. I think it is learned through the hurly burly, ups and downs, and knocks of early childhood development

Today in the UK, the lifestyle that my generation experienced growing up in the '60s has changed. Urbanisation, social practices and, fear, occasionally real, but often perceived, have meant that we approach life differently. I have three children who have shared my own love of the great outdoors for the entirety of their short lives. My wife and I both believe that the outdoor experience brings a sense of wellbeing and fulfilment that can exceed the short-term fix associated with materialism. We try to encourage our children to learn, to value these experiences, but I still observe how easy and addictive modern technology is. Computers and social networking sites seduce them away from the raw natural environment. This leaves me to speculate what path my own kids will take in the future.

As a parent I try and balance our own children's appreciation of the world by exposing them to the pleasures of our natural environment. I think that this is made a little easier because I live in rural England, on the very backbone of the Pennines surrounded by fields and wild moorland. Yet it is clear by talking to our children, that many of their peers are being encouraged by an increasingly materialistic culture to place stuff, rather than experience at the top of their values list. It would seem that the next generation are destined to lead increasingly virtual lives. As soon as they come in from school my own children gravitate to the computer and can, if allowed, immerse themselves in a virtual world for hours on end.

I'm certainly no Luddite. I use most technological innovations to make my life easier, but I also think that there is a danger in that these supposed advancements could denude us of knowledge and inherent abilities built up over generations. How long will it be before we lose our innate sense of direction, or our learned ability to navigate as the sexy voice on the Sat Nav system continues to advise us to turn left and right. It's a fact of life that things advance. Few people today still use the stars to navigate. I'm not opposed to change. The point I'm making is that there is the risk that heavy dependence on modern technologies can impact on the way our minds actually work. I can foresee a future where we lose the ability to problem solve, or become oblivious of danger, or bring up kids with no common sense.

Today in the UK we seem to be adopting an American litigation culture. At school our children are being denied long time traditions. Playing conkers, throwing snowballs, or playing out if it becomes too icy is now considered too risky. This winter my own kids were sent home from school because it was deemed too icy and the poor little blighters might slip over and hurt themselves. Fear is driving policy and common sense is being thrown out of the window. I'm not saying that the Health and Safety Executive doesn't have a place in today's society, far from it. It has undoubtedly saved countless lives and injuries and continues to protect many from unacceptable risk. The critical thing for me, is that we need to accept that the environment we live in does have hazards. Rather than creating a culture that thinks it can cocoon itself in a world that is free from danger, let us learn to tune in to these hazards.

In my view, risk assessment should be an intrinsic and well-developed mental process, something that becomes an instinctive or intuitive part of our cognition. For this to happen we need to experience the mishaps, near misses and knocks that are associated with danger first-hand. This can be a powerful survival mechanism particularly if developed during our childhood. To deny it, I think we are depriving ourselves of an important human attribute. I think there is a caveat to add, however. We need to heighten our inner radar, recognise when our intuition is at work and know when to listen to it. I think this is easy to say, but even with practice it's by no means foolproof. I think my intuition was at work when I broke my arm and damaged my shoulder at *Troller's Gill*. I was aware that something didn't feel right, but chose to override these feelings. In simple terms, on that occasion I let my head rule my gut.

When I talk about intuition, I'm not referring to what coaches term the inner game. The inner game is about all the things going on that interfere with performance. Things like fear, self-doubt, trying too hard etc. It's the internal dialogue that goes on in our heads and this can often have a negative impact on performance, particularly in sport. The job of the Coach is to help the athlete understand what the interference is and then help them to devise tactics to eliminate it. Unlike golfers, or tennis players, climbers sometimes have additional issues to deal with. On occasion, climbers sometimes find themselves in situations where they've pushed the boat out a little too far and overstepped their ability. In these situations it's not just worry about the state of your game. Here a mistake can result in real injury. I've found myself in such situations and it can be very frightening indeed when you suddenly become aware of the place you're in. In such situations you either learn to deal with the internal dialogue, or suffer the consequences. The key difference between the inner game and intuition is that usually we are very aware of mental interference. Intuition is much more subtle.

The great psychologist, Carl Gustav Jung, described intuition as the sixth sense. But clearly we only have five senses, so what was Jung talking about? In nature we are bombarded with information. Our brain receives this information simultaneously, things we see; smells; noises etc., I'm sure many of us are familiar with the smell of newly mown grass experience. The sensation can transport us to another place and time. The olfactory stimulus appears to trigger patterns in the brain that evoke stored memories. I think this is an example of the intuition at work. Maybe climbing experiences are stored as memory bundles, or neural patterns in the brain. When these are triggered by a related, or associated external stimulus it might influence how we evaluate the situation and ultimately our choice of decision. It's all speculative stuff, of course, but when I look back and reflect on a lifetime of climbing, the evidence seems to substantiate that for me at least, there is something tangible about intuition.

A real incident springs to mind here. Back in the mid '80s, Adrian Ledgway and I were intent on climbing the Cordier Pillar on the Grand Charmoz. We checked the Météo in Chamonix's high street. The barometer arrow was green, the pressure was rising and the outlook was for fair weather. We gathered our gear and caught the cable car in the afternoon, deciding to bivouac below the pillar and make a rapid lightweight ascent the following day. At first light we crossed the bergschrund and started on the route. We'd not been going long when I turned to Ledge, 'This might sound a bit weird, but things just don't feel right'.

'Yeah I know what you mean,' agreed Ledge.

With that we bailed out and abseiled back to the base of the route. It looked like it was going to be a beautiful sunny summer's day. Our decision to abandon the climb was very irrational, but that's what we did. Back in Chamonix we rued our decision as we sat drinking beer under a clear blue sky. Later that day a storm blew in and the whole of the Aiguilles disappeared under a blanket of thick cloud and the heavens opened. We calculated that had we continued our climb that day, we would have been nearing the top of the pillar when the storm struck. It raged for the next twenty four hours and when it finally cleared the Aiguilles were plastered in snow, had we been caught I think it would have been pretty ugly. Was our decision to bail out luck? Or was something else at play on this occasion?

I work with industries that, rightly so, major on health and safety at work. I've worked with young apprentices and new graduate recruits who, as part of their induction, are taught how to make risk assessments. At times I have been shocked at the lack of common sense that certain individuals demonstrate. When I've spoken to them at length it's often transpired that these individuals have led what might be called sheltered upbringings. I'm not knocking the practice of teaching risk assessment; it is necessary. What I'm highlighting is the natural instinctive approach to risk that is developed as we grow and interact with our environment.

My experiences through climbing suggest that we are often safer in the presence of overt hazard, than in situations which on the surface appear safe. This is because we are usually acutely tuned-in when danger is apparent and we manage the situation as best we can with the knowledge and skills available to us at the time. If, in addition, we also listen to our gut feel, perhaps we not only make analytically sound decisions, but also emotionally intelligent ones. We manage the stress and fear rather than letting the fear dictate our path. There is a paradox with this of course. If we are to be acutely tuned in to danger, we also need to experience it first-hand and this is counter-intuitive.

In the mountains, no amount of intuition or previous experience can predict the maverick falling rock, avalanche or collapsing sérac, We might conclude from this, that when your number's up, it's simply down to the luck of the draw. Or is it? I recall one instance when we were climbing at Scimitar Ridge in the Llanberis Pass. We started to make base camp on a little level area directly below the crag. Dave Barton suddenly decided he didn't like our location and spoke up, 'I don't like it here, let's move over there where we'll get more sun.'

We all agreed with his observation and moved away from the crag to another convenient spot. No sooner had we'd moved, than a huge rock about the size of a breeze block fell from the top of the crag. It landed in the exact spot where we had been a few minutes earlier. I asked Dave what was behind his suggestion to move. He said he couldn't really explain it. It just didn't feel right where we were. I've shared many experiences with Dave, both in the mountains and in everyday life. I've learned that when he expresses that something doesn't feel right, then it's time to do something about it. Dave used to climb with the great mountaineer Don Whillans, and even made an early attempt on the Eiger's North Face with Don. Dave says that Whillans also had an uncanny knack of listening to his gut and not just in the beer swilling sense. Don's powerful intuition certainly influenced some of his mountaineering decisions.

Maybe as we've evolved over the eons as tool users and technologists, the mental processes that predispose us to these traits have come to dominate how our mind works. We prefer to listen to our more reliable mental processes to such an extent that reliance on our intuition, or gut feel, is overridden or squeezed out.

As we develop, hopefully we continue to strive to learn and discover new things. There are some clear motives after all, one of them being that we need everything going for us in order to survive in a competitive and sometimes hostile environment. So can climbing help with our own personal development? I think it can and it also relates to how we make decisions, how we behave and the consequences of that behaviour.

Research highlights the importance that emotions play in our behaviour. An obvious and simple example is the part played by adrenaline in fight or flight survival response. Simplistically speaking this is an evolutionary mechanism that enables us to assess whether, am I its prey or is it my prey?

In survival terms such situations warrant a speedy response. We certainly don't want to be mulling things over when faced with a big predator, or where a speedy response can provide us with a needy meal. It's useful to understand a little bit about our mental processes that govern such behaviour. A primitive part of the brain called the Amygdala plays a crucial role in emergency situations. Our prefrontal lobes house our decision-making centre and are connected to the Amygdala by a neural superhighway. The Amygdala is the brain's emotional memory bank and holds all our moments of triumph and failure, fear and frustration. It uses these stored memories in its function as the brain's alarm system, scanning information from moment to moment to assess for threats by matching what's happening now to the stored templates of our past experience. When the Amygdala is triggered the thinking brain is short-circuited and the hypothalamus stimulates the release of hormones. The result is a spontaneous behavioural reaction. Run like hell, or throw your spear. The point of relevance here is that the brain's ancient crisis response is not always appropriate to situations that we find ourselves in today and when triggered can have drawbacks. An extreme example might look something like this. A driver is ambling calmly along the road when suddenly another ca starts tailgating them and flashing its lights. Suddenly the driver in front slams on his brakes, stops the car and drags the other driver out and beats twelve bells out of him. Afterwards in police custody, the assailant can't explain his irrational behaviour, but feels a great sense of regret and also has to suffer a charge of GBH. What has happened in this example is that the Amygdala has interpreted the tailgating behaviour as a physical attack and the response is to attack back, before the thinking brain has had chance to take control. This is called an Amygdala Hijack and a whole range of factors can trigger such a response. There is a current school of thinking that suggests if we are able to identify our personal triggers and are in touch with our emotions, then we can use them to manage our behaviour and the behaviour of others to greater advantage. Simplistically this is called emotional intelligence.

In climbing we place ourselves in situations where raw emotion is an ever-present factor. Fear of falling, joy of success, depression from failure, frustration of being unable to do a move, climbing is capable of creating massive highs and lows. And to get on with climbing you've got to develop the ability to manage the emotional aspects well. I think the addictive nature of climbing, or indeed any extreme activity, is inextricably linked to emotions and the part that hormones and endorphins play. Whether climbers develop high levels of emotional intelligence is hard to say, but a lot of climbers who I've seen working under pressure and stress, outside their comfort zones, tend to manage themselves coolly and still make rational decisions. These are hallmarks of emotionally intelligent behaviour.

The concept of emotional intelligence is not a new one. As Aristotle put it in the Nichomachean Ethics written in 350 BC:

> Anyone can become angry, that is easy. But to be angry with the right person, to the right degree, at the right time, for the right purpose and in the right way – this is not easy.

Maybe another way of thinking about Aristotle's observation is that from time to time we all get shit scared. The key attribute is developing the ability to channel the fear in the right direction, at the right time to get the right result. This ability could be a real lifesaver, but I suspect it's also hard learned. Professionals working in the field of emotional intelligence advocate strongly that it can be learned and developed. I would concur with this view based simply on some of my own personal experiences whilst climbing. Whatever one's view about emotional intelligence, I think any attribute that tempers counter-productive irrational behaviour, or allows us to consciously fuel our passion, must complement our intellect and give us a more balanced and heightened level of overall intelligence.

Experiences growing up, undoubtedly etched my subconscious with values that hold important meaning for me today. I recognise that one of these values is freedom. As a child I was allowed considerable freedom to roam, as I explored, I chose to take risks, but it wasn't about courting danger it was more about breaking rules. I knew I shouldn't climb pylons, the signs at their base made that all too clear. When someone said you couldn't do something, a voice in my head said, who says so?

From an early age I think I had a clear sense of what was right and wrong, good and bad. I'd had good parenting and had witnessed first-hand what bad people could get up to, but if it felt like I wasn't hurting anyone else, then I wanted to break the rules. I think what caused me such angst when I ran away from school at the tender age of nine was authority. Fundamentally, I think I felt my liberty was under threat, I felt too scared at the time to fight back, so instead I ran. Psychologists still debate personality, speculating whether it has its origins in genetics, or whether it is a cognitive function. Personally, I think it has its rudiments in nature, looking around at other species suggests to me that most inherit strong genetic memories. Whatever its root, whether nature or nurture, I developed an anarchistic streak as part of my personality that still lives with me today. I also suspect that this in part drew me towards climbing. I think that part of the appeal of climbing and why I connected with it so strongly is because it embodies, or should embody, freedom. This sense of freedom can also liberate the mind. For me, climbing is sometimes about consciously choosing to break some of society's norms. These norms are the accepted unwritten rules that we adopt to maintain the status quo. They can be strongly linked to fundamental values such as safety, security and compliance, which are clearly important, but I think the world also needs rule breakers, people who will buck the trend.

I have witnessed considerable change in the world of rock-climbing in the UK over the last thirty odd years, some of it very progressive, but the actions of some individuals can, I think, have potentially regressive consequences. Looking back, climbing has evolved by following traditions. People lead by example and set standards of performance. Those who come after follow the example, but sometimes strive to raise the bar, do things better and so it evolves. Better, can be defined in many ways: standard of difficulty, style of ascent, concepts of boldness, etc. The interesting twist to the tale on some of our British cliffs has been the introduction and use of the bolt. On certain cliffs the bolt gained acceptance and a few individuals have really pushed the standards of sport climbing, and this has been a positive and progressive advance for this offshoot of climbing. Great feats of physical endurance and

Top: Joe Healey, Jerry Peel and Gaz Healey were a force to be reckoned with during the '80s captured here in 2000. *Photo: Mark Radtke.*

Below Left: Dawn Radtke and Donna Harridge enjoying the autumn colours of Fontainebleau. *Photo: Mark Radtke*

Below Right: Will Simm reaching for the pocket on the classic *Le Toit du Cul de Chien*, 7a. Fontainebleau. *Photo: Mark Radtke*

Top. Me and Ledge *Under the Influence*, E4 6a. The Castle, Pembroke.
Photo: Glenn Robbins c. 1990

Bottom Left: Atlanta Wall, Little Orme. I'm leading *Sacrifice* and to my left Mick Ryan is leading *Vitamin Sea*. *Photo: Glenn Robbins.*

Bottom Right: Glenn Robbins caught in front of the Camera c. 1991. *Photo: Mark Radtke.*

Top: Dave Barton on the classic *Forked Lightning Crack*, Heptonstall
Photo: Mark Radtke.

Bottom Left: Ian Cooksey on *A Step in the Light Green* during the first ascent.
Photo: Jane Cooksey.

Bottom Right. A young Geoff Hibbert committed on the bold *White Wand*, Stannage in the late '80s.
Photo: Mark Radtke.

Left to Right. Dave Barton wielding the drill, Chris Gibb, Jerry Peel and Grip the dog. Victoria Cave, Yorkshire. Taken during the sport climbing development of the crag in 1995. *Photo: Mark Radtke.*

Three photographs illustrating the shattered and sometimes loose rock that typifies parts of Gordale Scar.

Top: Roy Healey concentrating hard.
Photo: Mark Radtke.

Bottom Left: Jerry Peel and Mick Johnston making the second ascent of *The Thrivin'*. *Photo: Mark Radtke.*

Bottom Right: On the first ascent of *Revival* in 1991. *Photo: Craven Herald.*

Jerry Peel making the second ascent of Matt Troilett's *Washed Up*, E6 6b at Earl Crag. This was one of two variation finishes to Peel's original line of *Desert Island Arête* that were climbed by Troilett and Peel in 1999. *Photo: Mark Radtke.*

An ever expanding number of rock climbing destinations are available to the modern rock climber with styles and grades to suit everyone.

Above: Gilmore Peel enjoying 'holiday mode' climbing on the Greek island of Kalymnos. An attractive international climbing destination, but will it fall victim of its own success?
Photo: Mark Radtke.

Right: The spirits of old friends. Alan Bennett and Duncan Drake in heaven on the *Grande Arête*. Bellacombe. France.
Photo: Mark Radtke

I've always enjoyed taking pictures. This one capturing the sunrise over the Grande Jorrasses was one of my first to be published and graced the front cover of High magazine in May 1985. *Photo: Mark Radtke.*

athleticism are being demonstrated, mental stoicism and self-belief is evidence of personal development and this is all pioneering stuff. People continue to break records. We must remember, however, that this type of climbing is exactly what its name says, a sport.

In my humble personal opinion, I also think that the actions of a minority but influential group of climbers are also using the bolt regressively. Specifically on crags previously climbed by traditional methods that are now being bolted indiscriminately to produce sport climbing for the masses. I make no excuse for this personal view. It goes back to the point I raised earlier about social norms and rule breaking. People who wish to bolt crags wholesale are, I think, governed by a slightly different value set to me, values that nurture a sense of community, conformity and accessibility. There's nothing wrong with espousing such values of course, I think they are important guiding principles for civilisation. The issue for me is when these values are applied to climbing. It is here that I think they foster comfort zone mentality. This feeds a culture of pure recreation. Climbers feel that they are entitled to consume anything they want and this breeds an attitude that things ought to be easy. In such a culture, any real earned rite of passage achieved through hard work and fight, becomes secondary. Pioneering passion withers and ultimately people are destined to stagnate, happy to operate within their personal comfort zones. This is at odds with all the developmental, enlightening and creative benefits that climbing can yield.

Ironically, from my observations, the people who are at the forefront of these retro developments are the old stagers, some of who were real pioneers in their day. All I can think is that they now live on past memories and manipulate current climbing trends to satisfy weak wills. I think it's a matter of course that as we get older we also become softer, but we shouldn't allow this to undermine the potential for real progress.

Sport climbing is definitely more accessible than other forms of climbing. The novice sport climber can quickly get to grips with the challenge of climbing the rock without having to worry too much about hurting themselves. The skills required to reduce the hazards are learned easily compared to the craft needed by the trad climber for example. The safety apprenticeship can be short and the sport climber can focus on honing physical ability and technique. Gratification from success and achievement can be rapid. These are factors that in my opinion contribute to the appeal and popularity of sport climbing. The slight downside to this is the pressure that popularity exerts on our environment. More bolts, more climbers, more cars, more erosion, more damage. There is a real danger that the popularity of climbing can bring us into direct conflict with other stakeholders in our countryside. Farmers still work the land for a living and when lines of cars parked along country lanes begin interfering with their livelihood I understand their frustrations. Already in Yorkshire pressure from the sheer numbers of climbers visiting certain crags is jeopardising future access. I would argue that in a couple of cases at least, this is the direct result of recent bolting activity. I'm not arguing against sport climbing here, but making the more general point that sometimes we embark on a course of action without first considering the long term implications of our actions. Perhaps this is another example of the human trait that is consumerism.

Another concern about the negative impact of mass bolting is about the abstract concept of adventure as a finite resource. With modern transportation allowing speedy access across the globe and telecommunications that keep us abreast of current developments, we can argue that the world is becoming a smaller and smaller place. What used to be remote and wild places are increasingly accessible to more and more people and consequently people feel the need to look to remoter places to satisfy their desires. When I was a child natural inquisitiveness led me down the garden path into a natural world of adventure and discovery. I started climbing in Yorkshire and learned my craft, and craft it was, through a self-taught apprenticeship on crags where the only waymarkers were the features of the rock itself. This form of rock climbing was genuine exploration and I was able to satisfy my modest spirit for adventure with rewarding personal experiences. Many of these crags are now peppered with bolts and their character is changed. My view is that we are denuding ourselves of a precious resource that is adventure. I think we should preserve the potential for exploration that the crags in our own back yard offer us, rather than continuing to destroy it. Selfishly, I could say, why bother, I experienced it first-hand in my day and got my fair-share of self-fulfilment out of it. I could also argue that the kids graduating from indoor climbing walls today need to apply newly acquired skills outside, and these bolted crags with their moderately graded safe routes provide the perfect vehicle for this. I don't subscribe to this, however. On the contrary, I take the view that if we have attained some wisdom through our life experiences, then we have a duty to mentor those who follow rather than simply dictating what is available to them through our own short-sighted actions.

Regressive bolting is not confined to crags in Britain, examples can be found across the globe. In mainland Europe professional mountain guides advocate the placing of bolts at the belays of classic Alpine routes, like the *Cassin* on the Piz Badile. They justify this by saying it is in the interests of safety to themselves and their clients. In reality, commercialism and convenience is driving things here, and for good or bad, it is at risk of completely changing the nature of the climbing experience on such routes. When I climbed The Fire Tower in Spain and encountered retro bolts on a route that had been climbed over thirty years earlier without, I was glad of them. Similarly bolts that have been added to the belays of the *Hasse* on the Cima Grande gave us an extra degree of added comfort. Despite welcoming the presence of these bolts I still uphold the view that these routes would have provided a more rewarding experience without them. There is also another consideration. As human beings we need challenge and if we can prevail and overcome the challenges we set ourselves then it gives us the power to learn, develop and progress.

Bolts now protect sections of guided routes on Everest. I have read the arguments seeking to justify these actions. Personally, I can see and accept the pragmatic logic behind replacing the odd dodgy peg or frozen-in rope with a reliable anchor that can preserve life. Yet when I read advocates of such actions wrapping it all up by saying that, the mountain is now a COMMERCIAL mountain, then I am saddened. It would seem that some professional mountaineers hold the opinion that because they choose the mountain environment as their place of work, they also maintain the view that they have the right to alter it to suit their own needs. I don't think this is right and I think what these people are really saying is, 'We don't give a shit as long as we're lining our pockets.' Yet can I justify such opinion having just written several paragraphs espousing the value of personal freedom and the right to make individual choices? I think that when we take action in whatever walk of life, we need to consider whether it is progressive and can move us forward, or whether it is undermining or devaluing something that we have already achieved. Some people would argue that all this stuff about bolting and removing unnecessary risk is for the better, but I think we need to ask ourselves what does better mean and is better always right?

The sheer amount of time spent living outdoors, touching rock and getting dirty with the elements has undoubtedly brought me closer to nature. I know that I am a part of nature and not above it. Climbing has allowed me to explore my own fallibilities and shortcomings. Failure has occasionally resulted in one or two broken bones, but more often a bruised ego has been the more painful. It has provided the opportunity to satisfy creative urges as in my own mind's eye I have painted new routes on canvases of rock. Such self-expression is important to no one other than myself, but this has brought me inner satisfaction. Climbing has also taken me on a journey in a very physical sense. Without it, I'm sure my experience of counties, countries and continents would have been far less. It has also facilitated self-exploration and through this I have been fortunate to feel fleeting sensations of self-fulfilment. I have been privileged to experience first-hand what it feels like to place your life in someone else's hands and what it means when someone else trusts you implicitly. I think I understand why we have a sense of humour. It's a survival mechanism used to re-frame things when we're faced with situations of hopelessness, or unparalleled despair.

So what have I learned from climbing and what is the point of it? In answer to the latter question I would like to quote an elderly gentleman of about eighty years who I bumped into whilst on a road trip across North America. We were stocking up on some groceries from the local store at City of Rocks in Idaho. The elderly gent obviously intrigued by our English accents enquired about the purpose of our visit.

'We're here on a rock-climbing trip,' we dutifully informed the man. Without batting an eyelid he simply said, 'Well I guess that's what God put them rocks there for, to be climbed on.'

It seemed as good an observation as any to me.

My good friend Mick Johnston has a slightly broader, philosophical take on the value of climbing.

To quote Mick:

> 'We don't own anything in this world, we're just caretakers, renting and looking after things until we're gone, so why not just do something powerful that lets us enjoy the moment.'

It is easy to think of climbing as a pointless or futile activity, but from my experiences I can conclude that it is far from either. It is simply a very easy and very beautiful means to the end.

Postscript

'A Small Gift From Nature'

Arnaud Petit Spring 2011

Having completed this book, I felt that I couldn't put the pen down without first making some comments about the remarkable achievement of French rock-climbing ace, Arnaud Petit. His achievement was brought to my attention through a short documentary that I watched recently on the Internet. The film captures the man doing the sort of physical stuff that is fairly commonplace by today's climbing elite. It features great photography, beautiful rock and superb climbing, but what makes it remarkable is that Petit has chosen to make an ascent of a world-class sport route, but in traditional style. *Black Bean* is an impressive line at the French jewel of Céüse. It tackles an eighty metre overhanging wall, holds a grade of F8b and in Petit's own words 'is perhaps one of the best climbs of its grade in the world'. Petit had climbed the route in its original bolted form, but in so doing, became captured by the thought that he might be able to climb the route using only natural protection. In the spring of 2011 he fulfilled this personal quest leading the climb in one long pitch using modern cams, a sling and a few nuts to protect his passage. The film shows Petit in action on the route and as he climbs his voiceover provides great insight into the nature of the challenge.

I haven't reproduced the full transcript of the voiceover here, but just a few of my favourite sound bites.

'The route is 65 metres long and there are nine spots for protection.'
'The route is not a solo, but for sure there are places that you must not fall.'
'At 8 metres I place my first protection two small Totemcams, not bad.'

He climbs on, placing a further three cams at around the 15 metre mark

203

which are less than inspiring. Above these he finds…

'Here is a gift from nature, a small thread that is just solid enough.'

From here Petit has to run it out climbing on sloping holds. At around thirty metres Petit is about halfway up the climb. He arrives at a large handhold, places what he describes as the first truly solid protection and hanging from the large hold proceeds to haul more gear that he'll use on the upper part of the route. He then begins the crux of the climb, an intense fifteen metres section.

'I start the thirteen moves a really hard section, the first crux of *Black Bean.*'

He places a solitary cam in a hole that partially fills the best hold in the middle of this testing crux section and presses on to the second crux of the climb.

'This second crux ends in a delicate traverse on small footholds. It's a bit stressful because if I fall here and the cam below pops, I can touch the ground.'

Fortunately Petit manages the second crux and arrives at another large pocket.

'I arrive at a real rest and place two cams, really solid. It's important because the next piece of gear is fifteen metres higher.'

Petit duly arrives at a flake and places a couple of cams behind the hollow sounding feature, and sets off up to tackle the last bit of F7c climbing before the route eases back to a more amenable grade.

'The climbing is much easier only 7a, but I have to climb really carefully otherwise I'm in for a thirty metre fall… and that's if the flake holds.'

As I watched the film it evoked powerful emotions. Gut-wrenching fear as I fantasised about making that journey myself, pure excitement as I listened to his 'matter of fact' voiceover revealing the mettle of the man. Admiration not just for his prowess as a climber, but for what he appeared to value and believe in. I really connected with what Arnaud Petit was doing. I don't get the impression that Petit is trying to set some sort of ethical precedence with his boltless ascent, although he does confess that it would have been an even more exciting challenge had the route been 'virgin'. What interested me is how Petit took what might be construed as a pretty abstract concept and turned it into reality. This provides us with some insight into the question of why? I think here Petit demonstrates that by believing in possibility he is able to achieve something which transcends that which convention would normally dictate. Has he proved anything with his unconventional ascent of *Black Bean*? There are some crass observations that we can make about this climb, but if we look beyond the obvious, I think we can draw some more philosophical conclusions. I would even go as far as saying that by breaking with convention Arnaud Petit has provided a snippet of proof that one or two of the hypotheses presented in earlier chapters may hold some validity. Has he raised the bar and set an example that others will follow? I suspect that will all be down to the choices of an inquisitive few. What I think is important, is how we interpret Petit's motivation and what he has acheived. When people break with accepted norms and do something different, even if it is just an act of self-expression, it can give us great food for thought. In my opinion Petit has demonstrated a bit of creative inspiration, an attribute which I feel expands our thinking and if we allow it to, enables us to re-frame our take on the way we do things. I also take reassurance from the fact that such an inspirational guy like Arnaud Petit is willing to communicate so graphically, that he is really in touch with the fundamental essence of the climbing experience.

Glossary

A range of climbing related, or colloquial terms occur throughout the narrative. Some will be self explanatory when read in the context of the sentence in which they occur. Most seasoned climbers will be familiar with the terminology. This glossary and the explanatory notes in the following section, are included for the benefit of those readers less familiar with some of the climbing specific terminology.

Arête – Where two rock walls meet to form a sharp edge. An arête can be at any angle from horizontal through to overhanging. A particularly large or long arête could be described as a sharp ridge.

Bachar Ladder – A rope ladder strung under tension at an angle of about 120 degrees and used to train arm and upper body strength. The climber hangs on the underside of the ladder and makes upward progress between the rungs without using feet. In its purist form the exercise requiring the climber to make a series of repeated one-arm pull-ups alternating between arms. The process is repeated on the descent. The technique was adopted by many during the '80s, but overuse led to several noted climbers developing serious shoulder and elbow problems. Developed by legendary American rock climber and soloist – the late John Bachar.

Bergschrund – A crevasse that is formed where a glacier meets a cliff face

Beta – Information or knowledge sometimes collated by climbers prior to making an ascent of a traditional climb, usually to help improve safety. Obtaining beta about a sport route can increase the chances of making a flash ascent, but voids the concept of the on-sight flash.

Bolts, bolt runners, bolt belays – Permanent steel anchors drilled into the rock to which a metal plate called a bolt hanger is attached using a permanent locking nut, The hanger sits flush to the rock and a karabiner or a quickdraw can be clipped through it and attached to the rope. Various bolt designs and fixing mechanisms have been developed for rock-climbing most having their origins in the construction industry. In the UK 10mm diameter stainless steel expansion bolts are commonly used. These are known as mechanical fixings. In certain rock types bolts are glued in place using construction strength resin. These are referred to as chemical fixings. Generally bolts are regarded as bombproof.

Bomber, Bombproof – Used when referring to gear or protection that is unlikely to fail in the event of a long fall onto it. Derived from the concept of being strong enough to withstand the blast of a bomb, the complete opposite of poor, token, marginal, crap, or morale boosting.

Camming device – A piece of climbing equipment used as protection. The device can be inserted into cracks in the rock. It utilises spring loaded cams that expand against the sides of the crack holding it securely in place. The original versions were called Friends and came onto the market in the 1970s. Versions from different manufacturers are now available, such as Camalots. These devices come in different sizes ranging from those that will fit into cracks less than a centimetre wide increasing up to those that will fit into cracks of around 15cm wide.

Camalots – refer to camming device.

Campus – Used to describe a specific climbing move usually on overhanging rock which involves moving from one finger edge to another without using feet on the rock. The term originates from an indoor training facility used to develop finger and upper body strength.

Choss – Loose and broken, rubble-like. Used to denote poor quality rock.

Cragging – Used to describe rock-climbing on smaller cliffs as opposed to long multi-pitch climbs, or mountaineering. Can infer a less serious or committing form of rock-climbing.

Crash Pad – A portable matt filled with high density foam. It is usually about 20cm thick and used at the base of boulder problems to soften the impact of the climbers' fall.

Diedre – Where the rock walls meet to form a corner, or gully.

Dyno, Dynamic slap – An unconventional, but sometimes necessary climbing move. To move dynamically from one hold to another. To dyno means generating momentum of the body. A single dyno – to leap for and catch a hold with one hand. A double dyno – to leap for and catch a hold with both hands simultaneously. A slap could be described as a mini dyno.

Fingery – A term used to describe a passage over the rock where the holds are small, usually of fingertip size or less. Sometimes also referred to as, thin. Often associated with a difficult section of the climb.

Flashed – To have climbed a route bottom to top without falling, or using gear as direct assistance as a rest, or to assist progress.

Friends – Refer to Camming device.

Gear – Generic term used to describe the array of equipment carried by the climber. Often used in specific reference to those pieces of equipment used to place in the rock to protect the climber's passage. Also referred to as protection or pro. A vast array of ingenious designs from many manufacturers are now available on the market. Several are still commonly referred to by the names of the objects that gave rise to these contemporary pieces of equipment such as: Nuts, Wires, Stoppers, Chocks, RPs, Cams, Rocks, Hexentrics, Pegs.

Highball – Used in bouldering to denote that the problem is unusually high and the consequences of falling could be serious. The use of multiple crash pads can reduce the hazards.

Hilti Battery Drill – One brand of cordless electric hammer drill used for drilling holes in the rock to take permanent steel expansion bolts used as protection in sport climbs.

Hexentrics – Refer to Gear.

Ironmongery – An encompassing term used to describe permanent or semi permanent gear left in the rock by aid climbers. Also used to describe the metal pegs, or pitons that can be hammered into cracks in the rock used by aid climbers.

Jug – A large hold on the rock, derived from the concept of jug handle, therefore easy to hang from or pull up on.

Karabiner (also referred to as Carabiner) – An alloy link with a spring loaded gate used for clipping pieces of gear together. The karabiner is the piece of gear that is used to connect pieces of protection to the climbing rope allowing it to run fluidly between the lead climber and belayer.

Kevlar – The roped version of the polymer used as an alternative to wire for threading chocks. Refer to wires and gear.

Laybacking – A form of climbing move.

Living end – A quirky term that could be likened to living in hell.

Lucky stoppers – A term of affection bestowed on personal bits of gear that have earned the term on previous occasions.

Match, Matched – To share one hold with both hands simultaneously.

Météo – Weather forecast in France.

Névé – Hard, compact snow.

On-sight – To start a climb with no prior knowledge, or minimal knowledge about it.

One-arm Lock Off – The ability to hold the body statically in place at the end of a one-arm pull up. Requires considerable physical strength and power. On certain climbs and boulder problems where the terrain is so steep that feet become redundant, this ability may be the only way to do the move and could be the difference between success and failure.

Pegs, Pitons – Steel pegs with a circular hole or eye at one end that will accommodate a karabiner. They come in many different thicknesses and lengths and are hammered into cracks and holes on the rock. Commonly used pre and post WW2 before the development of modern protection devices. Still commonly used in aid climbing, or where they form a better, or more ethically acceptable alternative to other forms of protection.

Poff – A small porous cloth bag containing dried pine resin. Originated and still used in the bouldering areas around Fontainebleau. Is used to dry and add friction to finger tips.

Pumpy – When the nature of the climbing fills the forearms with lactic acid, making it increasingly difficult to hold on. See also Fingery.

Quickdraw – Two karabiners attached to each other with a short sewn sling. Used to connect the rope to protection in the rock. Originated in the '80s based on the concept of drawing a gun from a holster. It provides the climber with a more efficient method of clipping the rope into protection saving time and energy during the ascent. It also allows the rope to run freely between the lead climber and second, enabling more effective rope management.

Rack – The collective term used to describe the whole array of climbing equipment carried on the climber's harness during an ascent.

Rock over – A climbing move where one foot is placed on a high foothold usually above waist height and then the body is pulled dynamically up so that the centre of gravity is quickly transferred over the foot.

Runner, Running belay – Where the rope runs through a piece of protection in the rock or ice. See also Karabiner.

Redpoint – Where a route is climbed successfully after rehearsal and practice. Originated by the legendary German climber – the late Kurt Albert, who in the '70s was influential in promoting a free climbing ethic in Germany. When he climbed former aid routes free, he adopted the practice of painting a red dot on the rock at the base of the climb to denote that the route had been climbed free bottom to top in one single push. This was known as the Rot Punkt, and became accepted as a superior style of ascent to other forms that were commonly used during a period of changing ethics and standards.

Scree – The heaps of loose and shattered stone accumulated over the millennia that commonly litter the hillsides beneath mountain crags.

Sling – A loop of rope or sewn tape with a variety of versatile uses in safeguarding the climber's passage. Usually forms part of the climber's rack.

Sequency – Where a specific combination of holds or a set sequence of moves have to be followed in order to climb a section of the route.

Séracs – Large towers of ice of unpredictable stability usually found on glaciers where the ice is thrown into chaotic upheaval by the contours of the earth beneath it.

Set of cams – Refer to Camming device, gear.

Skyhook – A small steel hook that can be place over a sharp rock edge and can hold a climber's body weight. Designed for aiding climbers to enable them to hang on sections of rock that will not, other than by drilling, accommodate any other forms of protection.

Sloper – Description of a hold on the rock that has no positive attributes such as edges to it. Imagine an inflated balloon, if it were rock it might be described as a sloper.

Sloping layaway – A vertical sloping hold

Smearing – A technique of using the feet to create friction and prevent slippage on severely sloping foot holds. Refer to Sloper

Snarg – A brand of ice screw popular in the '80s. Now superseded by new alloys and improved designs

Sticht plate – A device that climbers use to belay each other.

Tat – Bits of rope or nylon tape threaded behind flakes of rock and left in place as permanent protection. Sometimes left attached to permanent fixed gear such as old pegs.

Thank God Nut – A piece of protection that offers sanctuary at the end of a particularly hard and hazardous section of a climb.

Thrutch, Thrutches, Thrutching – Colloquial climbing terminology often used to describe upward movement in rock features such as wide cracks and tight chimneys. These features often necessitate that the climber's whole body or a significant part of it is wedged within its depths. Upward progress often requires a sort of strenuous upward shuffling, more akin to techniques used when caving.

Topo – A Topographical guidebook. Climbing guides which illustrate the line taken by routes using diagrams, or photographs as opposed to narrative descriptions.

Udge, Udges – See Thrutch

Whipper – Colloquial term for a long or violent fall. Imagine the crack of whip.

Wires – Alloy wedges also called chocks and Rocks fixed to a wire loop about 14cm in length. With skill these can be inserted into cracks in the rock and used as temporary runners to safeguard the climber's passage. The alloy wedge end of the wires are manufactured in a range of sizes from micro versions of about 2mm in thickness to much stronger versions in excess of 4cm in thickness. Refer also to Gear

Explanatory Notes

Types of Climbing

I cover five types of climbing in this book, traditional rock-climbing, sport climbing, artificial climbing, bouldering and ice-climbing. I thought it would be helpful to highlight some of the unique characteristics of each.

Traditional Rock Climbing

Traditional rock-climbing is commonly referred to as *Trad*. This is the form of rock-climbing that most people will conjure up in their mind's eye when they visualise climbing. Imagine two climbers arriving at the base of a cliff face, armed with rope and an assortment of climbing gear. One climber ties into the rope and using hands and feet begins to climb, after ten feet or so the climber finds a natural flake, or spike of rock protruding from the wall. The climber carries specially designed slings that can be placed over such spikes and can be attached to the rope using lightweight karabiners of immense strength. Once the rope is clipped into one of these *runners* they are temporarily safe-guarded. If the lead climber happened to fall at this point their partner, or *belayer,* will hold them from below and prevent them falling to the ground, providing, of course, the rock spike is strong enough to hold the climber's weight. The climber has no wish to fall, since the aim in climbing is to progress up the rock as fluidly and safely as possible. The leader continues to climb on in the hope that they will find spikes, cracks and holes in the rock, that will accommodate not just slings, but also an array of other neat little devices specifically designed to provide temporary runners in the rock. This gear is referred to as *pro*. Sometimes pro is *bombproof* and the climber can judge that it would hold a considerable fall from above. At other times its security can be doubtful and the lead climber has to deal with the mental pressure posed by such risk. When the lead climber arrives at the top of the route they fasten themselves securely to the cliff at what is called a *belay* and bring the second climber up. As the second person climbs, safe-guarded by the rope from above he retrieves all the pro placed by the leader and arrives at the belay. This may be the top of the cliff and the climb is finished. Sometimes, however, climbs can be hundreds or even thousands of feet long. On such routes the climbers find intermediate ledges to belay on and in this fashion the climbers, if they are of equal ability, will share and alternate the lead and *leapfrog* up the face. This is a simple description of traditional or trad climbing, it is how rock-climbing started and evolved in the UK and, as the name implies, has some strong traditions associated with it. Unwritten rules and codes of practice govern climbers' attitudes, approaches and behaviour. Part of the appeal of trad climbing revolves around the subjective concepts of exploration, adventure and risk.

Sport Climbing

Sport climbing has its roots in mainland Europe and was introduced into the UK in the mid '80s. Sport climbing differs from trad climbing in a number of respects. Small rock anchors are placed as permanent fixtures in the rock. Specifically designed bolts are now commonly used that meet strict safety guidelines. Bolts are placed at regular intervals up the rock face and are regarded as bombproof. When the climber starts their chosen route they climb in the same manner as the trad climber, but rather than hoping they will find some pro on the climb, they embark in the knowledge they will pass bolt runners that will completely safeguard their passage. It is still the aim of the sport climber to get to the top of the route without falling off, but unlike the trad climber who sometimes risks the consequences of falling and fear of injury, sport climbing is considered to be much safer. If the sport climber falls, the consequences are merely that their attempt at the climb is temporarily thwarted. The attraction in this form of climbing comes from solving the physical and athletic challenge that the rock presents and is also derived from the aesthetics associated with movement over rock. It could be likened to a form of rock gymnastics, hence its terminology of *Sport Climbing*. In the UK sport climbing has been discouraged from crags where the frontiers of the sport have been pushed forward using traditional approaches. It has taken hold in those areas where it makes practical common sense to adopt the sport climbing approach.

Artificial Rock-Climbing

In trad climbing and sport climbing, the climber makes progress up the rock using hands and feet alone and only relies on pro and rope to stop them hitting the ground should they fall. Both these forms of climbing are referred to as *free climbing*. Imagine climbing a tree as a child, this constitutes free climbing.

Most people have climbed trees and invariably done so without a rope or other pro. In these cases not only have they climbed the tree free, they have done so in a style that would be described in rock-climbing terms as *free solo*. Artificial climbing is different from free climbing in that the climber actually pulls, hangs from, or rests on pro. Using such gear is described as aid climbing. In other words artificial aids are used to enable the climber to progress up the rock. This form of climbing is used in situations where the climber is physically unable, or not skilled enough to climb the rock free. In certain areas of the world, notably Yosemite Valley in California, the principles guiding the development of artificial climbing have created routes that embrace all the facets of adventure, risk and pioneering spirit. Such routes present extreme challenges, they demand the application of a different skill set to that of the free climber, but sometimes require the mental composure of the *free solo climber*.

Bouldering

Bouldering, as the name implies, is a genre of rock-climbing associated with climbing boulders or small pieces of rock as opposed to large cliffs and mountains. It was originally conceived as a means of testing how difficult moves on rock could be achieved. Practising such moves, which are at the limit of a persons' ability, near to the ground is useful preparation for overcoming such challenges on bigger routes such as trad climbs where the consequences of falling might be serious. Some climbers view bouldering as one of the purest forms of free rock-climbing that exists. Climbing without ropes or other gear to interrupt movement over rock. Success in this form of climbing requires application of strength, power, technique, and self-belief. The introduction of *the crash pad* in the early '90s meant that boulderers, more than ever before, could try ever-harder *boulder problems*. Today bouldering has progressed into an extremely popular sport in its own right. Its appeal lies in the challenge of trying to execute moves over rock that are at the limit of what is humanly possible. Like sport climbing some of the pleasure is derived from aesthetics.

Ice-Climbing

Ice-climbing employs all the principles associated in rock-climbing. In ice-climbing axes are used in the hands and crampons are attached to climbing boots. The *rack of gear*, or *pro*, is supplemented with sophisticated tubular screws that can be placed into the ice to act as runners. The hazards in ice climbing are determined by the weather, temperature, and condition of the ice itself. In perfect conditions ice-climbing can be likened to sport climbing, screws can be placed where one wishes and can be bombproof, making ascents for the skilled ice-climber fairly straightforward. In less favourable conditions, however, ice-climbing can have all the similarities of a very serious traditional climb with many hazards and real danger.

What's in a Grade

I refer to *grades* periodically within the narrative of this book and a little appreciation of what the grade of a climb conveys will provide some context for certain passages.

All climbs present challenges of varying difficulty and complexity. These can be physical, psychological, and technical, or a combination of all three. A particular climb or route may be obvious and relatively straightforward to follow. Like climbing a ladder. In climbing terminology this would be described as *easy to read*. The climb might have plenty of pro and be physically demanding. In this case it would be described as *safe, but strenuous*. Another route on the other hand could be less strenuous, but may be very bold and require strong psychological composure to deal with the risk. In this case the climb might be described as *delicate and serious*.

It may be obvious to *read* the moves on one particular sport climb, but its length and angle might demand lots of endurance by the climber, such a route would be described as *sustained*. Another may be less steep, but could be difficult to read, in this instance the route would be described as *technical*. Climbers have devised grading systems that aim to convey the combination of difficulties contained within the route. These grading systems differ depending on the type of climbing. Like language itself, they also vary from one country to the next.

Traditional Rock-Climbing Grades

The grading system used to describe traditional rock-climbing in the UK evolved as climbing developed. Imagine the early pioneers in the Victorian era seeking to challenge themselves by seeking steeper and ever steeper ways up mountains and cliffs. When the angle of the terrain demanded that hands had to be used to make upward progress it was described as steep scrambling. Where scrambles featured sections of steeper rock they were considered to be proper rock-climbs and were described, or graded as *Moderate or M*. The next category of difficulty was described as *Difficult or D*. As harder climbs were ascended a new classification called *Severe or S* was created. After this came *Very Severe or VS*. As climbers repeated established routes they discovered that there were variations within each category, some being slightly easier others slightly harder, so to encompass these variations, lower and upper levels of difficulty within each classification were created. Within the VS category for example, an easier VS climb was denoted with the prefix of *Mild*, whilst a

217

more difficult VS was given the prefix of *Hard*, so within the VS band there are three levels of ascending difficulty MVS, VS and HVS, this classification gives the experienced climber some idea of the likely difficulties they can encounter on the route. The grade attempts to provide an objective evaluation of the difficulty of a climb for the benefit of those wanting to attempt the route.

As described earlier, climbs vary in their *readability*, how to execute a particular move or sequence of moves is sometimes not obvious. This is referred to as the technical difficulty of the climb. Often a climb will have sections along the route, which are technically harder than others. A method of describing the technical difficulty within a climb was invented with the addition of a numerical system. This system was applied to easier graded climbs but really starts to add value at the VS grade where the moves start to become more complex to execute. The technical grading system currently runs from *1* increasing numerically to *7*. The number 4 roughly coincides with the VS category. Within each numeric banding there are three additional levels of technicality described as *a, b* or *c*. For illustrative purpose, when all this is put together around the Very Severe category of climb it gives the following combinations. MVS 4a, MVS 4b, MVS 4c, VS 4a, VS 4b, VS 4c. When we hit the HVS category the numeric grade increases to 5, so we get HVS 5a, HVS 5b, HVS 5c. This was the state of play up until ca 1940. In the '50s the levels of difficulty in rock climbing increased further and a new grade was required to describe these harder climbs. *The Extremely Difficult (ED)* grade was invented. As climbing standards were raised throughout the '50s '60s and '70s an open ended numeric system was adopted for the extreme grade starting at *E1* to describe the easiest extremes and increasing incrementally to E2, E3, E4 etc. The *E* grade attempts to describe elements such as the hazards within the climb as well as conveying factors such as the sustained or strenuous nature of the climbing. The numeric classification to describe the technical difficulty within the extreme category is retained, so as an example we might find a route given a grade of E5 5c or E5 6b or E6 6a or E6 6c. A climber about to tackle a climb with a grade of E5 5c might deduce the following: extreme difficulty at level five, but only 5c technically, since this is lower than what would normally be associated with an E5 climb it suggests that in all probability it is a serious route. On the other hand a climb of E5 6c might convey something like 6c suggests hard technical difficulties, yet the climb only gets the E5 grade. Conclusion, the most difficult bit of the climb is probably well-protected. This is a simplistic overview, but gives an indication that the climber can deduce quite a bit of information from the grade. Additional information about the climb is often provided with a brief narrative description contained within the guidebooks that log and record climbs. Any experienced climber will also gain a reasonable appraisal of the difficulties by looking up the route from below. Today the hardest extreme climbs in the UK are defined by a grade of E10 7a although such climbs can be counted on the fingers of one hand.

Sport Climbing Grades

Sport climbs adopt a similar grading principle to trad climbs. As suggested earlier, sport routes don't need to factor in the danger element and the grade aims to describe the overall difficulty of the route in terms of how sustained, powerful and technical it is. Easier sport routes start at grade 5 and currently the most difficult sport routes across the globe stand at grade 9. Once again there are three bands within each numeric category defined by letters a, b and c, but these letters do not have the same meaning as those used in the trad system. They simply represent a higher degree of overall difficulty within the numeric band. So we might encounter routes with grades 7a, 7b or 7c, the next incremental grade would be 8a and so on. The number in the sport grade is often prefixed with the letter F indicating *French*, which is largely accepted as the origin of the sport climb ing grade. The hardest sport climbs established to date are F9b and once again, like the top trad grade, they are still few and far between.

Artificial Rock-Climbing Grades

Artificial climbing uses a similar principle to the E grading system used in the trad classification. The letter A is used to represent artificial or *aid* and a number conveys the overall difficulty. Overall difficulty in artificial climbing embraces technical difficulty, seriousness and how strenuous the climbing is. A grade of A0 represents the easiest form of aid climbing, whilst a grade of A5 would suggest hard artificial climbing combining technical difficulty with serious hazards, such as the potential for long and dangerous falls. A6 and above would constitute climbing with risks on a par with, or sometimes greater than those faced by the free soloist.

Bouldering Grades

A number of different systems have been adopted for bouldering. Some people favour the *Font* numerical system that evolved in Fontainebleau, which is often viewed as the birthplace of modern bouldering whilst others prefer the *Vermin* or V grade from America. Both use an open-ended numerical system to give an indication of the overall difficulty of the boulder problem. The Vermin system starts at V0 and escalates in increments of 1. Current levels of difficulty have plateaued at about V15. The Font system starts at Font 3 and like the sport system uses three letter bands within the numeric grade. A V15 would equate to a Font 8c.

Ice-Climbing Grades

Ice-climbing follows a similar pattern to the UK E grade, but employs an open ended numeric system. Grade 1 and 2 would suggest steep angled snow, Grade 3 and 4 sections of steep ice, Grade 5 longer sections of vertical ice, Grade 6 sustained steep or overhanging ice, etc. Additional refinements to the grading system have been made to describe the seriousness and technicality of ice climbs.

Across Borders Grading

Different countries represent their grading with different letter or numeric representations, but all seek to achieve the same purpose. To give some insight into the likely challenges that might be found within the climb. This said, trying to create objectivity out of factors that can be very subjective presents a tough challenge in its own right. The saying 'one man's wine is another man's poison' springs to mind.

Climbing Styles – A Simple Overview

The style in which each individual chooses to undertake a climb is down to personal preference. However, some unwritten rules have evolved, as climbing has developed, that serve to set standards and guide the attitude and behaviour of the climber. Certain styles of ascent are deemed as being purer or superior than others and are based on the premise that the desire for personal challenge is a central motive of the climber. Overcoming challenge in a particular style is a reflection of standards.

There is some remarkable wildlife footage that shows baboons in Kenya. This particular troop of baboons has learned the skill of rock-climbing and the footage shows them ascending vertical cliffs over sixty feet in height. Clearly the apes have no ropes or gear used by their human counterparts yet they climb with skill, speed and agility. Their pursuit is not without risk and evidence suggests that accidents do happen and fatalities occur with these primates. What is their motivation? Escaping predators, search for food, pleasure, thrill seeking, who knows? This little example is a useful illustration of a form of rock-climbing mentioned earlier called *free soloing*. Some modern rock-climbers pursue this form of climbing and one or two talented individuals do so at the upper limits of possibility. The qualities of the climber operating at this level are impossible for me to describe here, but in my opinion this style of ascent is the one that might be described as *pure*. The risks associated with free soloing make it personally prohibitive for most and so many opt to use ropes and equipment that will reduce the risks of injury or death. I'm sure that many experienced climbers would agree that the purist approach in roped climbing when repeating established routes is to try the route armed only with the information that is provided in the guidebook. This approach is roughly described as *on sight* and is adopted so that wherever reasonably possible all the suspense and hidden challenge in a climb is retained and can be savoured by the would-be ascensionist. If this on-sight approach is followed and the climb is executed without falling off, or using pro to physically aid progress, then the style of ascent is roughly described as an *on-sight flash*. Once again the on-sight flash is regarded as a stylish form of ascent. If a climber falls or has to resort to resting on, or pulling on a piece of pro during the climb it is deemed as a failed or flawed attempt. The on-sight flash is relevant to all forms of climbing and is the standard to which serious climbers aspire.

Risk associated with falling is always present in climbing, but varies in degree. It could be slipping off the first move of a boulder problem and twisting an ankle, falling off between bolts on a sport route and bruising your body against the rock, taking a twenty foot fall on a trad route and breaking a leg, or falling to your death whilst soloing. What this tells us is that most climbers try at all costs not to fall and this is linked to peoples' personal choice of approach and style. If a proposed climb has inherent dangers then logic dictates that it is in the interest of the ascensionist to gain as much information, or *beta,* as possible to prevent them hurting themselves, so climbers tend to be a little more relaxed gaining prior knowledge about hazardous trad climbs.

Artificial climbing has undergone an interesting evolution and has over the years stimulated conflict with both free climbers and also the pioneers of adventurous aid climbing. The free climber would advocate that if it is possible to climb the rock free, then that is the way it should be done. Climbers from all disciplines recognise that with technology it is possible to engineer a safe passage up even the blankest and steepest sections of rock. It was recognised fairly early on in artificial climbing development that such engineering tactics devalued some of the challenge that climbing is meant to embrace. Today modern aid climbers try and hold true to some basic principles that aim to retain the risk, psychological, and technical elements that are central to pioneering adventure. Simply put, this means just using the natural features in the rock to aid upward progress and wherever possible refraining from drilling and placing bombproof permanent protection in the rock. This has resulted in the creation of some extremely bold artificially executed ascents.

In sport climbing and bouldering, where the risks of injury are greatly reduced, the pure on-sight concept is recognised by some as an important factor in the style of ascent. In sport climbing people operating *within their grade* will try the on-sight flash approach. If they fail by taking a fall they may resort to practising the moves and when they feel confident that they will succeed in climbing or *sending* the route they will make another attempt. This style is called a *redpoint* ascent and although it is perfectly acceptable it is widely regarded as inferior to the on-sight flash. In sport climbing a natural method of improving is to try routes that are beyond a person's *on-sight* grade. In these cases the climber will opt to practice, or *work* a route without even considering an on-sight attempt. This means rehearsing moves until the entire climb is within the person's grasp. The gap between the climbers on-sight grade and *working* grade will govern how long they will need to practice the route, but when they feel ready they will try to complete the climb in the redpoint style. This is a commonly used approach. I would suggest that in most cases in climbing, the more prior knowledge that a person has about a particular route the greater is their advantage in successfully completing it. Even a minute bit of additional, critical, beta, can mean the difference between success and failure. The lengths that any individual goes to obtain prior knowledge is down to personal choice, in climbing it is the individual who lays down the gauntlet to themselves. I think where prior knowledge about a climb does need to be considered is when onlookers, or even climbers themselves, start making comparative judgements about one person's ascent over another.

The Special Case of New Routes and First Ascents

A *first ascent* is quite simply that. It is when someone climbs a route for the first time, usually where no other climber has been before. A new route can take the form of a ten foot boulder problem, a fifty foot rock-climb, a thousand foot Alpine adventure or a route up Mount Everest that no one else has ever undertaken. Once again different approaches govern the style in which new routes are conceived. Some of these are bound up with traditions, but some are dictated by practical constraints. Perhaps the purest form of establishing a new route is on-sight, ground-up and free, indeed this approach is used and has resulted in some remarkable ascents. New routing in this style is about real pioneering, pushing into new ground where no one has been before, with no prior knowledge of whether it is feasible to overcome the ground ahead.

To appreciate some of the approaches to new routing that have become accepted of late we need to consider the concept that unclimbed rock is a finite and dwindling resource. We also need to think that as climbing evolves the standards of routes being established increases. This creates paradox. Each generation of climbers pick off their choice of new routes, the more new routes that are climbed means that the scope for any more decreases. Earlier generations select the more obvious lines or the best quality rock. It becomes increasingly difficult to establish new routes ground-up, on-sight simply because the potential routes that are left, tackle improbable ground, or are forced to climb over loose sections of rock. In certain situations a climber might envisage a new route up a section of a cliff, but from a wealth of previous climbing experience can see that the chance of climbing the route might be slim indeed. In this situation the climber might take the personal decision to abseil down the proposed line to inspect the rock in greater detail. In so doing they get a better appraisal of how to piece the moves together, what the pro is like, remove dirt and loose rock and establish whether the route will be climbable at all. Once they have made their assessment they will attempt the route ground-up. This is called *pre inspection and gardening* and whilst it is an inferior form of new routing to on-sight, it has gained acceptance simply because of the high degree of uncertainty that climbing uncharted rock can present the potential first ascensionist.

Establishing new sport routes can necessitate a simple pragmatic approach. Common practice is to abseil down the proposed line from above so that the route can be equipped with the bolts used to protect the passage. Once all

224

the bolts are in place the aspirant ascensionist will try and climb the route. If the terrain is within the climbers *on-sight grade* they will try to flash the route ground-up. Sometimes the proposed new route is at the upper end of the climbers ability and in these cases it might take many days of practice before the route is first climbed redpoint style.

In recent years a new practice has been adopted for establishing new routes in the UK on rock where the use of bolts is deemed unacceptable. On the gritstone edges and the mountain crags of the UK, climbers have started pioneering routes where there is no, or minimal, natural pro. Sometimes the proposed line covers ground of the utmost technical difficulty and even with knowledge of the moves gained by pre-inspection, falling is still mandatory. In effect such routes require a solo ascent. The potential first ascensionist is faced with a personal paradox. The desire to be first person to climb the route, versus the real consequences of failure, which can involve serious injury or even death. In these cases the climber will practise the route repeatedly on a top rope. If and when they feel that they have achieved the correct physical and mental state they will make an attempt at the route. This technique is called *Headpointing*. The terminology seems appropriate because of the mental state that is required to achieve success.

After any successful first ascent the climber responsible has the honour of naming their route. In the old days names were often chosen that simply described the features of the climb, like *Central Buttress* on Scafell, or *The Grooved Arête* on Tryfan. Occasionally the actual climber's name was associated with the feature like, *Sligsby's Chimney*, or the *Bonatti Pillar* in the Alps. Sometimes climbers have been a little quirkier with their names, like Yorkshireman Arthur Dolphin who in 1948 famously named a difficult climb on Gimmer Crag in the Lakes, *Kipling Groove*, because in his own words, *it was ruddy 'ard*. Some climbers derive great pleasure from their route names and it can give an insight into how they hold their first ascents in their own mind's eye.

This is a simple overview of some of the approaches and styles used in climbing. Different climbers adopt different approaches and this is down to personal preference. In my view certain styles are without doubt superior to others and, by deduction, climbers making ascents in superior style are simply, but importantly, defining higher standards. Human beings can be very competitive and sometimes display unbridled egos. History has shown us that climbers will bend principles to meet their own ends and it is known that certain individuals can be economical with the truth when recounting information about the style of their ascents. This is important context for an activity where there are no judges dishing out points, where strong personal values sit at the core and people rely on the honesty and transparency of their fellow climbers. To make false claims in climbing is recognised as deplorable, yet evidence suggests that it happens. In a pursuit that ultimately boils down to personal challenge and discovery, I would suggest that those who make such false claims are in the end simply deceiving themselves.

Acknowledgements

Acknowledgements

Many people have enriched my life over the years and a few have made it into the pages of this book. There are many more who have not been mentioned by name, yet they have played an equally important part. Some are now no longer with us. To all those who have shared in the adventure, I am eternally grateful, without you I would not have been able to tell this story.

My parents set the scene perfectly by creating a home that placed family and life's experiences at its heart. My dad's natural desire for travel undoubtedly lit a gypsy spark in me which has led me a merry dance and continues to burn to this day. My brother Nigel, ever the historian, sowed seeds of romantic adventure and exploration. In the early days these germinated into one or two naively conceived exploits, but with the ability to laugh at ourselves and each other, we were able to learn along the way.

Sharing a rope with someone is an expression of mutual trust and respect. Sharing that rope time and time again through thick and thin creates a bond between people that transcends that which words can describe. I have been privileged to experience this bond with a number of special friends over the years and all of you reading this, will know who you are. A few others deserve special mention, not only because of the adventure shared on the rock, but also for the time spent reminiscing and recounting tales over a pint in the bar. Andy Cave, Alan Firth, Chris Frost, Chris Gibb, Dave Green, Roy Healey, Roger Hindle, Terry Holmes, Bill Lukin, Jaysen Metcalf, Neil McCallum, Danny Morgan, Dave Peace, Gilmore Peel, Greg Rimmer, Mick Ryan, Will Simm and Jon Smoothy. Certain friendships go deeper still and the following have brought special meaning to my life; Dave Barton, Ian Cooksey, Mick Johnston, Adrian Ledgway and Jerry Peel you are all great men. I am also grateful to Pam Barton, Sarah Cooksey and Sharon Horry-Ledgway, whose company has been a joy all along the way.

The production of this book has been an organic and evolving process and I would like to thank the following who became involved with the project as it progressed; Catherine Cousins, head of 2QT publishing for accepting the project and providing a first class professional service throughout. My editor Robert Auty who as a non- climber, took on the challenge enthusiastically and dealt with the 'climbing speak' in his stride. I wanted to retain as much artistic license as possible with this work and enjoyed Rob's editorial style, both objective and encouraging. Maggie Body cast a critical eye over the initial rough script and gave some revealing feedback early on. This made me re think the focus of the narrative and whilst the input was small the advice was invaluable. Ian Smith proofed the script at the eleventh hour, providing important corrections to some of the climbing syntax. I am also grateful to Ian as one of the first climbers to read the book for his feedback and enthusiasm

I am from the era of the vinyl music album. In my day when a new record was released its cover and sleeve notes were greeted with as much excitement as the music within. In an age when the book as a physical product appears to be under threat by technology, I think it is important to appreciate the written word as a physical work of art. If books continue to look and feel good, maybe they will endure. I would like to thank Hilary Pitt who added finesse to the designs of both the cover and the end papers. We have endeavoured to produce something that is pleasing to the eye.

Andy Cave, I'm sure I'll be able to find some as yet unclimbed line for you. Seriously thank you very much for the foreword.

Many of the pictures in this book are my own work, but a number are the result of other climbers and friends who were kind enough to capture the action on my behalf using my own cameras. I have credited the person behind the lens wherever possible, but some of the climbing shots go back over thirty years and I have had to work from memory. I would like to thank Glenn Robbins, in particular, for supplying the excellent cover shot and numerous pictures used throughout the book, and for the energy and enthusiasm and humour that he displayed both on the crag and in the bar. Thanks also to Alan Firth (dedicated to the abolition of the climbing club) for the rear cover photograph.

Finally to Dawn, Lauren, Bryony and Molly who continue to let me look to the vertical without voicing too many objections, my love is with you always.

Mark Radtke.
November, 2011.

The Scent of a Woman. E4 5c. Cave, Radtke. 1995

Ward 10. F7a+. Peel, Radtke. 1995

Them Boyd Creatures. E4 6a. Radtke, Nadin. 1995
Ginny Greenteeth. E5 6a. Radtke, Peel. 1996

The Blood on the Shamrock. E6 6b. Peel, Radtke. 1996
Just in Time. E5 6b. Peel, Barton, Radtke. 1996
Canine Fruitbat. E5 6b. Radtke, Barton. 1996

Stepmother Jag. E4 6b. Radtke, Rimmer. 1996

The Crack of Dawn E3 5c, Radtke, Rimmer. 1996

The Dawning. E4 6b. Radtke, Peel, Barton. 1996
The Skryking. E5 6a. Radtke, Barton. 1997

Over the Top. E4 6a. Barton, Radtke. 1997

Cutting the Cord. E4 5c. Radtke, Barton. 1997
The Warriors of Hanuman. E5 6b. Radtke, Peel. 1997

Aye n Ard Crack. E2 6b. Radtke, Barton. 1997

The Kiss of Life. E5 6b. Radtke, Barton. 1997
Call of the Curlew. E4 6a. Radtke, Barton. 1998

Blull Gum Sloggitt. E3 6a. Radtke, Peel. 1998

Laurens Wall. E1 5c. Radtke. 1998
Bubba. E3 5c. Barton, Radtke. 1998
Sobieskis Winged Hussars. E4 6a. Radtke, Troilett. 1998

Cheeted. E6 6b. Peel, Radtke. 1998

Paintsripper Gritter. E4 6a, Peel, Radtke.1998
Sandersons Sorrow. E4 6a. Peel, Radtke.1998